Algernon Charles Swinburne

Tristram of Lyonesse

And Other Poems. Sixth Edition

Algernon Charles Swinburne

Tristram of Lyonesse
And Other Poems. Sixth Edition

ISBN/EAN: 9783744713931

Printed in Europe, USA, Canada, Australia, Japan

Cover: Foto ©Thomas Meinert / pixelio.de

More available books at **www.hansebooks.com**

TRISTRAM OF LYONESSE

AND OTHER POEMS

TRISTRAM OF LYONESSE

AND OTHER POEMS

BY

ALGERNON CHARLES SWINBURNE

SIXTH EDITION

LONDON
CHATTO & WINDUS
1899

PRINTED BY

SPOTTISWOODE AND CO., NEW-STREET SQUARE

LONDON

TO MY BEST FRIEND

THEODORE WATTS

I DEDICATE IN THIS BOOK

THE BEST I HAVE TO GIVE HIM

Spring speaks again, and all our woods are stirred,
  And all our wide glad wastes aflower around,
  That twice have heard keen April's clarion sound
Since here we first together saw and heard
Spring's light reverberate and reiterate word
  Shine forth and speak in season. Life stands crowned
  Here with the best one thing it ever found,
As of my soul's best birthdays dawns the third.

There is a friend that as the wise man saith
  Cleaves closer than a brother: nor to me
    Hath time not shown, through days like waves at
      strife,
This truth more sure than all things else but death,
  This pearl most perfect found in all the sea
    That washes toward your feet these waifs of life.

THE PINES,
  April 1882.

CONTENTS.

CONTENTS.

TRISTRAM OF LYONESSE

PRELUDE.

TRISTRAM AND ISEULT.

LOVE, that is first and last of all things made,
The light that has the living world for shade,
The spirit that for temporal veil has on
The souls of all men woven in unison,
One fiery raiment with all lives inwrought
And lights of sunny and starry deed and thought,
And alway through new act and passion new
Shines the divine same body and beauty through,
The body spiritual of fire and light
That is to worldly noon as noon to night
Love, that is flesh upon the spirit of man
And spirit within the flesh whence breath began
Love, that keeps all the choir of lives in chime ;
[Love, that is blood within the veins of time ;]
That wrought the whole world without stroke of hand,
Shaping the breadth of sea, the length of land,
And with the pulse and motion of his breath
Through the great heart of the earth strikes life and
     death,

The sweet twain chords that make the sweet tune live
Through day and night of things alternative,
Through silence and through sound of stress and
    strife,
And ebb and flow of dying death and life ;
Love, that sounds loud or light in all men's ears,
Whence all men's eyes take fire from sparks of tears,
That binds on all men's feet or chains or wings ;
Love, that is root and fruit of terrene things ;
Love, that the whole world's waters shall not drown,
The whole world's fiery forces not burn down ;
Love, that what time his own hands guard his head
The whole world's wrath and strength shall not strike
    dead ;
Love, that if once his own hands make his grave
The whole world's pity and sorrow shall not save ;
Love, that for very life shall not be sold,
Nor bought nor bound with iron nor with gold ;
So strong that heaven, could love bid heaven farewell,
Would turn to fruitless and unflowering hell ;
So sweet that hell, to hell could love be given,
Would turn to splendid and sonorous heaven ;
Love that is fire within thee and light above,
And lives by grace of nothing but of love ;
Through many and lovely thoughts and much desire
Led these twain to the life of tears and fire ;
Through many and lovely days and much delight
Led these twain to the lifeless life of night.
    Yea, but what then? albeit all this were thus,
And soul smote soul and left it ruinous,

And love led love as eyeless men lead men,
Through chance by chance to deathward—Ah, what
    then?
Hath love not likewise led them further yet,
Out through the years where memories rise and set,
Some large as suns, some moon-like warm and pale,
Some starry-sighted, some through clouds that sail
Seen as red flame through spectral float of fume,
Each with the blush of its own special bloom
On the fair face of its own coloured light,
Distinguishable in all the host of night,
Divisible from all the radiant rest
And separable in splendour?   Hath the best
Light of love's all, of all that burn and move,
A better heaven than heaven is?   Hath not love
Made for all these their sweet particular air
To shine in, their own beams and names to bear,
Their ways to wander and their wards to keep,
Till story and song and glory and all things sleep?
Hath he not plucked from death of lovers dead
Their musical soft memories, and kept red
The rose of their remembrance in men's eyes,
The sunsets of their stories in his skies,
The blush of their dead blood in lips that speak
Of their dead lives, and in the listener's cheek
That trembles with the kindling pity lit
In gracious hearts for some sweet fever-fit,
A fiery pity enkindled of pure thought
By tales that make their honey out of nought,

The faithless faith that lives without belief
Its light life through, the griefless ghost of grief?
Yea, as warm night refashions the sere blood
In storm-struck petal or in sun-struck bud,
With tender hours and tempering dew to cure
The hunger and thirst of day's distemperature
And ravin of the dry discolouring hours,
Hath he not bid relume their flameless flowers
With summer fire and heat of lamping song,
And bid the short-lived things, long dead, live long,
And thought remake their wan funereal fames,
And the sweet shining signs of women's names
That mark the months out and the weeks anew
He moves in changeless change of seasons through
To fill the days up of his dateless year
Flame from Queen Helen to Queen Guenevere?
For first of all the sphery signs whereby
Love severs light from darkness, and most high,
In the white front of January there glows
The rose-red sign of Helen like a rose :
And gold-eyed as the shore-flower shelterless
Whereon the sharp-breathed sea blows bitterness,
A storm-star that the seafarers of love
Strain their wind-wearied eyes for glimpses of,
Shoots keen through February's grey frost and damp
The lamplike star of Hero for a lamp ;
The star that Marlowe sang into our skies
With mouth of gold, and morning in his eyes ;
And in clear March across the rough blue sea
The signal sapphire of Alcyone

Makes bright the blown brows of the wind-foot year ;
And shining like a sunbeam-smitten tear
Full ere it fall, the fair next sign in sight
Burns opal-wise with April-coloured light
When air is quick with song and rain and flame,
My birth-month star that in love's heaven hath name
Iseult, a light of blossom and beam and shower,
My singing sign that makes the song-tree flower ;
Next like a pale and burning pearl beyond
The rose-white sphere of flower-named Rosamond
Signs the sweet head of Maytime ; and for June
Flares like an angered and storm-reddening moon
Her signal sphere, whose Carthaginian pyre
Shadowed her traitor's flying sail with fire ;
Next, glittering as the wine-bright jacinth-stone,
A star south-risen that first to music shone,
The keen girl-star of golden Juliet bears
Light northward to the month whose forehead wears
Her name for flower upon it, and his trees
Mix their deep English song with Veronese ;
And like an awful sovereign chrysolite
Burning, the supreme fire that blinds the night,
The hot gold head of Venus kissed by Mars,
A sun-flower among small sphered flowers of stars,
The light of Cleopatra fills and burns
The hollow of heaven whence ardent August yearns ;
And fixed and shining as the sister-shed
Sweet tears for Phaethon disorbed and dead,
The pale bright autumn's amber-coloured sphere,
That through September sees the saddening year

As love sees change through sorrow, hath to name
Francesca's; and the star that watches flame
The embers of the harvest overgone
Is Thisbe's, slain of love in Babylon,
Set in the golden girdle of sweet signs
A blood-bright ruby; last save one light shines
An eastern wonder of sphery chrysopras,
The star that made men mad, Angelica's;
And latest named and lordliest, with a sound
Of swords and harps in heaven that ring it round,
Last love-light and last love-song of the year's,
Gleams like a glorious emerald Guenevere's.
These are the signs wherethrough the year sees move,
Full of the sun, the sun-god which is love,
A fiery body blood-red from the heart
Outward, with fire-white wings made wide apart,
That close not and unclose not, but upright
Steered without wind by their own light and might
Sweep through the flameless fire of air that rings
From heaven to heaven with thunder of wheels and
    wings
And antiphones of motion-moulded rhyme
Through spaces out of space and timeless time.
   So shine above dead chance and conquered change
The spherèd signs, and leave without their range
Doubt and desire, and hope with fear for wife,
Pale pains, and pleasures long worn out of life.
Yea, even the shadows of them spiritless,
Through the dim door of sleep that seem to press,

Forms without form, a piteous people and blind
Men and no men, whose lamentable kind
The shadow of death and shadow of life compel
Through semblances of heaven and false-faced hell,
Through dreams of light and dreams of darkness tost
On waves innavigable, are these so lost?
Shapes that wax pale and shift in swift strange wise,
Void faces with unspeculative eyes,
Dim things that gaze and glare, dead mouths that
    move,
Featureless heads discrowned of hate and love,
Mockeries and masks of motion and mute breath,
Leavings of life, the superflux of death—
If these things and no more than these things be
Left when man ends or changes, who can see?
Or who can say with what more subtle sense
Their subtler natures taste in air less dense
A life less thick and palpable than ours,
Warmed with faint fires and sweetened with dead
    flowers
And measured by low music? how time fares
In that wan time-forgotten world of theirs,
Their pale poor world too deep for sun or star
To live in, where the eyes of Helen are,
And hers who made as God's own eyes to shine
The eyes that met them of the Florentine,
Wherein the godhead thence transfigured lit
All time for all men with the shadow of it?
Ah, and these too felt on them as God's grace
The pity and glory of this man's breathing face;

For these too, these my lovers, these my twain,
Saw Dante, saw God visible by pain,
With lips that thundered and with feet that trod
Before men's eyes incognisable God ;
Saw love and wrath and light and night and fire
Live with one life and at one mouth respire,
And in one golden sound their whole soul heard
Sounding, one sweet immitigable word.
 They have the night, who had like us the day ;
We, whom day binds, shall have the night as they.
We, from the fetters of the light unbound,
Healed of our wound of living, shall sleep sound.
All gifts but one the jealous God may keep
From our soul's longing, one he cannot—sleep.
This, though he grudge all other grace to prayer,
This grace his closed hand cannot choose but spare.
This, though his ear be sealed to all that live,
Be it lightly given or lothly, God must give.
We, as the men whose name on earth is none,
We too shall surely pass out of the sun ;
Out of the sound and eyeless light of things,
Wide as the stretch of life's time-wandering wings,
Wide as the naked world and shadowless,
And long-lived as the world's own weariness.
Us too, when all the fires of time are cold,
The heights shall hide us and the depths shall hold.
Us too, when all the tears of time are dry,
The night shall lighten from her tearless eye.
Blind is the day and eyeless all its light,
But the large unbewildered eye of night

Hath sense and speculation; and the sheer
Limitless length of lifeless life and clear,
The timeless space wherein the brief worlds move
Clothed with light life and fruitful with light love,
With hopes that threaten, and with fears that cease,
Past fear and hope, hath in it only peace.
Yet of these lives inlaid with hopes and fears,
Spun fine as fire and jewelled thick with tears,
These lives made out of loves that long since were,
Lives wrought as ours of earth and burning air,
Fugitive flame, and water of secret springs,
And clothed with joys and sorrows as with wings,
Some yet are good, if aught be good, to save
Some while from washing wreck and wrecking wave.
Was such not theirs, the twain I take, and give
Out of my life to make their dead life live
Some days of mine, and blow my living breath
Between dead lips forgotten even of death?
So many and many of old have given my twain
Love and live song and honey-hearted pain,
Whose root is sweetness and whose fruit is sweet,
So many and with such joy have tracked their feet,
What should I do to follow? yet I too,
I have the heart to follow, many or few
Be the feet gone before me ; for the way,
Rose-red with remnant roses of the day
Westward, and eastward white with stars that break,
Between the green and foam is fair to take
For any sail the sea-wind steers for me
From morning into morning, sea to sea.

THE SAILING OF THE SWALLOW.

About the middle music of the spring
Came from the castled shore of Ireland's king
A fair ship stoutly sailing, eastward bound
And south by Wales and all its wonders round
To the loud rocks and ringing reaches home
That take the wild wrath of the Cornish foam,
Past Lyonesse unswallowed of the tides
And high Carlion that now the steep sea hides
To the wind-hollowed heights and gusty bays
Of sheer Tintagel, fair with famous days.
Above the stem a gilded swallow shone,
Wrought with straight wings and eyes of glittering
    stone
As flying sunward oversea, to bear
Green summer with it through the singing air.
And on the deck between the rowers at dawn,
As the bright sail with brightening wind was drawn,
Sat with full face against the strengthening light
Iseult, more fair than foam or dawn was white.

Her gaze was glad past love's own singing of,
And her face lovely past desire of love.
Past thought and speech her maiden motions were,
And a more golden sunrise was her hair.
The very veil of her bright flesh was made
As of light woven and moonbeam-coloured shade
More fine than moonbeams ; white her eyelids shone
As snow sun-stricken that endures the sun,
And through their curled and coloured clouds of deep
Luminous lashes thick as dreams in sleep
Shone as the sea's depth swallowing up the sky's
The springs of unimaginable eyes.
As the wave's subtler emerald is pierced through
With the utmost heaven's inextricable blue,
And both are woven and molten in one sleight
Of amorous colour and implicated light
Under the golden guard and gaze of noon,
So glowed their awless amorous plenilune,
Azure and gold and ardent grey, made strange
With fiery difference and deep interchange
Inexplicable of glories multiform ;
Now as the sullen sapphire swells toward storm
Foamless, their bitter beauty grew acold,
And now afire with ardour of fine gold.
Her flower-soft lips were meek and passionate,
For love upon them like a shadow sate
Patient, a foreseen vision of sweet things,
A dream with eyes fast shut and plumeless wings
That knew not what man's love or life should be,
Nor had it sight nor heart to hope or see

What thing should come, but childlike satisfied
Watched out its virgin vigil in soft pride
And unkissed expectation ; and the glad
Clear cheeks and throat and tender temples had
Such maiden heat as if a rose's blood
Beat in the live heart of a lily-bud.
Between the small round breasts a white way led
Heavenward, and from slight foot to slender head
The whole fair body flower-like swayed and shone
Moving, and what her light hand leant upon
Grew blossom-scented : her warm arms began
To round and ripen for delight of man
That they should clasp and circle : her fresh hands,
Like regent lilies of reflowering lands
Whose vassal firstlings, crown and star and plume,
Bow down to the empire of that sovereign bloom,
Shone sceptreless, and from her face there went
A silent light as of a God content ;
Save when, more swift and keen than love or shame,
Some flash of blood, light as the laugh of flame,
Broke it with sudden beam and shining speech,
As dream by dream shot through her eyes, and each
Outshone the last that lightened, and not one
Showed her such things as should be borne and done.
Though hard against her shone the sunlike face
That in all change and wreck of time and place
Should be the star of her sweet living soul.
Nor had love made it as his written scroll
For evil will and good to read in yet ;
But smooth and mighty, without scar or fret,

Fresh and high-lifted was the helmless brow
As the oak-tree flower that tops the topmost bough,
Ere it drop off before the perfect leaf ;
And nothing save his name he had of grief,
The name his mother, dying as he was born,
Made out of sorrow in very sorrow's scorn,
And set it on him smiling in her sight,
Tristram ; who now, clothed with sweet youth and
    might,
As a glad witness wore that bitter name,
The second symbol of the world for fame.
Famous and full of fortune was his youth
Ere the beard's bloom had left his cheek unsmooth,
And in his face a lordship of strong joy
And height of heart no chance could curb or cloy
Lightened, and all that warmed them at his eyes
Loved them as larks that kindle as they rise
Toward light they turn to music love the blue strong
    skies.
So like the morning through the morning moved
Tristram, a light to look on and be loved.
Song sprang between his lips and hands, and shone
Singing, and strengthened and sank down thereon
As a bird settles to the second flight,
Then from beneath his harping hands with might
Leapt, and made way and had its fill and died,
And all whose hearts were fed upon it sighed
Silent, and in them all the fire of tears
Burned as wine drunken not with lips but ears.
And gazing on his fervent hands that made
The might of music all their souls obeyed

With trembling strong subservience of delight,
Full many a maid that had him once in sight
Thought in the secret rapture of her heart
In how dark onset had these hands borne part
How oft, and were so young and sweet of skill ;
And those red lips whereon the song burned still,
What words and cries of battle had they flung
Athwart the swing and shriek of swords, so young ;
And eyes as glad as summer, what strange youth
Fed them so full of happy heart and truth,
That had seen sway from side to sundering side
The steel flow of that terrible springtide
That the moon rules not, but the fire and light
Of men's hearts mixed in the mid mirth of fight.
Therefore the joy and love of him they had
Made thought more amorous in them and more glad
For his fame's sake remembered, and his youth
Gave his fame flowerlike fragrance and soft growth
As of a rose requickening, when he stood
Fair in their eye, a flower of faultless blood.
And that sad queen to whom his life was death,
A rose plucked forth of summer in mid breath,
A star fall'n out of season in mid throe
Of that life's joy that makes the star's life glow,
Made their love sadder toward him and more strong.
And in mid change of time and fight and song
Chance cast him westward on the low sweet strand
Where songs are sung of the old green Irish land,
And the sky loves it, and the sea loves best,
And as a bird is taken to man's breast

c

The sweet-souled land where sorrow sweetest sings
Is wrapt round with them as with hands and wings
And taken to the sea's heart as a flower.
There in the luck and light of his good hour
Came to the king's court like a noteless man
Tristram, and while some half a season ran
Abode before him harping in his hall,
And taught sweet craft of new things musical
To the dear maiden mouth and innocent hands
That for his sake are famous in all lands.
Yet was not love between them, for their fate
Lay wrapt in its appointed hour at wait,
And had no flower to show yet, and no sting.
But once being vexed with some past wound the king
Bade give him comfort of sweet baths, and then
Should Iseult watch him as his handmaiden,
For his more honour in men's sight, and ease
The hurts he had with holy remedies
Made by her mother's magic in strange hours
Out of live roots and life-compelling flowers.
And finding by the wound's shape in his side
This was the knight by whom their strength had died
And all their might in one man overthrown
Had left their shame in sight of all men shown,
She would have slain him swordless with his sword ;
Yet seemed he to her so great and fair a lord
She heaved up hand and smote not ; then said he,
Laughing—'What comfort shall this dead man be,
Damsel ? what hurt is for my blood to heal ?
But set your hand not near the toothèd steel

Lest the fang strike it.'—'Yea, the fang,' she said,
' Should it not sting the very serpent dead
That stung mine uncle? for his slayer art thou,
And half my mother's heart is bloodless now
Through thee, that mad'st the veins of all her kin
Bleed in his wounds whose veins through thee ran thin.'
Yet thought she how their hot chief's violent heart
Had flung the fierce word forth upon their part
Which bade to battle the best knight that stood
On Arthur's, and so dying of his wild mood
Had set upon his conqueror's flesh the seal
Of his mishallowed and anointed steel,
Whereof the venom and enchanted might
Made the sign burn here branded in her sight.
These things she stood recasting, and her soul
Subsiding till its wound of wrath were whole
Grew smooth again, as thought still softening stole
Through all its tempered passion ; nor might hate
Keep high the fire against him lit of late ;
But softly from his smiling sight she passed.
And peace thereafter made between them fast
Made peace between two kingdoms, when he went
Home with hands reconciled and heart content,
To bring fair truce 'twixt Cornwall's wild bright strand
And the long wrangling wars of that loud land.
And when full peace was struck betwixt them twain
Forth must he fare by those green straits again,
And bring back Iseult for a plighted bride
And set to reign at Mark his uncle's side.

So now with feast made and all triumphs done
They sailed between the moonfall and the sun
Under the spent stars eastward ; but the queen
Out of wise heart and subtle love had seen
Such things as might be, dark as in a glass,
And lest some doom of these should come to pass
Bethought her with her secret soul alone
To work some charm for marriage unison
And strike the heart of Iseult to her lord
With power compulsive more than stroke of sword.
Therefore with marvellous herbs and spells she
    wrought
To win the very wonder of her thought,
And brewed it with her secret hands and blest
And drew and gave out of her secret breast
To one her chosen and Iseult's handmaiden,
Brangwain, and bade her hide from sight of men
This marvel covered in a golden cup,
So covering in her heart the counsel up
As in the gold the wondrous wine lay close ;
And when the last shout with the last cup rose
About the bride and bridegroom bound to bed,
Then should this one word of her will be said
To her new-married maiden child, that she
Should drink with Mark this draught in unity,
And no lip touch it for her sake but theirs :
For with long love and consecrating prayers
The wine was hallowed for their mouths to pledge ;
And if a drop fell from the beaker's edge

That drop should Iseult hold as dear as blood
Shed from her mother's heart to do her good.
And having drunk they twain should be one heart
Who were one flesh till fleshly death should part—
Death, who parts all.   So Brangwain swore, and kept
The hid thing by her while she waked or slept.
And now they sat to see the sun again
Whose light of eye had looked on no such twain
Since Galahault in the rose-time of the year
Brought Launcelot first to sight of Guenevere.
    And Tristram caught her changing eyes and said :
' As this day raises daylight from the dead
Might not this face the life of a dead man ? '
    And Iseult, gazing where the sea was wan
Out of the sun's way, said : ' I pray you not
Praise me, but tell me there in Camelot,
Saving the queen, who hath most name of fair ?
I would I were a man and dwelling there,
That I might win me better praise than yours,
Even such as you have ; for your praise endures,
That with great deeds ye wring from mouths of men,
But ours—for shame, where is it ?   Tell me then,
Since woman may not wear a better here,
Who of this praise hath most save Guenevere ? '
    And Tristram, lightening with a laugh held in—
' Surely a little praise is this to win,
A poor praise and a little ! but of these
Hapless, whom love serves only with bowed knees,
Of such poor women fairer face hath none
That lifts her eyes alive against the sun

Than Arthur's sister, whom the north seas call
Mistress of isles ; so yet majestical
Above the crowns on younger heads she moves,
Outlightening with her eyes our late-born loves.'
    ' Ah,' said Iseult, ' is she more tall than I?
Look, I am tall ;' and struck the mast hard by,
With utmost upward reach of her bright hand ;
' And look, fair lord, now, when I rise and stand,
How high with feet unlifted I can touch
Standing straight up ; could this queen do thus much?
Nay, over tall she must be then, like me ;
Less fair than lesser women.   May this be,
That still she stands the second stateliest there,
So more than many so much younger fair,
She, born when yet the king your lord was not,
And has the third knight after Launcelot
And after you to serve her ? nay, sir, then
God made her for a godlike sign to men.'
    ' Ay,' Tristram answered, ' for a sign, a sign—
Would God it were not ! for no planets shine
With half such fearful forecast of men's fate
As a fair face so more unfortunate.'
    Then with a smile that lit not on her brows
But moved upon her red mouth tremulous
Light as a sea-bird's motion oversea,
' Yea,' quoth Iseult, ' the happier hap for me,
With no such face to bring men no such fate.
Yet her might all we women born too late
Praise for good hap, who so enskied above
Not more in age excels us than man's love.'

There came a glooming light on Tristram's face
Answering : 'God keep you better in his grace
Than to sit down beside her in men's sight.
For if men be not blind whom God gives light
And lie not in whose lips he bids truth live,
Great grief shall she be given, and greater give,
For Merlin witnessed of her years ago
That she should work woe and should suffer woe
Beyond the race of women : and in truth
Her face, a spell that knows nor age nor youth,
Like youth being soft, and subtler-eyed than age,
With lips that mock the doom her eyes presage,
Hath on it such a light of cloud and fire,
With charm and change of keen or dim desire,
And over all a fearless look of fear
Hung like a veil across its changing cheer,
Made up of fierce foreknowledge and sharp scorn,
That it were better she had not been born.
For not love's self can help a face which hath
Such insubmissive anguish of wan wrath,
Blind prescience and self-contemptuous hate
Of her own soul and heavy-footed fate,
Writ broad upon its beauty : none the less
Its fire of bright and burning bitterness
Takes with as quick a flame the sense of men
As any sunbeam, nor is quenched again
With any drop of dewfall ; yea, I think
No herb of force or blood-compelling drink
Would heal a heart that ever it made hot.
Ay, and men too that greatly love her not,

Seeing the great love of her and Lamoracke,
Make no great marvel, nor look strangely back
When with his gaze about her she goes by
Pale as a breathless and star-quickening sky
Between moonrise and sunset, and moves out
Clothed with the passion of his eyes about
As night with all her stars, yet night is black ;
And she, clothed warm with love of Lamoracke,
Girt with his worship as with girdling gold,
Seems all at heart anhungered and acold,
Seems sad at heart and loveless of the light,
As night, star-clothed or naked, is but night.'
     And with her sweet eyes sunken, and the mirth
Dead in their look as earth lies dead in earth
That reigned on earth and triumphed, Iseult said :
' Is it her shame of something done and dead
Or fear of something to be born and done
That so in her soul's eye puts out the sun ? '
     And Tristram answered : 'Surely, as I think,
This gives her soul such bitterness to drink,
The sin born blind, the sightless sin unknown,
Wrought when the summer in her blood was blown,
But scarce aflower, and spring first flushed her will
With bloom of dreams no fruitage should fulfil,
When out of vision and desire was wrought
The sudden sin that from the living thought
Leaps a live deed and dies not : then there came
On that blind sin swift eyesight like a flame
Touching the dark to death, and made her mad
With helpless knowledge that too late forbade

What was before the bidding; and she knew
How sore a life dead love should lead her through
To what sure end how fearful; and though yet
Nor with her blood nor tears her way be wet
And she look bravely with set face on fate,
Yet she knows well the serpent hour at wait
Somewhere to sting and spare not; ay, and he,
Arthur'——

      'The king,' quoth Iseult suddenly,
'Doth the king too live so in sight of fear?
They say sin touches not a man so near
As shame a woman; yet he too should be
Part of the penance, being more deep than she
Set in the sin.'

      'Nay,' Tristram said, 'for thus
It fell by wicked hap and hazardous,
That wittingly he sinned no more than youth
May sin and be assoiled of God and truth,
Repenting; since in his first year of reign
As he stood splendid with his foemen slain
And light of new-blown battles, flushed and hot
With hope and life, came greeting from King Lot
Out of his wind-worn islands oversea,
And homage to my king and fealty
Of those north seas wherein the strange shapes swim,
As from his man; and Arthur greeted him
As his good lord and courteously, and bade
To his high feast; who coming with him had
This Queen Morgause of Orkney, his fair wife,
In the green middle Maytime of her life,

And scarce in April was our king's as then,
And goodliest was he of all flowering men,
And of what graft as yet himself knew not ;
But cold as rains in autumn was King Lot
And grey-grown out of season : so there sprang
Swift love between them, and all spring through sang
Light in their joyous hearing ; for none knew
The bitter bond of blood between them two,
Twain fathers but one mother, till too late
The sacred mouth of Merlin set forth fate
And brake the secret seal on Arthur's birth,
And showed his ruin and his rule on earth
Inextricable, and light on lives to be.
For surely, though time slay us, yet shall we
Have such high name and lordship of good days
As shall sustain us living, and men's praise
Shall burn a beacon lit above us dead.
And of the king how shall not this be said
When any of us from any mouth has praise,
That such were men in only this king's days,
In Arthur's ? yea, come shine or shade, no less
His name shall be one name with knightliness,
His fame one light with sunlight.   Yet in sooth
His age shall bear the burdens of his youth
And bleed from his own bloodshed ; for indeed
Blind to him blind his sister brought forth seed,
And of the child between them shall be born
Destruction : so shall God not suffer scorn,
Nor in men's souls and lives his law lie dead.'
    And as one moved and marvelling Iseult said :

'Great pity it is and strange it seems to me
God could not do them so much right as we,
Who slay not men for witless evil done ;
And these the noblest under God's glad sun
For sin they knew not he that knew shall slay,
And smite blind men for stumbling in fair day.
What good is it to God that such should die ?
Shall the sun's light grow sunnier in the sky
Because their light of spirit is clean put out ? '
    And sighing, she looked from wave to cloud about,
And even with that the full-grown feet of day
Sprang upright on the quivering water-way,
And his face burned against her meeting face
Most like a lover's thrilled with great love's grace
Whose glance takes fire and gives ; the quick sea
        shone
And shivered like spread wings of angels blown
By the sun's breath before him ; and a low
Sweet gale shook all the foam-flowers of thin snow .
As into rainfall of sea-roses shed
Leaf by wild leaf on that green garden-bed
Which tempests till and sea-winds turn and plough :
For rosy and fiery round the running prow
Fluttered the flakes and feathers of the spray,
And bloomed like blossoms cast by God away
To waste on the ardent water ; swift the moon
Withered to westward as a face in swoon
Death-stricken by glad tidings : and the height
Throbbed and the centre quivered with delight

And the depth quailed with passion as of love,
Till like the heart of some new-mated dove
Air, light, and wave seemed full of burning rest,
With motion as of one God's beating breast.

  And her heart sprang in Iseult, and she drew
With all her spirit and life the sunrise through,
And through her lips the keen triumphant air
Sea-scented, sweeter than land-roses were,
And through her eyes the whole rejoicing east
Sun-satisfied, and all the heaven at feast
Spread for the morning; and the imperious mirth
Of wind and light that moved upon the earth,
Making the spring, and all the fruitful might
And strong regeneration of delight
That swells the seedling leaf and sapling man,
Since the first life in the first world began
To burn and burgeon through void limbs and veins,
And the first love with sharp sweet procreant pains
To pierce and bring forth roses; yea, she felt
Through her own soul the sovereign morning melt,
And all the sacred passion of the sun;
And as the young clouds flamed and were undone
About him coming, touched and burnt away
In rosy ruin and yellow spoil of day,
The sweet veil of her body and corporal sense
Felt the dawn also cleave it, and incense
With light from inward and with effluent heat
The kindling soul through fleshly hands and feet.
And as the august great blossom of the dawn
Burst, and the full sun scarce from sea withdrawn

Seemed on the fiery water a flower afloat,
Sc as a fire the mighty morning smote
Throughout her, and incensed with the influent hour
Her whole soul's one great mystical red flower
Burst, and the bud of her sweet spirit broke
Rose-fashion, and the strong spring at a stroke
Thrilled, and was cloven, and from the full sheath
    came
The whole rose of the woman red as flame :
And all her Mayday blood as from a swoon
Flushed, and May rose up in her and was June.
So for a space her heart as heavenward burned :
Then with half summer in her eyes she turned,
And on her lips was April yet, and smiled,
As though the spirit and sense unreconciled
Shrank laughing back, and would not ere its hour
Let life put forth the irrevocable flower.
    And the soft speech between them grew again
With questionings and records of what men
Rose mightiest, and what names for love or fight
Shone starriest overhead of queen or knight.
There Tristram spake of many a noble thing,
High feast and storm of tournay round the king,
Strange quest by perilous lands of marsh and brake
And circling woods branch-knotted like a snake
And places pale with sins that they had seen
Where was no life of red fruit or of green
But all was as a dead face wan and dun ;
And bowers of evil builders whence the sun

Turns silent, and the moon holds hardly light
Above them through the sick and star-crossed night;
And of their hands through whom such holds lay
    waste,
And all their strengths dishevelled and defaced
Fell ruinous, and were not from north to south :
And of the might of Merlin's ancient mouth,
The son of no man's loins, begot by doom
In speechless sleep out of a spotless womb;
For sleeping among graves where none had rest
And ominous houses of dead bones unblest
Among the grey grass rough as old rent hair
And wicked herbage whitening like despair
And blown upon with blasts of dolorous breath
From gaunt rare gaps and hollow doors of death,
A maid unspotted, senseless of the spell,
Felt not about her breathe some thing of hell
Whose child and hers was Merlin ; and to him
Great light from God gave sight of all things dim
And wisdom of all wondrous things, to say
What root should bear what fruit of night or day,
And sovereign speech and counsel higher than man;
Wherefore his youth like age was wise and wan,
And his age sorrowful and fain to sleep ;
Yet should sleep never, neither laugh nor weep,
Till in some depth of deep sweet land or sea
The heavenly hands of holier Nimue,
That was the nurse of Launcelot, and most sweet
Of all that move with magical soft feet

Among us, being of lovelier blood and breath,
Should shut him in with sleep as kind as death:
For she could pass between the quick and dead:
And of her love toward Pelleas, for whose head
Love-wounded and world-wearied she had won
A place beyond all pain in Avalon;
And of the fire that wasted afterward
The loveless eyes and bosom of Ettarde,
In whose false love his faultless heart had burned;
And now being rapt from her, her lost heart yearned
To seek him, and passed hungering out of life:
And after all the thunder-hours of strife
That roared between King Claudas and King Ban
How Nimue's mighty nursling waxed to man,
And how from his first field such grace he got
That all men's hearts bowed bown to Launcelot,
And how the high prince Galahault held him dear
And led him even to love of Guenevere
And to that kiss which made break forth as fire
The laugh that was the flower of his desire,
The laugh that lightened at her lips for bliss
To win from Love so great a lover's kiss:
And of the toil of Balen all his days
To reap but thorns for fruit and tears for praise,
Whose hap was evil as his heart was good,
And all his works and ways by wold and wood
Led through much pain to one last labouring day
When blood for tears washed grief with life away:
And of the kin of Arthur, and their might;
The misborn head of Mordred, sad as night,

With cold waste cheeks and eyes as keen as pain,
And the close angry lips of Agravaine ;
And gracious Gawain, scattering words as flowers,
The kindliest head of worldly paramours ;
And the fair hand of Gareth, found in fight
Strong as a sea-beast's tushes and as white ;
And of the king's self, glorious yet and glad
For all the toil and doubt of doom he had,
Clothed with men's loves and full of kingly days.

Then Iseult said : ' Let each knight have his praise
And each good man good witness of his worth ;
But when men laud the second name on earth,
Whom would they praise to have no worldly peer
Save him whose love makes glorious Guenevere ? '

' Nay,' Tristram said, ' such man as he is none.'

' What,' said she, ' there is none such under sun
Of all the large earth's living ? yet I deemed
Men spake of one—but maybe men that dreamed,
Fools and tongue-stricken, witless, babbler's breed—
That for all high things was his peer indeed
Save this one highest, to be so loved and love.'

And Tristram : ' Little wit had these thereof ;
For there is none such in the world as this.'

' Ay, upon land,' quoth Iseult, ' none such is,
I doubt not, nor where fighting folk may be ;
But were there none such between sky and sea,
The world's whole worth were poorer than I wist.'

And Tristram took her flower-white hand and kissed,
Laughing ; and through his fair face as in shame
The light blood lightened. ' Hear they no such name ? '

She said ; and he, ' If there be such a word,
I wot the queen's poor harper hath not heard.'
Then, as the fuller-feathered hours grew long,
He holp to speed their warm slow feet with song.

' Love, is it morning risen or night deceased
  That makes the mirth of this triumphant east ?
    Is it bliss given or bitterness put by
  That makes most glad men's hearts at love's high feast ?
    Grief smiles, joy weeps, that day should live and die.

' Is it with soul's thirst or with body's drouth
  That summer yearns out sunward to the south,
    With all the flowers that when thy birth drew nigh
  Were molten in one rose to make thy mouth ?
    O love, what care though day should live and die ?

' Is the sun glad of all the love on earth,
  The spirit and sense and work of things and worth ?
    Is the moon sad because the month must fly
  And bring her death that can but bring back birth ?
    For all these things as day must live and die.

' Love, is it day that makes thee thy delight
  Or thou that seest day made out of thy light ?
    Love, as the sun and sea are thou and I,
  Sea without sun dark, sun without sea bright ;
    The sun is one though day should live and die.

' O which is elder, night or light, who knows ?
  And life or love, which first of these twain grows ?
    For life is born of love to wail and cry,
  And love is born of life to heal his woes,
    And light of night, that day should live and die.

' O sun of heaven above the worldly sea,
  O very love, what light is this of thee !
    My sea of soul is deep as thou art high,
  But all thy light is shed through all of me,
    As love's through love, while day shall live and die.'

D

'Nay,' said Iseult, 'your song is hard to read.'
'Ay?' said he : ' or too light a song to heed,
Too slight to follow, it may be ?   Who shall sing
Of love but as a churl before a king
If by love's worth men rate his worthiness ?
Yet as the poor churl's worth to sing is less,
Surely the more shall be the great king's grace
To show for churlish love a kindlier face.'
    ' No churl,' she said, 'but one in soothsayer's wise
Who tells but truths that help no more than lies.
I have heard men sing of love a simpler way
Than these wrought riddles made of night and day,
Like jewelled reins whereon the rhyme-bells hang.'
    And Tristram smiled and changed his song and sang

' The breath between my lips of lips not mine,
  Like spirit in sense that makes pure sense divine,
    Is as life in them from the living sky
  That entering fills my heart with blood of thine
    And thee with me, while day shall live and die.

' Thy soul is shed into me with thy breath,
  And in my heart each heartbeat of thee saith
    How in thy life the lifesprings of me lie,
  Even one life to be gathered of one death
    In me and thee, though day may live and die.

' Ah, who knows now if in my veins it be
  My blood that feels life sweet, or blood of thee,
    And this thine eyesight kindled in mine eye
  That shows me in thy flesh the soul of me,
    For thine made mine, while day may live and die ?

' Ah, who knows yet if one be twain or one,
  And sunlight separable again from sun,
    And I from thee with all my lifesprings dry,
  And thou from me with all thine heartbeats done,
    Dead separate souls while day shall live and die ?

' I see my soul within thine eyes, and hear
My spirit in all thy pulses thrill with fear,
   And in my lips the passion of thee sigh,
And music of me made in mine own ear ;
   Am I not thou while day shall live and die ?

' Art thou not I as I thy love am thou ?
So let all things pass from us ; we are now,
   For all that was and will be, who knows why ?
And all that is and is not, who knows how ?
   Who knows ?   God knows why day should live and die.'

And Iseult mused and spake no word, but sought
Through all the hushed ways of her tongueless though
What face or covered likeness of a face
In what veiled hour or dream-determined place
She seeing might take for love's face, and believe
This was the spirit to whom all spirits cleave.
For that sweet wonder of the twain made one
And each one twain, incorporate sun with sun,
Star with star molten, soul with soul imbued,
And all the soul's works, all their multitude,
Made one thought and one vision and one song,
Love—this thing, this, laid hand on her so strong
She could not choose but yearn till she should see.
So went she musing down her thoughts ; but he,
Sweet-hearted as a bird that takes the sun
With clear strong eyes, and feels the glad god run
Bright through his blood and wide rejoicing wings,
And opens all himself to heaven and sings,
Made her mind light and full of noble mirth
With words and songs the gladdest grown on earth,

D 2

Till she was blithe and high of heart as he.
So swam the Swallow through the springing sea.
   And while they sat at speech as at a feast,
Came a light wind fast hardening forth of the east
And blackening till its might had marred the skies ;
And the sea thrilled as with heart-sundering sighs
One after one drawn, with each breath it drew,
And the green hardened into iron blue,
And the soft light went out of all its face.
Then Tristram girt him for an oarsman's place
And took his oar and smote, and toiled with might
In the east wind's full face and the strong sea's spite
Labouring ; and all the rowers rowed hard, but he
More mightily than any wearier three.
And Iseult watched him rowing with sinless eyes
That loved him but in holy girlish wise   .
For noble joy in his fair manliness
And trust and tender wonder ; none the less
She thought if God had given her grace to be
Man, and make war on danger of earth and sea,
Even such a man she would be ; for his stroke
Was mightiest as the mightier water broke,
And in sheer measure like strong music drave
Clean through the wet weight of the wallowing wave,
And as a tune before a great king played
For triumph was the tune their strong strokes made,
And sped the ship through with smooth strife of oars
Over the mid sea's grey foam-paven floors,
For all the loud breach of the waves at will.
So for an hour they fought the storm out still,

And the shorn foam spun from the blades, and high
The keel sprang from the wave-ridge, and the sky
Glared at them for a breath's space through the rain ;
Then the bows with a sharp shock plunged again
Down, and the sea clashed on them, and so rose
The bright stem like one panting from swift blows,
And as a swimmer's joyous beaten head
Rears itself laughing, so in that sharp stead
The light ship lifted her long quivering bows
As might the man his buffeted strong brows
Out of the wave-breach ; for with one stroke yet
Went all men's oars together, strongly set
As to loud music, and with hearts uplift
They smote their strong way through the drench and
      drift.
Till the keen hour had chafed itself to death
And the east wind fell fitfully, breath by breath,
Tired ; and across the thin and slackening rain
Sprang the face southward of the sun again.
Then all they rested and were eased at heart ;
And Iseult rose up where she sat apart,
And with her sweet soul deepening her deep eyes
Cast the furs from her and subtle embroideries
That wrapped her from the storming rain and spray,
And shining like all April in one day,
Hair, face, and throat dashed with the straying
      showers,
She stood the first of all the whole world's flowers,
And laughed on Tristram with her eyes, and said,
' I too have heart then, I was not afraid.'

And answering some light courteous word of grace
He saw her clear face lighten on his face
Unwittingly, with unenamoured eyes,
For the last time. A live man in such wise
Looks in the deadly face of his fixed hour
And laughs with lips wherein he hath no power
To keep the life yet some five minutes' space.
So Tristram looked on Iseult face to face
And knew not, and she knew not. The last time—
The last that should be told in any rhyme
Heard anywhere on mouths of singing men
That ever should sing praise of them again ;
The last hour of their hurtless hearts at rest,
The last that peace should touch them breast to
    breast,
The last that sorrow far from them should sit,
This last was with them, and they knew not it.
    For Tristram being athirst with toil now spake,
Saying, ' Iseult, for all dear love's labour's sake
Give me to drink, and give me for a pledge
The touch of four lips on the beaker's edge.'
And Iseult sought and would not wake Brangwain
Who slept as one half dead with fear and pain,
Being tender-natured ; so with hushed light feet
Went Iseult round her, with soft looks and sweet
Pitying her pain ; so sweet a spirited thing
She was, and daughter of a kindly king.
And spying what strange bright secret charge was
    kept
Fast in that maid's white bosom while she slept,

She sought and drew the gold cup forth and smiled
Marvelling, with such light wonder as a child
That hears of glad sad life in magic lands ;
And bare it back to Tristram with pure hands
Holding the love-draught that should be for flame
To burn out of them fear and faith and shame,
And lighten all their life up in men's sight,
And make them sad for ever.   Then the knight
Bowed toward her and craved whence had she this
      strange thing
That might be spoil of some dim Asian king,
By starlight stolen from some waste place of sands,
And a maid bore it here in harmless hands.
And Iseult, laughing—'Other lords that be
Feast, and their men feast after them ; but we,
Our men must keep the best wine back to feast
Till they be full and we of all men least
Feed after them and fain to fare so well :
So with mine handmaid and your squire it fell
That hid this bright thing from us in a wile :'
And with light lips yet full of their swift smile
And hands that wist not though they dug a grave,
Undid the hasps of gold, and drank, and gave,
And he drank after, a deep glad kingly draught :
And all their life changed in them, for they quaffed
Death ; if it be death so to drink, and fare
As men who change and are what these twain were.
And shuddering with eyes full of fear and fire
And heart-stung with a serpentine desire

He turned and saw the terror in her eyes
That yearned upon him shining in such wise
As a star midway in the midnight fixed.
 Their Galahault was the cup, and she that mixed;
Nor other hand there needed, nor sweet speech
To lure their lips together; each on each
Hung with strange eyes and hovered as a bird
Wounded, and each mouth trembled for a word;
Their heads neared, and their hands were drawn in
  one,
And they saw dark, though still the unsunken sun
Far through fine rain shot fire into the south;
And their four lips became one burning mouth.

II

THE QUEEN'S PLEASANCE.

OUT of the night arose the second day,
And saw the ship's bows break the shoreward spray.
As the sun's boat of gold and fire began
To sail the sea of heaven unsailed of man,
And the soft waves of sacred air to break
Round the prow launched into the morning's lake,
They saw the sign of their sea-travel done.
 Ah, was not something seen of yester-sun,
When the sweet light that lightened all the skies
Saw nothing fairer than one maiden's eyes,
That whatsoever in all time's years may be
To-day's sun nor to-morrow's sun shall see?
Not while she lives, not when she comes to die
Shall she look sunward with that sinless eye.
 Yet fairer now than song may show them stand
Tristram and Iseult, hand in amorous hand,
Soul-satisfied, their eyes made great and bright
With all the love of all the livelong night;
With all its hours yet singing in their ears

No mortal music made of thoughts and tears,
But such a song, past conscience of man's thought,
As hearing he grows god and knows it not.
Nought else they saw nor heard but what the night
Had left for seal upon their sense and sight,
Sound of past pulses beating, fire of amorous light.
Enough, and overmuch, and never yet
Enough, though love still hungering feed and fret,
To fill the cup of night which dawn must overset.
For still their eyes were dimmer than with tears
And dizzier from diviner sounds their ears
Than though from choral thunders of the quiring
     spheres.
They heard not how the landward waters rang,
Nor saw where high into the morning sprang,
Riven from the shore and bastioned with the sea,
Toward summits where the north wind's nest might be,
A wave-walled palace with its eastern gate
Full of the sunrise now and wide at wait,
And on the mighty-moulded stairs that clomb
Sheer from the fierce lip of the lapping foam
The knights of Mark that stood before the wall.
So with loud joy and storm of festival
They brought the bride in up the towery way
That rose against the rising front of day,
Stair based on stair, between the rocks unhewn,
To those strange halls wherethrough the tidal tune
Rang loud or lower from soft or strengthening sea,
Tower shouldering tower, to windward and to lee,

With change of floors and stories, flight on flight,
That clomb and curled up to the crowning height
Whence men might see wide east and west in one
And on one sea waned moon and mounting sun.
And severed from the sea-rock's base, where stand
Some worn walls yet, they saw the broken strand,
The beachless cliff that in the sheer sea dips,
The sleepless shore inexorable to ships,
And the straight causeway's bare gaunt spine between
The sea-spanned walls and naked mainland's green.
 On the mid stairs, between the light and dark,
Before the main tower's portal stood King Mark,
Crowned : and his face was as the face of one
Long time athirst and hungering for the sun
In barren thrall of bitter bonds, who now
Thinks here to feel its blessing on his brow.
A swart lean man, but kinglike, still of guise,
With black streaked beard and cold unquiet eyes,
Close-mouthed, gaunt-cheeked, wan as a morning
      moon,
Though hardly time on his worn hair had strewn
The thin first ashes from a sparing hand :
Yet little fire there burnt upon the brand,
And way-worn seemed he with life's wayfaring.
So between shade and sunlight stood the king,
And his face changed nor yearned not toward his bride;
But fixed between mild hope and patient pride
Abode what gift of rare or lesser worth
This day might bring to all his days on earth.

But at the glory of her when she came
His heart endured not : very fear and shame
Smote him, to take her by the hand and kiss,
Till both were molten in the burning bliss,
And with a thin flame flushing his cold face
He led her silent to the bridal place.
There were they wed and hallowed of the priest ;
And all the loud time of the marriage feast
One thought within three hearts was as a fire,
Where craft and faith took counsel with desire.
For when the feast had made a glorious end
They gave the new queen for her maids to tend
At dawn of bride-night, and thereafter bring
With marriage music to the bridegroom king.
Then by device of craft between them laid
To him went Brangwain delicately, and prayed
That this thing even for love's sake might not be,
But without sound or light or eye to see
She might come in to bride-bed : and he laughed,
As one that wist not well of wise love's craft,
And bade all bridal things be as she would.
Yet of his gentleness he gat not good ;
For clothed and covered with the nuptial dark
Soft like a bride came Brangwain to King Mark,
And to the queen came Tristram ; and the night
Fled, and ere danger of detective light
From the king sleeping Brangwain slid away,
And where had lain her handmaid Iseult lay.
And the king waking saw beside his head
That face yet passion-coloured, amorous red

From lips not his, and all that strange hair shed
Across the tissued pillows, fold on fold,
Innumerable, incomparable, all gold,
To fire men's eyes with wonder, and with love
Men's hearts ; so shone its flowering crown above
The brows enwound with that imperial wreath,
And framed with fragrant radiance round the face
     beneath.
  And the king marvelled, seeing with sudden start
Her very glory, and said out of his heart ;
'What have I done of good for God to bless
That all this he should give me, tress on tress,
All this great wealth and wondrous ? Was it this
That in mine arms I had all night to kiss,
And mix with me this beauty ? this that seems
More fair than heaven doth in some tired saint's
     dreams,
Being part of that same heaven ? yea, more, for he,
Though loved of God so, yet but seems to see,
But to me sinful such great grace is given
That in mine hands I hold this part of heaven
Not to mine eyes lent merely. Doth God make
Such things so godlike for man's mortal sake ?
Have I not sinned, that in this fleshly life
Have made of her a mere man's very wife ?'
  So the king mused and murmured ; and she heard
The faint sound trembling of each breathless word
And laughed into the covering of her hair.
  And many a day for many a month as fair
Slid over them like music ; and as bright
Burned with love's offerings many a secret night.

And many a dawn to many a fiery noon
Blew prelude, when the horn's heart-kindling tune
Lit the live woods with sovereign sound of mirth
Before the mightiest huntsman hailed on earth
Lord of its lordliest pleasure, where he rode
Hard by her rein whose peerless presence glowed
Not as that white queen's of the virgin hunt
Once, whose crown-crescent braves the night-wind's
      brunt,
But with the sun for frontlet of a queenlier front.
For where the flashing of her face was turned
As lightning was the fiery light that burned
From eyes and brows enkindled more with speed
And rapture of the rushing of her steed
Than once with only beauty ; and her mouth
Was as a rose athirst that pants for drouth
Even while it laughs for pleasure of desire,
And all her heart was as a leaping fire.
Yet once more joy they took of woodland ways
Than came of all those flushed and fiery days
When the loud air was mad with life and sound,
Through many a dense green mile, of horn and hound
Before the king's hunt going along the wind,
And ere the timely leaves were changed or thinned,
Even in mid maze of summer.   For the knight
Forth was once ridden toward some frontier fight
Against the lewd folk of the Christless lands
That warred with wild and intermittent hands
Against the king's north border ; and there came
A knight unchristened yet of unknown name,

Swart Palamede, upon a secret quest,
To high Tintagel, and abode as guest
In likeness of a minstrel with the king.
Nor was there man could sound so sweet a string,
Save Tristram only, of all held best on earth.
And one loud eve, being full of wine and mirth,
Ere sunset left the walls and waters dark,
To that strange minstrel strongly swore King Mark,
By all that makes a knight's faith firm and strong,
That he for guerdon of his harp and song
Might crave and have his liking. Straight there came
Up the swart cheek a flash of swarthier flame,
And the deep eyes fulfilled of glittering night
Laughed out in lightnings of triumphant light
As the grim harper spake : ' O king, I crave
No gift of man that king may give to slave,
But this thy crowned queen only, this thy wife,
Whom yet unseen I loved, and set my life
On this poor chance to compass, even as here,
Being fairer famed than all save Guenevere.'
Then as the noise of seaward storm that mocks
With roaring laughter from reverberate rocks
The cry from ships near shipwreck, harsh and high
Rose all the wrath and wonder in one cry
Through all the long roof's hollow depth and length
That hearts of strong men kindled in their strength
May speak in laughter lion-like, and cease,
Being wearied : only two men held their peace
And each glared hard on other : but King Mark
Spake first of these : ' Man, though thy craft be dark

And thy mind evil that begat this thing,
Yet stands the word once plighted of a king
Fast : and albeit less evil it were for me
To give my life up than my wife, or be
A landless man crowned only with a curse,
Yet this in God's and all men's sight were worse,
To live soul-shamed, a man of broken troth,
Abhorred of men as I abhor mine oath
Which yet I may forswear not.'   And he bowed
His head, and wept : and all men wept aloud,
Save one, that heard him weeping : but the queen
Wept not : and statelier yet than eyes had seen
That ever looked upon her queenly state
She rose, and in her eyes her heart was great
And full of wrath seen manifest and scorn
More strong than anguish to go thence forlorn
Of all men's comfort and her natural right.
And they went forth into the dawn of night.
Long by wild ways and clouded light they rode,
Silent ; and fear less keen at heart abode
With Iseult than with Palamede : for awe
Constrained him, and the might of love's high law,
That can make lewd men loyal ; and his heart
Yearned on her, if perchance with amorous art
And soothfast skill of very love he might
For courtesy find favour in her sight
And comfort of her mercies : for he wist
More grace might come of that sweet mouth unkissed
Than joy for violence done it, that should make
His name abhorred for shame's disloyal sake.

And in the stormy starlight clouds were thinned
And thickened by short gusts of changing wind
That panted like a sick man's fitful breath:
And like a moan of lions hurt to death
Came the sea's hollow noise along the night.
But ere its gloom from aught but foam had light
They halted, being aweary : and the knight
As reverently forbore her where she lay
As one that watched his sister's sleep till day.
Nor durst he kiss or touch her hand or hair
For love and shamefast pity, seeing how fair
She slept, and fenceless from the fitful air.
And shame at heart stung nigh to death desire,
But grief at heart burned in him like a fire
For hers and his own sorrowing sake, that had
Such grace for guerdon as makes glad men sad,
To have their will and want it.   And the day
Sprang : and afar along the wild waste way
They heard the pulse and press of hurrying horse-
    hoofs play :
And like the rushing of a ravenous flame
Whose wings make tempest of the darkness, came
Upon them headlong as in thunder borne
Forth of the darkness of the labouring morn
Tristram: and up forthright upon his steed
Leapt, as one blithe of battle, Palamede,
And mightily with shock of horse and man
They lashed together : and fair that fight began
As fair came up that sunrise : to and fro,
With knees nigh staggered and stout heads bent low

E

From each quick shock of spears on either side,
Reeled the strong steeds heavily, haggard-eyed
And heartened high with passion of their pride
As sheer the stout spears shocked again, and flew
Sharp-splintering: then, his sword as each knight drew,
They flashed and foined full royally, so long
That but to see so fair a strife and strong
A man might well have given out of his life
One year's void space forlorn of love or strife.
As when a bright north-easter, great of heart,
Scattering the strengths of squadrons, hurls apart
Ship from ship labouring violently, in such toil
As earns but ruin—with even so strong recoil
Back were the steeds hurled from the spear-shock, fain
And foiled of triumph : then with tightened rein
And stroke of spur, inveterate, either knight
Bore in again upon his foe with might,
Heart-hungry for the hot-mouthed feast of fight
And all athirst of mastery : but full soon
The jarring notes of that tempestuous tune
Fell, and its mighty music made of hands
Contending, clamorous through the loud waste lands,
Broke at once off ; and shattered from his steed
Fell, as a mainmast ruining, Palamede,
Stunned : and those lovers left him where he lay,
And lightly through green lawns they rode away.
   There was a bower beyond man's eye more fair
Than ever summer dews and sunniest air
Fed full with rest and radiance till the boughs
Had wrought a roof as for a holier house

Than aught save love might breathe in ; fairer far
Than keeps the sweet light back of moon and star
From high kings' chambers: there might love and sleep
Divide for joy the darkling hours, and keep
With amorous alternation of sweet strife
The soft and secret ways of death and life
Made smooth for pleasure's feet to rest and run
Even from the moondawn to the kindling sun,
Made bright for passion's feet to run and rest
Between the midnight's and the morning's breast,
Where hardly though her happy head lie down
It may forget the hour that wove its crown ;
Where hardly though her joyous limbs be laid
They may forget the mirth that midnight made.
And thither, ere sweet night had slain sweet day,
Iseult and Tristram took their wandering way,
And rested, and refreshed their hearts with cheer
In hunters' fashion of the woods ; and here
More sweet it seemed, while this might be, to dwell
And take of all world's weariness farewell
Than reign of all world's lordship queen and king.
Nor here would time for three moons' changes bring
Sorrow nor thought of sorrow ; but sweet earth
Fostered them like her babes of eldest birth,
Reared warm in pathless woods and cherished well
And the sun sprang above the sea and fell,
And the stars rose and sank upon the sea ;
And outlaw-like, in forest wise and free,
The rising and the setting of their lights
Found those twain dwelling all those days and nights

And under change of sun and star and moon
Flourished and fell the chaplets woven of June,
And fair through fervours of the deepening sky
Panted and passed the hours that lit July,
And each day blessed them out of heaven above,
And each night crowned them with the crown of love.
Nor till the might of August overhead
Weighed on the world was yet one roseleaf shed
Of all their joy's warm coronal, nor aught
Touched them in passing ever with a thought
That ever this might end on any day
Or any night not love them where they lay ;
But like a babbling tale of barren breath
Seemed all report and rumour held of death,
And a false bruit the legend tear-impearled
That such a thing as change was in the world.
And each bright song upon his lips that came,
Mocking the powers of change and death by name,
Blasphemed their bitter godhead, and defied
Time, though clothed round with ruin as kings with
   pride,
To blot the glad life out of love : and she
Drank lightly deep of his philosophy
In that warm wine of amorous words which is
Sweet with all truths of all philosophies.
For well he wist all subtle ways of song,
And in his soul the secret eye was strong
That burns in meditation, till bright words
Break flamelike forth as notes from fledgeling birds

That feel the soul speak through them of the spring.
So fared they night and day as queen and king
Crowned of a kingdom wide as day and night.
Nor ever cloudlet swept or swam in sight
Across the darkling depths of their delight
Whose stars no skill might number, nor man's art
Sound the deep stories of its heavenly heart.
Till, even for wonder that such life should live,
Desires and dreams of what death's self might give
Would touch with tears and laughter and wild speech
The lips and eyes of passion, fain to reach,
Beyond all bourne of time or trembling sense,
The verge of love's last possible eminence.
Out of the heaven that storm nor shadow mars,
Deep from the starry depth beyond the stars,
A yearning ardour without scope or name
Fell on them, and the bright night's breath of flame
Shot fire into their kisses; and like fire
The lit dews lightened on the leaves, as higher
Night's heart beat on toward midnight. Far and fain
Somewhiles the soft rush of rejoicing rain
Solaced the darkness, and from steep to steep
Of heaven they saw the sweet sheet lightning leap
And laugh its heart out in a thousand smiles,
When the clear sea for miles on glimmering miles
Burned as though dawn were strewn abroad astray,
Or, showering out of heaven, all heaven's array
Had paven instead the waters : fain and far
Somewhiles the burning love of star for star

Spake words that love might wellnigh seem to hear
In such deep hours as turn delight to fear
Sweet as delight's self ever.　So they lay
Tranced once, nor watched along the fiery bay
The shine of summer darkness palpitate and play.
She had nor sight nor voice ; her swooning eyes
Knew not if night or light were in the skies ;
Across her beauty sheer the moondawn shed
Its light as on a thing as white and dead ;
Only with stress of soft fierce hands she prest
Between the throbbing blossoms of her breast
His ardent face, and through his hair her breath
Went quivering as when life is hard on death ;
And with strong trembling fingers she strained fast
His head into her bosom ; till at last,
Satiate with sweetness of that burning bed,
His eyes afire with tears, he raised his head
And laughed into her lips ; and all his heart
Filled hers ; then face from face fell, and apart
Each hung on each with panting lips, and felt
Sense into sense and spirit in spirit melt.

　'Hast thou no sword? I would not live till day ;
O love, this night and we must pass away,
It must die soon, and let not us die late.'

　'Take then my sword and slay me ; nay, but wait
Till day be risen ; what, wouldst thou think to die
Before the light take hold upon the sky ? '

　'Yea, love ; for how shall we have twice, being
　　twain,
This very night of love's most rapturous reign ?

Live thou and have thy day, and year by year
Be great, but what shall I be? Slay me here;
Let me die not when love lies dead, but now
Strike through my heart : nay, sweet, what heart hast
    thou ?
Is it so much I ask thee, and spend my breath
In asking? nay, thou knowest it is but death.
Hadst thou true heart to love me, thou wouldst give
This : but for hate's sake thou wilt let me live.'

    Here he caught up her lips with his, and made
The wild prayer silent in her heart that prayed,
And strained her to him till all her faint breath sank
And her bright light limbs palpitated and shrank
And rose and fluctuated as flowers in rain
That bends them and they tremble and rise again
And heave and straighten and quiver all through with
    bliss
And turn afresh their mouths up for a kiss,
Amorous, athirst of that sweet influent love ;
So, hungering toward his hovering lips above,
Her red-rose mouth yearned silent, and her eyes
Closed, and flashed after, as through June's darkest
    skies
The divine heartbeats of the deep live light
Make open and shut the gates of the outer night.
    Long lay they still, subdued with love, nor knew
If cloud or light changed colour as it grew,
If star or moon beheld them; if above
The heaven of night waxed fiery with their love,

Or earth beneath were moved at heart and root
To burn as they, to burn and bring forth fruit
Unseasonable for love's sake ; if tall trees
Bowed, and close flowers yearned open, and the breeze
Failed and fell silent as a flame that fails :
And all that hour unheard the nightingales
Clamoured, and all the woodland soul was stirred,
And depth and height were one great song unheard,
As though the world caught music and took fire
From the instant heart alone of their desire.
  So sped their night of nights between them : so,
For all fears past and shadows, shine and snow,
That one pure hour all-golden where they lay
Made their life perfect and their darkness day.
And warmer waved its harvest yet to reap,
Till in the lovely fight of love and sleep
At length had sleep the mastery ; and the dark
Was lit with soft live gleams they might not mark,
Fleet butterflies, each like a dead flower's ghost,
White, blue, and sere leaf-coloured ; but the most
White as the sparkle of snow-flowers in the sun
Ere with his breath they lie at noon undone
Whose kiss devours their tender beauty, and leaves
But raindrops on the grass and sere thin leaves
That were engraven with traceries of the snow
Flowerwise ere any flower of earth's would blow ;
So swift they sprang and sank, so sweet and light
They swam the deep dim breathless air of night.
Now on her rose-white amorous breast half bare,
Now on her slumberous love-dishevelled hair,

The white wings lit and vanished, and afresh
Lit soft as snow lights on her snow-soft flesh,
On hand or throat or shoulder ; and she stirred
Sleeping, and spake some tremulous bright word,
And laughed upon some dream too sweet for truth,
Yet not so sweet as very love and youth
That there had charmed her eyes to sleep at last.
Nor woke they till the perfect night was past,
And the soft sea thrilled with blind hope of light.
But ere the dusk had well the sun in sight
He turned and kissed her eyes awake and said,
Seeing earth and water neither quick nor dead
And twilight hungering toward the day to be,
'As the dawn loves the sunlight I love thee.'
And even as rays with cloudlets in the skies
Confused in brief love's bright contentious wise,
Sleep strove with sense rekindling in her eyes ;
And as the flush of birth scarce overcame
The pale pure pearl of unborn light with flame
Soft as may touch the rose's heart with shame
To break not all reluctant out of bud,
Stole up her sleeping cheek her waking blood ;
And with the lovely laugh of love that takes
The whole soul prisoner ere the whole sense wakes,
Her lips for love's sake bade love's will be done.
And all the sea lay subject to the sun.

III.

TRISTRAM IN BRITTANY.

*" As the dawn loves the sunlight I love thee ; "
As men that shall be swallowed of the sea
Love the sea's lovely beauty ; as the night
That wanes before it loves the young sweet light,
And dies of loving ; as the worn-out noon
Loves twilight, and as twilight loves the moon
That on its grave a silver seal shall set—
We have loved and slain each other, and love yet.
Slain ; for we live not surely, being in twain :
In her I lived, and in me she is slain,
Who loved me that I brought her to her doom,
Who loved her that her love might be my tomb.
As all the streams on earth and all fresh springs
And sweetest waters, every brook that sings,
Each fountain where the young year dips its wings
First, and the first-fledged branches of it wave,
Even with one heart's love seek one bitter grave.
From hills that first see bared the morning's breast
And heights the sun last yearns to from the west,

All tend but toward the sea, all born most high
Strive downward, passing all things joyous by,
Seek to it and cast their lives in it and die.
So strive all lives for death which all lives win ;
So sought her soul to my soul, and therein
Was poured and perished : O my love, and mine
Sought to thee and died of thee and died as thine.
As the dawn loves the sunlight that must cease
Ere dawn again may rise and pass in peace ;
Must die that she being dead may live again,
To be by his new rising nearly slain.
So rolls the great wheel of the great world round,
And no change in it and no fault is found,
And no true life of perdurable breath,
And surely no irrevocable death.
Day after day night comes that day may break,
And day comes back for night's reiterate sake.
Each into each dies, each of each is born :
Day past is night, shall night past not be morn ?
Out of this moonless and faint-hearted night
That love yet lives in, shall there not be light ?
Light strong as love, that love may live in yet ?
Alas, but how shall foolish hope forget
How all these loving things that kill and die
Meet not but for a breath's space and pass by ?
Night is kissed once of dawn and dies, and day
But touches twilight and is rapt away.
So may my love and her love meet once more,
And meeting be divided as of yore.

Yea, surely as the day-star loves the sun
And when he hath risen is utterly undone,
So is my love of her and hers of me—
And its most sweetness bitter as the sea.
Would God yet dawn might see the sun and die !'
   Three years had looked on earth and passed it by
Since Tristram looked on Iseult, when he stood
So communing with dreams of evil and good,
And let all sad thoughts through his spirit sweep
As leaves through air or tears through eyes that weep
Or snowflakes through dark weather : and his soul,
That had seen all those sightless seasons roll
One after one, wave over weary wave,
Was in him as a corpse is in its grave.
Yet, for his heart was mighty, and his might
Through all the world as a great sound and light,
The mood was rare upon him ; save that here
In the low sundawn of the lightening year
With all last year's toil and its triumph done
He could not choose but yearn for that set sun
Which at this season saw the firstborn kiss
That made his lady's mouth one fire with his.
Yet his great heart being greater than his grief
Kept all the summer of his strength in leaf
And all the rose of his sweet spirit in flower;
Still his soul fed upon the sovereign hour
That had been or that should be ; and once more
He looked through drifted sea and drifting shore
That crumbled in the wave-breach, and again
Spake sad and deep within himself : ' What pain

Should make a man's soul wholly break and die,
Sapped as weak sand by water?   How shall I
Be less than all less things are that endure
And strive and yield when time is?   Nay, full sure
All these and we are parts of one same end ;
And if through fire or water we twain tend
To that sure life where both must be made one,
If one we be, what matter?   Thou, O sun,
The face of God, if God thou be not—nay,
What but God should I think thee, what should say,
Seeing thee rerisen, but very God?—should I,
I fool, rebuke thee sovereign in thy sky,
The clouds dead round thee and the air alive,
The winds that lighten and the waves that strive
Toward this shore as to that beneath thy breath,
Because in me my thoughts bear all towards death?
O sun, that when we are dead wilt rise as bright,
Air deepening up toward heaven, and nameless light,
And heaven immeasurable, and faint clouds blown
Between us and the lowest aerial zone
And each least skirt of their imperial state—
Forgive us that we held ourselves so great !
What should I do to curse you?   I indeed
Am a thing meaner than this least wild seed
That my foot bruises and I know not—yet
Would not be mean enough for worms to fret
Before their time and mine was.
                              ' Ah, and ye
Light washing weeds, blind waifs of dull blind sea,

Do ye so thirst and hunger and aspire,
Are ye so moved with such long strong desire
In the ebb and flow of your sad life, and strive
Still toward some end ye shall not see alive—
But at high noon ye know it by light and heat
Some half-hour, till ye feel the fresh tide beat
Up round you, and at night's most bitter noon
The ripples leave you naked to the moon?
And this dim dusty heather that I tread,
These half-born blossoms, born at once and dead,
Sere brown as funeral cloths, and purple as pall,
What if some life and grief be in them all?
  'Ay, what of these? but, O strong sun! O sea!
I bid not you, divine things! comfort me,
I stand not up to match you in your sight—
Who hath said ye have mercy toward us, ye who have
    might?
And though ye had mercy, I think I would not pray
That ye should change your counsel or your way
To make our life less bitter : if such power
Be given the stars on one deciduous hour,
And such might be in planets to destroy
Grief and rebuild, and break and build up joy,
What man would stretch forth hand on them to make
Fate mutable, God foolish, for his sake?
For if in life or death be aught of trust,
And if some unseen just God or unjust
Put soul into the body of natural things
And in time's pauseless feet and worldwide wings

Some spirit of impulse and some sense of will
That steers them through the seas of good and ill
To some incognizable and actual end,
Be it just or unjust, foe to man or friend,
How should we make the stable spirit to swerve,
How teach the strong soul of the world to serve,
The imperious will in time and sense in space
That gives man life turn back to give man place—
The conscious law lose conscience of its way,
The rule and reason fail from night and day,
The streams flow back toward whence the springs
    began,
That less of thirst might sear the lips of man?
Let that which is be, and sure strengths stand sure,
And evil or good and death or life endure,
Not alterable and rootless, but indeed
A very stem born of a very seed
That brings forth fruit in season: how should this
Die that was sown, and that not be which is,
And the old fruit change that came of the ancient
    root,
And he that planted bid it not bear fruit,
And he that watered smite his vine with drouth
Because its grapes are bitter in our mouth,
And he that kindled quench the sun with night
Because its beams are fire against our sight,
And he that tuned untune the sounding spheres
Because their song is thunder in our ears?
How should the skies change and the stars, and time
Break the large concord of the years that chime,

Answering, as wave to wave beneath the moon
That draws them shoreward, mar the whole tide's tune
For the instant foam's sake on one turning wave—
For man's sake that is grass upon a grave?
How should the law that knows not soon or late,
For whom no time nor space is—how should fate,
That is not good nor evil, wise nor mad,
Nor just nor unjust, neither glad nor sad—
How should the one thing that hath being, the one
That moves not as the stars move or the sun
Or any shadow or shape that lives or dies
In likeness of dead earth or living skies,
But its own darkness and its proper light
Clothe it with other names than day. or night,
And its own soul of strength and spirit of breath
Feed it with other powers than life or death—
How should it turn from its great way to give
Man that must die a clearer space to live?
Why should the waters of the sea be cleft,
The hills be molten to his right and left,
That he from deep to deep might pass dry-shod,
Or look between the viewless heights on God?
Hath he such eyes as, when the shadows flee,
The sun looks out with to salute the sea?
Is his hand bounteous as the morning's hand?
Or where the night stands hath he feet to stand?
Will the storm cry not when he bids it cease?
Is it his voice that saith to the east wind, Peace?
Is his breath mightier than the west wind's breath?
Doth his heart know the things of life and death?

F

Can his face bring forth sunshine and give rain,
Or his weak will that dies and lives again
Make one thing certain or bind one thing fast,
That as he willed it shall be at the last?
How should the storms of heaven and kindled lights
And all the depths of things and topless heights
And air and earth and fire and water change
Their likeness, and the natural world grow strange,
And all the limits of their life undone
Lose count of time and conscience of the sun,
And that fall under which was fixed above,
That man might have a larger hour for love?'
    So musing with close lips and lifted eyes
That smiled with self-contempt to live so wise,
With silent heart so hungry now so long,
So late grown clear, so miserably made strong,
About the wolds a banished man he went,
The brown wolds bare and sad as banishment,
By wastes of fruitless flowerage, and grey downs
That felt the sea-wind shake their wild-flower crowns
As though fierce hands would pluck from some grey
        head
The spoils of majesty despised and dead,
And fill with crying and comfortless strange sound
Their hollow sides and heights of herbless ground.
Yet as he went fresh courage on him came,
Till dawn rose too within him as a flame,
The heart of the ancient hills and his were one ;
The winds took counsel with him, and the sun

Spake comfort; in his ears the shout of birds
Was as the sound of clear sweet-spirited words,
The noise of streams as laughter from above
Of the old wild lands, and as a cry of love
Spring's trumpet-blast blown over moor and lea :
The skies were red as love is, and the sea
Was as the floor of heaven for love to tread.
So went he as with light about his head,
And in the joyous travail of the year
Grew April-hearted; since nor grief nor fear
Can master so a young man's blood so long
That it shall move not to the mounting song
Of that sweet hour when earth replumes her wings
And with fair face and heart set heavenward sings
As an awakened angel unaware
That feels his sleep fall from him, and his hair
By some new breath of wind and music stirred,
Till like the sole song of one heavenly bird
Sounds all the singing of the host of heaven,
And all the glories of the sovereign Seven
Are as one face of one incorporate light.
And as that host of singers in God's sight
Might draw toward one that slumbered, and arouse
The lips requickened and rekindling brows,
So seemed the earthly host of all things born
In sight of spring and eyeshot of the morn,
All births of land or waifs of wind and sea,
To draw toward him that sorrowed, and set free
From presage and remembrance of all pains
The life that leapt and lightened in his veins.

So with no sense abashed nor sunless look,
But with exalted eyes and heart, he took
His part of sun or storm-wind, and was glad,
For all things lost, of these good things he had.
   And the spring loved him surely, being from birth
One made out of the better part of earth,
A man born as at sunrise ; one that saw
Not without reverence and sweet sense of awe
But wholly without fear or fitful breath
The face of life watched by the face of death ;
And living took his fill of rest and strife,
Of love and change, and fruit and seed of life,
And when his time to live in light was done
With unbent head would pass out of the sun :
A spirit as morning, fair and clear and strong,
Whose thought and work were as one harp and song
Heard through the world as in a strange king's hall
Some great guest's voice that sings of festival.
So seemed all things to love him, and his heart
In all their joy of life to take such part,
That with the live earth and the living sea
He was as one that communed mutually
With naked heart to heart of friend to friend :
And the star deepening at the sunset's end,
And the moon fallen before the gate of day
As one sore wearied with vain length of way,
And the winds wandering, and the streams and skies,
As faces of his fellows in his eyes.
Nor lacked there love where he was evermore
Of man and woman, friend of sea or shore,

Not measurable with weight of graven gold,
Free as the sun's gift of the world to hold
Given each day back to man's reconquering sight
That loses but its lordship for a night.
And now that after many a season spent
In barren ways and works of banishment,
Toil of strange fights and many a fruitless field,
Ventures of quest and vigils under shield,
He came back to the strait of sundering sea
That parts green Cornwall from grey Brittany,
Where dwelt the high king's daughter of the lands,
Iseult, named alway from her fair white hands,
She looked on him and loved him ; but being young
Made shamefastness a seal upon her tongue,
And on her heart, that none might hear its cry,
Set the sweet signet of humility.
Yet when he came a stranger in her sight,
A banished man and weary, no such knight
As when the Swallow dipped her bows in foam
Steered singing that imperial Iseult home,
This maiden with her sinless sixteen years
Full of sweet thoughts and hopes that played at fears
Cast her eyes on him but in courteous wise,
And lo, the man's face burned upon her eyes
As though she had turned them on the naked sun :
And through her limbs she felt sweet passion run
As fire that flowed down from her face, and beat
  Soft through stirred veins on even to her hands and
    feet

As all her body were one heart on flame,
Athrob with love and wonder and sweet shame.
And when he spake there sounded in her ears
As 'twere a song out of the graves of years
Heard, and again forgotten, and again
Remembered with a rapturous pulse of pain.
But as the maiden mountain snow sublime
Takes the first sense of April's trembling time
Soft on a brow that burns not though it blush
To feel the sunrise hardly half aflush,
So took her soul the sense of change, nor thought
That more than maiden love was more than nought.
Her eyes went hardly after him, her cheek
Grew scarce a goodlier flower to hear him speak,
Her bright mouth no more trembled than a rose
May for the least wind's breathless sake that blows
Too soft to sue save for a sister's kiss,
And if she sighed in sleep she knew not this.
Yet in her heart hovered the thoughts of things
Past, that with lighter or with heavier wings
Beat round about her memory, till it burned
With grief that brightened and with hope that yearned,
Seeing him so great and sad, nor knowing what fate
Had bowed and crowned a head so sad and great.
Nor might she guess but little, first or last,
Though all her heart so hung upon his past,
Of what so bowed him for what sorrow's sake :
For scarce of aught at any time he spake
That from his own land oversea had sent
His lordly life to barren banishment.

Yet still or soft or keen remembrance clung
Close round her of the least word from his tongue
That fell by chance of courtesy, to greet
With grace of tender thanks her pity, sweet
As running streams to men's way-wearied feet.
And when between strange words her name would fall
Suddenly straightway to that lure's recall
Back would his heart bound as the falconer's bird
And tremble and bow down before the word.
'Iseult'—and all the cloudlike world grew flame,
And all his heart flashed lightning at her name;
'Iseult'—and all the wan waste weary skies
Shone as his queen's own love-enkindled eyes.
And seeing the bright blood in his face leap up
As red wine mantling in a royal cup
To hear the sudden sweetness of the sound
Ring, but ere well his heart had time to bound
His cheek would change, and grief bow down his
    head,
'Haply,' the girl's heart, though she spake not, said,
'This name of mine was worn of one long dead,
Some sister that he loved:' and therewithal
Would pity bring her heart more deep in thrall.
But once, when winds about the world made mirth,
And March held revel hard on April's birth
Till air and sea were jubilant as earth,
Delight and doubt in sense and soul began,
And yearning of the maiden toward the man,
Harping on high before her : for his word
Was fire that kindled in her heart that heard,

And alway through the rhymes reverberate came
The virginal soft burden of her name.
And ere the full song failed upon her ear
Joy strove within her till it cast out fear,
And all her heart was. as his harp, and rang
Swift music, made of hope whose birthnote sprang
Bright in the blood that kindled as he sang.

‘ Stars know not how we call them, nor may flowers
Know by what happy name the hovering hours
   Baptize their new-born heads with dew and flame :
And Love, adored of all time as of ours,
   Iseult, knew nought for ages of his name.

‘With many tongues men called on him, but he
Wist not which word of all might worthiest be
   To sound for ever in his ear the same,
Till heart of man might hear and soul might see,
   Iseult, the radiance ringing from thy name.

‘ By many names men called him, as the night
By many a name calls many a starry light,
   Her several sovereigns of dividual fame ;
But day by one name only calls aright,
   Iseult, the sun that bids men praise his name.

‘ In many a name of man his name soared high
And song shone round it soaring, till the sky
   Rang rapture, and the world’s fast-founded·frame
Trembled with sense of triumph, even as I,
   Iseult, with sense of worship at thy name.

‘ In many a name of woman smiled his power
Incarnate, as all summer in a flower,
   Till winter bring forgetfulness or shame :
But thine, the keystone of his topless tower,
   Iseult, is one with Love’s own lordliest name.

'Iseult my love, Iseult my queen twice crowned,
  In thee my death, in thee my life lies bound :
    Names are there yet that all men's hearts acclaim,
  But Love's own heart rings answer to the sound,
    Iseult, that bids it bow before thy name.'

There ceased his voice yearning upon the word,
Struck with strong passion dumb : but she that heard
Quailed to the heart, and trembled ere her eyes
Durst let the loving light within them rise,
And yearn on his for answer : yet at last,
Albeit not all her fear was overpast,
Hope, kindling even the frost of fear apace
With sweet fleet bloom and breath of gradual grace,
Flushed in the changing roses of her face.
And ere the strife took truce of white with red,
Or joy for soft shame's sake durst lift up head,
Something she would and would not fain have said,
And wist not what the fluttering word would be,
But rose and reached forth to him her hand : and he,
Heart-stricken, bowed his head and dropped his knee,
And on her fragrant hand his lips were fire ;
And their two hearts were as one trembling lyre
Touched by the keen wind's kiss with brief desire
And music shuddering at its own delight.
So dawned the moonrise of their marriage night.

IV

THE MAIDEN MARRIAGE.

SPRING watched her last moon burn and fade with
    May
While the days deepened toward a bridal day.
And on her snowbright hand the ring was set
While in the maiden's ear the song's word yet
Hovered, that hailed as love's own queen by name
Iseult : and in her heart the word was flame ;
A pulse of light, a breath of tender fire,
Too dear for doubt, too driftless for desire.
Between her father's hand and brother's led
From hall to shrine, from shrine to marriage-bed,
She saw not how by hap at home-coming
Fell from her new lord's hand a royal ring,
Whereon he looked, and felt the pulse astart
Speak passion in his faith-forsaken heart.
For this was given him of the hand wherein
That heart's pledge lay for ever : so the sin
That should be done if truly he should take
This maid to wife for strange love's faithless sake

Struck all his mounting spirit abashed, and fear
Fell cold for shame's sake on his changing cheer.
Yea, shame's own fire that burned upon his brow
To bear the brand there of a broken vow
Was frozen again for very fear thereof
That wrung his heart with keener pangs than love.
And all things rose upon him, all things past
Ere last they parted, cloven in twain at last,
Iseult from Tristram, Tristram from the queen;
And how men found them in the wild woods green
Sleeping, but sundered by the sword between,
Dividing breast from amorous breast a span,
But scarce in heart the woman from the man
As far as hope from joy or sleep from truth,
And Mark that saw them held for sacred sooth
These were no fleshly lovers, by that sign
That severed them, still slumbering ; so divine
He deemed it : how at waking they beheld
The king's folk round the king, and uncompelled
Were fain to follow and fare among them home
Back to the towers washed round with rolling foam
And storied halls wherethrough sea-music rang :
And how report thereafter swelled and sprang,
A full-mouthed serpent, hissing in men's ears
Word of their loves : and one of all his peers
That most he trusted, being his kinsman born,
A man base-moulded for the stamp of scorn,
Whose heart with hate was keen and cold and dark,
Gave note by midnight whisper to King Mark

Where he might take them sleeping ; how ere day
Had seen the grim next morning all away
Fast bound they brought him down a weary way
With forty knights about him, and their chief
That traitor who for trust had given him grief,
To the old hoar chapel, like a strait stone tomb
Sheer on the sea-rocks, there to take his doom :
How, seeing he needs must die, he bade them yet
Bethink them if they durst for shame forget
What deeds for Cornwall had he done, and wrought
For all their sake what rescue, when he fought
Against the fierce foul Irish foe that came
To take of them for tribute in their shame
Three hundred heads of children ; whom in fight
His hand redeeming slew Moraunt the knight
That none durst lift his eyes against, not one
Had heart but he, who now had help of none,
To take the battle ; whence great shame it were
To knighthood, yea, foul shame on all men there,
To see him die so shamefully : nor durst
One man look up, nor one make answer first,
Save even the very traitor, who defied
And would have slain him naked in his pride,
But he, that saw the sword plucked forth to slay,
Looked on his hands, and wrenched their bonds
    away,
Haling those twain that he went bound between
Suddenly to him, and kindling in his mien
Shone lion-fashion forth with eyes alight,

And lion-wise leapt on that kinsman knight
And wrung forth of his felon hands with might
The sword that should have slain him weaponless
And smote him sheer down : then came all the press
All raging in upon him; but he wrought
So well for his deliverance as they fought
That ten strong knights rejoicingly he slew,
And took no wound, nor wearied : then the crew
Waxed greater, and their cry on him ; but he
Had won the chapel now above the sea
That chafed right under : then the heart in him
Sprang, seeing the low cliff clear to leap, and swim
Right out by the old blithe way the sea-mew takes
Across the bounding billow-belt that breaks
For ever, but the loud bright chain it makes
To bind the bridal bosom of the land
Time shall unlink not ever, till his hand
Fall by its own last blow dead : thence again
Might he win forth into the green great main
Far on beyond, and there yield up his breath
At least, with God's will, by no shameful death,
Or haply save himself, and come anew
Some long day later, ere sweet life were through.
And as the sea-gull hovers high, and turns
With eyes wherein the keen heart glittering yearns
Down toward the sweet green sea whereon the broad
    noon burns,
And suddenly, soul-stricken with delight,
Drops, and the glad wave gladdens, and the light
Sees wing and wave confuse their fluttering white,

So Tristram one brief breathing-space apart
Hung, and gazed down ; then with exulting heart
Plunged : and the fleet foam round a joyous head
Flashed, that shot under, and ere a shaft had sped
Rose again radiant, a rejoicing star,
And high along the water-ways afar
Triumphed : and all they deemed he needs must die ;
But Gouvernayle his squire, that watched hard by,
Sought where perchance a man might win ashore,
Striving, with strong limbs labouring long and sore,
And there abode an hour : till as from fight
Crowned with hard conquest won by mastering might,
Hardly, but happier for the imperious toil,
Swam the knight in forth of the close waves' coil,
Sea-satiate, bruised with buffets of the brine,
Laughing, and flushed as one afire with wine :
All this came hard upon him in a breath ;
And how he marvelled in his heart that death
Should be no bitterer than it seemed to be
There, in the strenuous impulse of the sea
Borne as to battle deathward : and at last
How all his after seasons overpast
Had brought him darkling to this dark sweet hour,
Where his foot faltered nigh the bridal bower.
And harder seemed the passage now to pass,
Though smoother-seeming than the still sea's glass,
More fit for very manhood's heart to fear,
Than all straits past of peril.   Hardly here
Might aught of all things hearten him save one,
Faith : and as men's eyes quail before the sun

So quailed his heart before the star whose light
Put out the torches of his bridal night,
So quailed and shrank with sense of faith's keen star
That burned as fire beheld by night afar
Deep in the darkness of his dreams ; for all
The bride-house now seemed hung with heavier pall
Than clothes the house of mourning.   Yet at last,
Soul sick with trembling at the heart, he passed
Into the sweet light of the maiden bower
Where lay the lonely lily-featured flower
That, lying within his hand to gather, yet
Might not be gathered of it.   Fierce regret
And bitter loyalty strove hard at strife
With amorous pity toward the tender wife
That wife indeed might never be, to wear
The very crown of wedlock ; never bear
Children, to watch and worship her white hair
When time should change, with hand more soft than
    snow,
The fashion of its glory ; never know
The loveliness of laughing love that lives
On little lips of children : all that gives
Glory and grace and reverence and delight
To wedded woman by her bridal right,
All praise and pride that flowers too fair to fall,
Love that should give had stripped her of them all
And left her bare for ever.   So his thought
Consumed him, as a fire within that wrought
Visibly, ravening till its wrath were spent :
So pale he stood, so bowed and passion-rent,
Before the blithe-faced bride-folk, ere he went

Within the chamber, heavy-eyed : and there
Gleamed the white hands and glowed the glimmering
    hair
That might but move his memory more of one more
    fair,
More fair than all this beauty : but in sooth
So fair she too shone in her flower of youth
That scarcely might man's heart hold fast its truth,
Though strong, who gazed upon her : for her eyes
Were emerald-soft as evening-coloured skies,
And a smile in them like the light therein
Slept, or shone out in joy that knew not sin,
Clear as a child's own laughter : and her mouth,
Albeit no rose full-hearted from the south
And passion-coloured for the perfect kiss
That signs the soul for love and stamps it his,
Was soft and bright as any bud new-blown ;
And through her cheek the gentler lifebloom shone
Of mild wild roses nigh the northward sea.
So in her bride-bed lay the bride : and he
Drew nigh, and all the high sad heart in him
Yearned on her, seeing the twilight meek and dim
Through all the soft alcove tremblingly lit
With hovering silver, as a heart in it
Beating, that burned from one deep lamp above,
Fainter than fire of torches, as the love
Within him fainter than a bridegroom's fire,
No marriage-torch red with the heart's desire,
But silver-soft, a flameless light that glowed
Starlike along night's dark and starry road

G

Wherein his soul was traveller.   And he sighed,
Seeing, and with eyes set sadly toward his bride
Laid him down by her, and spake not : but within
His heart spake, saying how sore should be the sin
To break toward her, that of all womankind
Was faithfullest, faith plighted, or unbind
The bond first linked between them when they drank
The love-draught : and his quick blood sprang and
    sank,
Remembering in the pulse of all his veins
That red swift rapture, all its fiery pains
And all its fierier pleasures : and he spake
Aloud, one burning word for love's keen sake—
' Iseult ; ' and full of love and lovelier fear
A virgin voice gave answer—' I am here.'
And a pang rent his heart at root : but still,
For spirit and flesh were vassals to his will,
Strong faith held mastery on them : and the breath
Felt on his face did not his will to death,
Nor glance nor lute-like voice nor flower-soft touch
Might so prevail upon it overmuch
That constancy might less prevail than they,
For all he looked and loved her as she lay
Smiling ; and soft as bird alights on bough
He kissed her maiden mouth and blameless brow,
Once, and again his heart within him sighed :
But all his young blood's yearning toward his bride,
How hard soe'er it held his life awake
For passion, and sweet nature's unforbidden sake,
And will that strove unwillingly with will it might not
    break,

Fell silent as a wind abashed, whose breath
Dies out of heaven, suddenly done to death,
When in between them on the dumb dusk air
Floated the bright shade of a face more fair
Than hers that hard beside him shrank and smiled
And wist of all no more than might a child.
So had she all her heart's will, all she would,
For love's sake that sufficed her, glad and good,
All night safe sleeping in her maidenhood.

ISEULT AT TINTAGEL.

BUT that same night in Cornwall oversea
Couched at Queen Iseult's hand, against her knee,
With keen kind eyes that read her whole heart's pain
Fast at wide watch lay Tristram's hound Hodain,
The goodliest and the mightiest born on earth,
That many a forest day of fiery mirth
Had plied his craft before them ; and the queen
Cherished him, even for those dim years between,
More than of old in those bright months far flown
When ere a blast of Tristram's horn was blown
Each morning as the woods rekindled, ere
Day gat full empire of the glimmering air,
Delight of dawn would quicken him, and fire
Spring and pant in his breath with bright desire
To be among the dewy ways on quest :
But now perforce at restless-hearted rest
He chafed through days more barren than the sand,
Soothed hardly but soothed only with her hand,
Though fain to fawn thereon and follow, still
With all his heart and all his loving will

Desiring one divided from his sight,
For whose lost sake dawn was as dawn of night
And noon as night's noon in his eyes was dark.
But in the halls far under sat King Mark,
Feasting, and full of cheer, with heart uplift,
As on the night that harper gat his gift :
And music revelled on the fitful air,
And songs came floated up the festal stair,
And muffled roar of wassail, where the king
Took heart from wine-cups and the quiring string
Till all his cold thin veins rejoiced and ran
Strong as with lifeblood of a kinglier man.
But the queen shut from sound her wearied ears,
Shut her sad eyes from sense of aught save tears,
And wrung her hair with soft fierce hands, and
    prayed :
  ' O God, God born of woman, of a maid,
Christ, once in flesh of thine own fashion clad ;
O very love, so glad in heaven and sad
On earth for earth's sake alway ; since thou art
Pure only, I only impure of spirit and heart,
Since thou for sin's sake and the bitter doom
Didst as a veil put on a virgin's womb,
I that am none, and cannot hear or see
Or shadow or likeness or a sound of thee
Far off, albeit with man's own speech and face
Thou shine yet and thou speak yet, showing forth
    grace—
Ah me ! grace only shed on souls that are
Lit and led forth of shadow by thy star—

Alas! to these men only grace, to these,
Lord, whom thy love draws Godward, to thy knees—
I, can I draw thee me-ward, can I seek,
Who love thee not, to love me? seeing how weak,
Lord, all this little love I bear thee is,
And how much is my strong love more than this,
My love that I love man with, that I bear
Him sinning through me sinning? wilt thou care,
God, for this love, if love be any, alas,
In me to give thee, though long since there was,
How long, when I too, Lord, was clean, even I,
That now am unclean till the day I die—
Haply by burning, harlot-fashion, made
A horror in all hearts of wife and maid,
Hateful, not knowing if ever in these mine eyes
Shone any light of thine in any wise
Or this were love at all that I bore thee?'
    And the night spake, and thundered on the sea,
Ravening aloud for ruin of lives : and all
The bastions of the main cliff's northward wall
Rang response out from all their deepening length,
As the east wind girded up his godlike strength
And hurled in hard against that high-towered hold
The fleeces of the flock that knows no fold,
The rent white shreds of shattering storm : but she
Heard not nor heeded wind or storming sea,
Knew not if night were mild or mad with wind.
    'Yea, though deep lips and tender hair be thinned,
Though cheek wither, brow fade, and bosom wane,
Shall I change also from this heart again

To maidenhood of heart and holiness?
Shall I more love thee, Lord, or love him less—
Ah miserable ! though spirit and heart be rent,
Shall I repent, Lord God? shall I repent?
Nay, though thou slay me ! for herein I am blest,
That as I loved him yet I love him best—
More than mine own soul or thy love or thee,
Though thy love save and my love save not me.
Blest am I beyond women even herein,
That beyond all born women is my sin,
And perfect my transgression : that above
All offerings of all others is my love,
Who have chosen it only, and put away for this
Thee, and my soul's hope, Saviour, of the kiss
Wherewith thy lips make welcome all thine own
When in them life and death are overthrown ;
The sinless lips that seal the death of sin,
The kiss wherewith their dumb lips touched begin
Singing in heaven.
     'Where we shall never, love,
Never stand up nor sing ! for God above
Knows us, how too much more than God to me
Thy sweet love is, my poor love is to thee !
Dear, dost thou see now, dost thou hear to-night,
Sleeping, my waste wild speech, my face worn white,
—Speech once heard soft by thee, face once kissed
  red !—
In such a dream as when men see their dead
And know not if they know if dead these be?
Ah love, are thy days my days, and to thee

Are all nights like as my nights? does the sun
Grieve thee? art thou soul-sick till day be done,
And weary till day rises? is thine heart
Full of dead things as mine is? Nay, thou art
Man, with man's strength and praise and pride of life,
No bondwoman, no queen, no loveless wife
That would be shamed albeit she had not sinned.'
   And swordlike was the sound of the iron wind,
And as a breaking battle was the sea.
   ' Nay, Lord, I pray thee let him love not me,
Love me not any more, nor like me die,
And be no more than such a thing as I.
Turn his heart from me, lest my love too lose
Thee as I lose thee, and his fair soul refuse
For my sake thy fair heaven, and as I fell
Fall, and be mixed with my soul and with hell.
Let me die rather, and only; let me be
Hated of him so he be loved of thee,
Lord : for I would not have him with me there
Out of thy light and love in the unlit air,
Out of thy sight in the unseen hell where I
Go gladly, going alone, so thou on high
Lift up his soul and love him—Ah, Lord, Lord,
Shalt thou love as I love him? she that poured
From the alabaster broken at thy feet
An ointment very precious, not so sweet
As that poured likewise forth before thee then
From the rehallowed heart of Magdalen,
From a heart broken, yearning like the dove,
An ointment very precious which is love—

Couldst thou being holy and God, and sinful she,
Love her indeed as surely she loved thee?
Nay, but if not, then as we sinners can
Let us love still in the old sad wise of man.
For with less love than my love, having had
Mine, though God love him he shall not be glad.
And with such love as my love, I wot well,
He shall not lie disconsolate in hell:
Sad only as souls for utter love's sake be
Here, and a little sad, perchance, for me—
Me happy, me more glad than God above,
In the utmost hell whose fires consume not love!
For in the waste ways emptied of the sun
He would say—" Dear, thy place is void, and one
Weeps among angels for thee, with his face
Veiled, saying, *O sister, how thy chosen place*
Stands desolate, that God made fair for thee!
Is heaven not sweeter, and we thy brethren, we
Fairer than love on earth and life in hell? "
And I—with me were all things then not well?
Should I not answer—" O love, be well content;
Look on me, and behold if I repent."
This were more to me than an angel's wings.
Yea, many men pray God for many things,
But I pray that this only thing may be.'
    And as a full field charging was the sea,
And as the cry of slain men was the wind.
    ' Yea, since I surely loved him, and he sinned
Surely, though not as my sin his be black,
God, give him to me—God, God, give him back!

For now how should we live in twain or die?
I am he indeed, thou knowest, and he is I.
Not man and woman several as we were,
But one thing with one life and death to bear.
How should one love his own soul overmuch?
And time is long since last I felt the touch,
The sweet touch of my lover, hand and breath,
In such delight as puts delight to death,
Burn my soul through, till spirit and soul and sense,
In the sharp grasp of the hour, with violence
Died, and again through pangs of violent birth
Lived, and laughed out with refluent might of mirth;
Laughed each on other and shuddered into one,
As a cloud shuddering dies into the sun.
Ah, sense is that or spirit, soul or flesh,
That only love lulls or awakes afresh?
Ah, sweet is that or bitter, evil or good,
That very love allays not as he would?
Nay, truth is this or vanity, that gives
No love assurance when love dies or lives?
This that my spirit is wrung withal, and yet
No surelier knows if haply thine forget,
Thou that my spirit is wrung for, nor can say
Love is not in thee dead as yesterday?
Dost thou feel, thou, this heartbeat whence my heart
Would send thee word what life is mine apart,
And know by keen response what life is thine?
Dost thou not hear one cry of all of mine?
O Tristram's heart, have I no part in thee?'
   And all her soul was as the breaking sea,

And all her heart anhungered as the wind.

   ' Dost thou repent thee of the sin we sinned?
Dost thou repent thee of the days and nights
That kindled and that quenched for us their lights,
The months that feasted us with all their hours,
The ways that breathed of us in all their flowers,
The dells that sang of us with all their doves?
Dost thou repent thee of the wildwood loves?
Is thine heart changed, and hallowed? art thou
    grown
God's, and not mine?   Yet, though my heart make
    moan,
Fain would my soul give thanks for thine, if thou
Be saved—yea, fain praise God, and knows not how.
How should it know thanksgiving? nay, or learn
Aught of the love wherewith thine own should burn,
God's, that should cast out as an evil thing
Mine? yea, what hand of prayer have I to cling,
What heart to prophesy, what spirit of sight
To strain insensual eyes toward increate light,
Who look but back on life wherein I sinned?'

   And all their past came wailing in the wind,
And all their future thundered in the sea.

   ' But if my soul might touch the time to be,
If hand might handle now or eye behold
My life and death ordained me from of old,
Life palpable, compact of blood and breath,
Visible, present, naked, very death,
Should I desire to know before the day
These that I know not, nor is man that may?

For haply, seeing, my heart would break for fear,
And my soul timeless cast its load off here,
Its load of life too bitter, love too sweet,
And fall down shamed and naked at thy feet,
God, who wouldst take no pity of it, nor give
One hour back, one of all its hours to live
Clothed with my mortal body, that once more,
Once, on this reach of barren beaten shore,
This stormy strand of life, ere sail were set,
Had haply felt love's arms about it yet—
Yea, ere death's bark put off to seaward, might
With many a grief have bought me one delight
That then should know me never. Ah, what years
Would I endure not, filled up full with tears,
Bitter like blood and dark as dread of death,
To win one amorous hour of mingling breath,
One fire-eyed hour and sunnier than the sun,
For all these nights and days like nights but one?
One hour of heaven born once, a stormless birth,
For all these windy weary hours of earth?
One, but one hour from birth of joy to death,
For all these hungering hours of feverish breath?
And I should lose this, having died and sinned.'

And as man's anguish clamouring cried the wind,
And as God's anger answering rang the sea.

' And yet what life—Lord God, what life for me
Has thy strong wrath made ready? Dost thou think
How lips whose thirst hath only tears to drink
Grow grey for grief untimely? Dost thou know,
O happy God, how men wax weary of woe—

Yea, for their wrong's sake that thine hand hath done
Come even to hate thy semblance in the sun?
Turn back from dawn and noon and all thy light
To make their souls one with the soul of night?
Christ, if thou hear yet or have eyes to see,
Thou that hadst pity, and hast no pity on me.
Know'st thou no more, as in this life's sharp span,
What pain thou hadst on earth, what pain hath man?
Hast thou no care, that all we suffer yet?
What help is ours of thee if thou forget?
What profit have we though thy blood were given,
If we that sin bleed and be not forgiven?
Not love but hate, thou bitter God and strange,
Whose heart as man's heart hath grown cold with
    change,
Not love but hate thou showest us that have sinned.'
  And like a world's cry shuddering was the wind,
And like a God's voice threatening was the sea.
  'Nay, Lord, for thou wast gracious; nay, in thee
No change can come with time or varying fate,
No tongue bid thine be less compassionate,
No sterner eye rebuke for mercy thine,
No sin put out thy pity—no, not mine.
Thou knowest us, Lord, thou knowest us, all we are,
He, and the soul that hath his soul for star:
Thou knowest as I know, Lord, how much more
    worth
Than all souls clad and clasped about with earth,
But most of all, God, how much more than I,
Is this man's soul that surely shall not die.

What righteousness, what judgment, Lord most
    high,
Were this, to bend a brow of doom as grim
As threats me, me the adulterous wife, on him?
There lies none other nightly by his side :
He hath not sought, he shall not seek a bride.
Far as God sunders earth from heaven above,
So far was my love born beneath his love.
I loved him as the sea-wind loves the sea,
To rend and ruin it only and waste : but he,
As the sea loves a sea-bird loved he me,
To foster and uphold my tired life's wing,
And bounteously beneath me spread forth spring,
A springtide space whereon to float or fly,
A world of happy water, whence the sky
Glowed goodlier, lightening from so glad a glass,
Than with its own light only.   Now, alas !
Cloud hath come down and clothed it round with
    storm,
And gusts and fits of eddying winds deform
The feature of its glory.   Yet be thou,
God, merciful : nay, show but justice now,
And let the sin in him that scarce was his
Stand expiated with exile : and be this
The price for him, the atonement this, that I
With all the sin upon me live, and die
With all thy wrath on me that most have sinned.'
    And like man's heart relenting sighed the wind,
And as God's wrath subsiding sank the sea.
    ' But if such grace be possible—if it be

Not sin more strange than all sins past, and worse
Evil, that cries upon thee for a curse,
To pray such prayers from such a heart, do thou
Hear, and make wide thine hearing toward me now ;
Let not my soul and his for ever dwell
Sundered : though doom keep always heaven and hell
Irreconcilable, infinitely apart,
Keep not in twain for ever heart and heart
That once, albeit by not thy law, were one ;
Let this be not thy will, that this be done.
Let all else, all thou wilt of evil, be,
But no doom, none, dividing him and me.'

By this was heaven stirred eastward, and there came
Up the rough ripple a labouring light like flame ;
And dawn, sore trembling still and grey with fear,
Looked hardly forth, a face of heavier cheer
Than one which grief or dread yet half enshrouds,
Wild-eyed and wan, across the cleaving clouds.
And Iseult, worn with watch long held on pain,
Turned, and her eye lit on the hound Hodain,
And all her heart went out in tears : and he
Laid his kind head along her bended knee,
Till round his neck her arms went hard, and all
The night past from her as a chain might fall :
But yet the heart within her, half undone,
Wailed, and was loth to let her see the sun.

And ere full day brought heaven and earth to flower,
Far thence, a maiden in a marriage bower,
That moment, hard by Tristram, oversea,
Woke with glad eyes Iseult of Brittany.

VI.

JOYOUS GARD.

A LITTLE time, O Love, a little light,
A little hour for ease before the night.
Sweet Love, that art so bitter ; foolish Love,
Whom wise men know for wiser, and thy dove
More subtle than the serpent ; for thy sake
These pray thee for a little beam to break,
A little grace to help them, lest men think
Thy servants have but hours like tears to drink.
O Love, a little comfort, lest they fear
To serve as these have served thee who stand here.
 For these are thine, thy servants these, that stand
Here nigh the limit of the wild north land,
At margin of the grey great eastern sea,
Dense-islanded with peaks and reefs, that see
No life but of the fleet wings fair and free
Which cleave the mist and sunlight all day long
With sleepless flight and cries more glad than song.
Strange ways of life have led them hither, here
To win fleet respite from desire and fear

With armistice from sorrow ; strange and sweet
Ways trodden by forlorn and casual feet
Till kindlier chance woke toward them kindly will
In happier hearts of lovers, and their ill
Found rest, as healing surely might it not,
By gift and kingly grace of Launcelot
At gracious bidding given of Guenevere.
For in the trembling twilight of this year
Ere April sprang from hope to certitude
Two hearts of friends fast linked had fallen at feud
As they rode forth on hawking, by the sign
Which gave his new bride's brother Ganhardine
To know the truth of Tristram's dealing, how
Faith kept of him against his marriage vow
Kept virginal his bride-bed night and morn ;
Whereat, as wroth his blood should suffer scorn,
Came Ganhardine to Tristram, saying, ' Behold,
We have loved thee, and for love we have shown of old
Scorn hast thou shown us : wherefore is thy bride
Not thine indeed, a stranger at thy side,
Contemned? what evil hath she done, to be
Mocked with mouth-marriage and despised of thee,
Shamed, set at nought, rejected?'   But there came
On Tristram's brow and eye the shadow and flame
Confused of wrath and wonder, ere he spake,
Saying, ' Hath she bid thee for thy sister's sake
Plead with me, who believed of her in heart
More nobly than to deem such piteous part
Should find so fair a player? or whence hast thou
Of us this knowledge?'   ' Nay,' said he, ' but now,

Riding beneath these whitethorns overhead,
There fell a flower into her girdlestead
Which laughing she shook out, and smiling said—
" Lo, what large leave the wind hath given this stray,
To lie more near my heart than till this day
Aught ever since my mother lulled me lay
Or even my lord came ever ; " whence I wot
We are all thy scorn, a race regarded not
Nor held as worth communion of thine own,
Except in her be found some fault alone
To blemish our alliance.' Then replied
Tristram, ' Nor blame nor scorn may touch my bride,
Albeit unknown of love she live, and be
Worth a man worthier than her love thought me.
Faith only, faith withheld me, faith forbade
The blameless grace wherewith love's grace makes
      glad
All lives linked else in wedlock ; not that less
I loved the sweet light of her loveliness,
But that my love toward faith was more : and thou,
Albeit thine heart be keen against me now,
Couldst thou behold my very lady, then
No more of thee than of all other men
Should this my faith be held a faithless fault.'
And ere that day their hawking came to halt
Being sore of him entreated for a sign,
He sware to bring his brother Ganhardine
To sight of that strange Iseult : and thereon
Forth soon for Cornwall are these brethren gone,

Even to that royal pleasance where the hunt
Rang ever of old with Tristram's horn in front
Blithe as the queen's horse bounded at his side:
And first of all her dames forth pranced in pride
That day before them, with a ringing rein
All golden-glad, the king's false bride Brangwain,
The queen's true handmaid ever : and on her
Glancing, 'Be called for all time truth-teller,
O Tristram, of all true men's tongues alive,'
Quoth Ganhardine ; 'for may my soul so thrive
As yet mine eye drank never sight like this.'
'Ay?' Tristram said, 'and she thou look'st on is
So great in grace of goodliness, that thou
Hast less thought left of wrath against me now,
Seeing but my lady's handmaid? Nay, behold ;
See'st thou no light more golden than of gold
Shine where she moves in midst of all, above
All, past all price or praise or prayer of love?
Lo, this is she.'　But as one mazed with wine
Stood, stunned in spirit and stricken, Ganhardine,
And gazed out hard against them : and his heart
As with a sword was cloven, and rent apart
As with strong fangs of fire ; and scarce he spake,
Saying how his life for even a handmaid's sake
Was made a flame within him.　And the knight
Bade him, being known of none that stood in sight,
Bear to Brangwain his ring, that she unseen
Might give in token privily to the queen
And send swift word where under moon or sun
They twain might yet be no more twain but one.

And that same night, under the stars that rolled
Over their warm deep wildwood nights of old
Whose hours for grains of sand shed sparks of fire,
Such way was made anew for their desire
By secret wile of sickness feigned, to keep
The king far off her vigils or her sleep,
That in the queen's pavilion midway set
By glimmering moondawn were those lovers met,
And Ganhardine of Brangwain gat him grace.
And in some passionate soft interspace
Between two swells of passion, when their lips
Breathed, and made room for such brief speech as
    slips
From tongues athirst with draughts of amorous wine
That leaves them thirstier than the salt sea's brine,
Was counsel taken how to fly, and where
Find covert from the wild world's ravening air
That hunts with storm the feet of nights and days
Through strange thwart lines of life and flowerless
    ways.
Then said Iseult : 'Lo, now the chance is here
Foreshown me late by word of Guenevere,
To give me comfort of thy rumoured wrong,
My traitor Tristram, when report was strong
Of me forsaken and thine heart estranged :
Nor should her sweet soul toward me yet be changed
Nor all her love lie barren, if mine hand
Crave harvest of it from the flowering land.
See therefore if this counsel please thee not,
That we take horse in haste for Camelot

And seek that friendship of her plighted troth
Which love shall be full fain to lend, nor loth
Shall my love be to take it.'   So next night
The multitudinous stars laughed round their flight,
Fulfilling far with laughter made of light
The encircling deeps of heaven : and in brief space
At Camelot their long love gat them grace
Of those fair twain whose heads men's praise im-
     pearled
As love's two lordliest lovers in the world :
And thence as guests for harbourage past they forth
To win this noblest hold of all the north.
Far by wild ways and many days they rode,
Till clear across June's kingliest sunset glowed
The great round girth of goodly wall that showed
Where for one clear sweet season's length should be
Their place of strength to rest in, fain and free,
By the utmost margin of the loud lone sea.
    And now, O Love, what comfort?   God most
     high,
Whose life is as a flower's to live and die,
Whose light is everlasting : Lord, whose breath
Speaks music through the deathless lips of death
Whereto time's heart rings answer : Bard, whom time
Hears, and is vanquished with a wandering rhyme
That once thy lips made fragrant : Seer, whose sooth
Joy knows not well, but sorrow knows for truth,
Being priestess of thy soothsayings : Love, what grace
Shall these twain find at last before thy face?

This many a year they have served thee, and
    deserved,
If ever man might yet of all that served,
Since the first heartbeat bade the first man's knee
Bend, and his mouth take music, praising thee,
Some comfort ; and some honey indeed of thine
Thou hast mixed for these with life's most bitter wine
Commending to their passionate lips a draught
No deadlier than thy chosen of old have quaffed
And blessed thine hand, their cupbearer's : for not
On all men comes the grace that seals their lot
As holier in thy sight, for all these feuds
That rend it, than the light-souled multitude's,
Nor thwarted of thine hand nor blessed ; but these
Shall see no twilight, Love, nor fade at ease,
Grey-grown and careless of desired delight,
But lie down tired and sleep before the night.
These shall not live till time or change may chill
Or doubt divide or shame subdue their will,
Or fear or slow repentance work them wrong,
Or love die first : these shall not live so long.
Death shall not take them drained of dear true life
Already, sick or stagnant from the strife,
Quenched : not with dry-drawn veins and lingering
    breath
Shall these through crumbling hours crouch down to
    death.
Swift, with one strong clean leap, ere life's pulse tire,
Most like the leap of lions or of fire,

Sheer death shall bound upon them : one pang past,
The first keen sense of him shall be their last,
Their last shall be no sense of any fear,
More than their life had sense of anguish here.
　　Weeks and light months had fled at swallow's
　　　speed
Since here their first hour sowed for them the seed
Of many sweet as rest or hope could be ;
Since on the blown beach of a glad new sea
Wherein strange rocks like fighting men stand scarred
They saw the strength and help of Joyous Gard.
Within the full deep glorious tower that stands
Between the wild sea and the broad wild lands
Love led and gave them quiet: and they drew
Life like a God's life in each wind that blew,
And took their rest, and triumphed.　Day by day
The mighty moorlands and the sea-walls grey,
The brown bright waters of green fells that sing
One song to rocks and flowers and birds on wing,
Beheld the joy and glory that they had,
Passing, and how the whole world made them glad,
And their great love was mixed with all things great,
As life being lovely, and yet being strong like fate.
For when the sun sprang on the sudden sea
Their eyes sprang eastward, and the day to be
Was lit in them untimely : such delight
They took yet of the clear cold breath and light
That goes before the morning, and such grace
Was deathless in them through their whole life's
　　space

As dies in many with their dawn that dies
And leaves in pulseless hearts and flameless eyes
No light to lighten and no tear to weep
For youth's high joy that time has cast on sleep.
Yea, this old grace and height of joy they had,
To lose no jot of all that made them glad
And filled their springs of spirit with such fire
That all delight fed in them all desire ;
And no whit less than in their first keen prime
The spring's breath blew through all their summer
    time,
And in their skies would sunlike Love confuse
Clear April colours with hot August hues,
And in their hearts one light of sun and moon
Reigned, and the morning died not of the noon :
Such might of life was in them, and so high
Their heart of love rose higher than fate could fly.
And many a large delight of hawk and hound
The great glad land that knows no bourne or bound,
Save the wind's own and the outer sea-bank's, gave
Their days for comfort ; many a long blithe wave
Buoyed their blithe bark between the bare bald rocks,
Deep, steep, and still, save for the swift free flocks
Unshepherded, uncompassed, unconfined,
That when blown foam keeps all the loud air blind
Mix with the wind's their triumph, and partake
The joy of blasts that ravin, waves that break,
All round and all below their mustering wings,
A clanging cloud that round the cliff's edge clings

On each bleak bluff breaking the strenuous tides
That rings reverberate mirth when storm bestrides
The subject night in thunder : many a noon
They took the moorland's or the bright sea's boon
With all their hearts into their spirit of sense,
Rejoicing, where the sudden dells grew dense
With sharp thick flight of hillside birds, or where
On some strait rock's ledge in the intense mute air
Erect against the cliff's sheer sunlit white
Blue as the clear north heaven, clothed warm with
    light,
Stood neck to bended neck and wing to wing
With heads fast hidden under, close as cling
Flowers on one flowering almond-branch in spring,
Three herons deep asleep against the sun,
Each with one bright foot downward poised, and one
Wing-hidden hard by the bright head, and all
Still as fair shapes fixed on some wondrous wall
Of minster-aisle or cloister-close or hall
To take even time's eye prisoner with delight.
Or, satisfied with joy of sound and sight,
They sat and communed of things past : what state
King Arthur, yet unwarred upon by fate,
Held high in hall at Camelot, like one
Whose lordly life was as the mounting sun
That climbs and pauses on the point of noon,
Sovereign : how royal rang the tourney's tune
Through Tristram's three days' triumph, spear to
    spear,
When Iseult shone enthroned by Guenevere,

Rose against rose, the highest adored on earth,
Imperial : yet with subtle notes of mirth
Would she bemock her praises, and bemoan
Her glory by that splendour overthrown
Which lightened from her sister's eyes elate ;
Saying how by night a little light seems great,
But less than least of all things, very nought,
When dawn undoes the web that darkness wrought ;
How like a tower of ivory well designed
By subtlest hand subserving subtlest mind,
Ivory with flower of rose incarnadined
And kindling with some God therein revealed,
A light for grief to look on and be healed,
Stood Guenevere : and all beholding her
Were heartstruck even as earth at midsummer
With burning wonder, hardly to be borne.
So was that amorous glorious lady born,
A fiery memory for all storied years :
Nor might men call her sisters crowned her peers,
Her sister queens, put all by her to scorn :
She had such eyes as are not made to mourn ;
But in her own a gleaming ghost of tears
Shone, and their glance was slower than Guenevere's,
And fitfuller with fancies grown of grief ;
Shamed as a Mayflower shames an autumn leaf
Full well she wist it could not choose but be
If in that other's eyeshot standing she
Should lift her looks up ever : wherewithal
Like fires whose light fills heaven with festival

Flamed her eyes full on Tristram's ; and he laughed,
Answering, ' What wile of sweet child-hearted craft
That children forge for children, to beguile
Eyes known of them not witless of the wile
But fain to seem for sport's sake self-deceived,
Wilt thou find out now not to be believed ?
Or how shall I trust more than ouphe or elf
Thy truth to me-ward, who beliest thyself ? '
' Nor elf nor ouphe or aught of airier kind,'
Quoth she, ' though made of moonbeams moist and
    blind,
Is light if weighed with man's winged weightless mind.
Though thou keep somewise troth with me, God wot,
When thou didst wed, I doubt, thou thoughtest not
So charily to keep it.'   ' Nay,' said he,
' Yet am not I rebukable by thee
As Launcelot, erring, held me ere he wist
No mouth save thine of mine was ever kissed
Save as a sister's only, since we twain
Drank first the draught assigned our lips to drain
That Fate and Love with darkling hands commixt
Poured, and no power to part them came betwixt,
But either's will, howbeit they seem at strife,
Was toward us one, as death itself and life
Are one sole doom toward all men, nor may one
Behold not darkness, who beholds the sun.'

   ' Ah, then,' she said, ' what word is this men hear
Of Merlin, how some doom too strange to fear
Was cast but late about him oversea,
Sweet recreant, in thy bridal Brittany ?

Is not his life sealed fast on him with sleep,
By witchcraft of his own and love's, to keep
Till earth be fire and ashes?'

                    'Surely,' said
Her lover, ' not as one alive or dead
The great good wizard, well beloved and well
Predestinate of heaven that casts out hell
For guerdon gentler far than all men's fate,
Exempt alone of all predestinate,
Takes his strange rest at heart of slumberland,
More deep asleep in green Broceliande
Than shipwrecked sleepers in the soft green sea
Beneath the weight of wandering waves : but he
Hath for those roofing waters overhead
Above him always all the summer spread
Or all the winter wailing : or the sweet
Late leaves marked red with autumn's burning feet,
Or withered with his weeping, round the seer
Rain, and he sees not, nor may heed or hear
The witness of the winter : but in spring
He hears above him all the winds on wing
Through the blue dawn between the brightening
    boughs,
And on shut eyes and slumber-smitten brows
Feels ambient change in the air and strengthening
    sun,
And knows the soul that was his soul at one
With the ardent world's, and in the spirit of earth
His spirit of life reborn to mightier birth
And mixed with things of elder life than ours ;
With cries of birds, and kindling lamps of flowers,

And sweep and song of winds, and fruitful light
Of sunbeams, and the far faint breath of night,
And waves and woods at morning : and in all,
Soft as at noon the slow sea's rise and fall,
He hears in spirit a song that none but he
Hears from the mystic mouth of Nimue
Shed like a consecration ; and his heart,
Hearing, is made for love's sake as a part
Of that far singing, and the life thereof
Part of that life that feeds the world with love :
Yea, heart in heart is molten, hers and his,
Into the world's heart and the soul that is
Beyond or sense or vision ; and their breath
Stirs the soft springs of deathless life and death,
Death that bears life, and change that brings forth
        seed
Of life to death and death to life indeed,
As blood recircling through the unsounded veins
Of earth and heaven with all their joys and pains.
Ah, that when love shall laugh no more nor weep
We too, we too might hear that song and sleep ! '
    ' Yea,' said Iseult, 'some joy it were to be
Lost in the sun's light and the all-girdling sea,
Mixed with the winds and woodlands, and to bear
Part in the large life of the quickening air,
And the sweet earth's, our mother : yet to pass
More fleet than mirrored faces from the glass
Out of all pain and all delight, so far
That love should seem but as the furthest star
Sunk deep in trembling heaven, scarce seen or known.

As a dead moon forgotten, once that shone
Where now the sun shines—nay, not all things yet,
Not all things always, dying, would I forget.'
   And Tristram answered amorously, and said :
'O heart that here art mine, O heavenliest head
That ever took men's worship here, which art
Mine, how shall death put out the fire at heart,
Quench in men's eyes the head's remembered light
That time shall set but higher in more men's sight ?
Think thou not much to die one earthly day,
Being made not in their mould who pass away
Nor who shall pass for ever.'
                      'Ah,' she said,
'What shall it profit me, being praised and dead?
What profit have the flowers of all men's praise ?
What pleasure of our pleasure have the days
That pour on us delight of life and mirth?
What fruit of all our joy on earth has earth?
Nor am I—nay, my lover, am I one
To take such part in heaven's enkindling sun
And in the inviolate air and sacred sea
As clothes with grace that wondrous Nimue ?
For all her works are bounties, all her deeds
Blessings ; her days are scrolls wherein love reads
The record of his mercies ; heaven above
Hath not more heavenly holiness of love
Than earth beneath, wherever pass or pause
Her feet that move not save by love's own laws,
In gentleness of godlike wayfaring
To heal men's hearts as earth is healed by spring

Of all such woes as winter : what am I,
Love, that have strength but to desire and die,
That have but grace to love and do thee wrong,
What am I that my name should live so long,
Save as the star that crossed thy star-struck lot,
With hers whose light was life to Launcelot?
Life gave she him, and strength, and fame to be
For ever : I, what gift can I give thee?
Peril and sleepless watches, fearful breath
Of dread more bitter for my sake than death
When death came nigh to call me by my name,
Exile, rebuke, remorse, and—O, not shame.
Shame only, this I gave thee not, whom none
May give that worst thing ever—no, not one.
Of all that hate, all hateful hearts that see
Darkness for light and hate where love should be,
None for my shame's sake may speak shame of thee.'
    And Tristram answering ere he kissed her smiled:
' O very woman, god at once and child,
What ails thee to desire of me once more
The assurance that thou hadst in heart before?
For all this wild sweet waste of sweet vain breath,
Thou knowest I know thou hast given me life, not
        death.
The shadow of death, informed with shows of strife,
Was ere I won thee all I had of life.
Light war, light love, light living, dreams in sleep,
Joy slight and light, not glad enough to weep,
Filled up my foolish days with sound and shine,
Vision and gleam from strange men's cast on mine,
Reverberate light from eyes presaging thine

That shed but shadowy moonlight where thy face
Now sheds forth sunshine in the deep same place,
The deep live heart half dead and shallower then
Than summer fords which thwart not wandering men.
For how should I, signed sorrow's from my birth,
Kiss dumb the loud red laughing lips of mirth?
Or how, sealed thine to be, love less than heaven on earth?
My heart in me was held at restless rest,
Presageful of some prize beyond its quest,
Prophetic still with promise, fain to find the best.
For one was fond and one was blithe and one
Fairer than all save twain whose peers are none ;
For third on earth is none that heaven hath seen
To stand with Guenevere beside my queen.
Not Nimue, girt with blessing as a guard :
Not the soft lures and laughters of Ettarde :
Not she, that splendour girdled round with gloom,
Crowned as with iron darkness of the tomb,
And clothed with clouding conscience of a monstrous
    doom,
Whose blind incestuous love brought forth a fire
To burn her ere it burn its darkling sire,
Her mother's son, King Arthur : yet but late
We saw pass by that fair live shadow of fate,
The queen Morgause of Orkney, like a dream
That scares the night when moon and starry beam
Sicken and swoon before some sorcerer's eyes
Whose wordless charms defile the saintly skies,
Bright still with fire and pulse of blood and breath,
Whom her own sons have doomed for shame to death.'

I

'Death — yea,' quoth she, ' there is not said or heard
So oft aloud on earth so sure a word.
Death, and again death, and for each that saith
Ten tongues chime answer to the sound of death.
Good end God send us ever—so men pray.
But I—this end God send me, would I say,
To die not of division and a heart
Rent or with sword of severance cloven apart,
But only when thou diest and only where thou art,
O thou my soul and spirit and breath to me,
O light, life, love! yea, let this only be,
That dying I may praise God who gave me thee,
Let hap what will thereafter.'

                        So that day
They communed, even till even was worn away,
Nor aught they said seemed strange or sad to say,
But sweet as night's dim dawn to weariness.
Nor loved they life or love for death's sake less,
Nor feared they death for love's or life's sake more.
And on the sounding soft funereal shore
They, watching till the day should wholly die,
Saw the far sea sweep to the far grey sky,
Saw the long sands sweep to the long grey sea.
And night made one sweet mist of moor and lea,
And only far off shore the foam gave light.
And life in them sank silent as the night.

VII.

THE WIFE'S VIGIL.

BUT all that year in Brittany forlorn,
More sick at heart with wrath than fear of scorn
And less in love with love than grief, and less
With grief than pride of spirit and bitterness,
Till all the sweet life of her blood was changed
And all her soul from all her past estranged
And all her will with all itself at strife
And all her mind at war with all her life,
Dwelt the white-handed Iseult, maid and wife,
A mourner that for mourning robes had on
Anger and doubt and hate of things foregone.
For that sweet spirit of old which made her sweet
Was parched with blasts of thought as flowers with
     heat
And withered as with wind of evil will ;
Though slower than frosts or fires consume or kill
That bleak black wind vexed all her spirit still.
As ripples reddening in the roughening breath
Of the eager east when dawn does night to death,

So rose and stirred and kindled in her thought
Fierce barren fluctuant fires that lit not aught,
But scorched her soul with yearning keen as hate
And dreams that left her wrath disconsolate.
When change came first on that first heaven where all
Life's hours were flowers that dawn's light hand let fall,
The sun that smote her dewy cloud of days
Wrought from its showery folds his rainbow's rays,
For love the red, for hope the gentle green,
But yellow jealousy glared pale between.
Ere yet the sky grew heavier, and her head
Bent flowerwise, chill with change and fancies fled,
She saw but love arch all her heaven across with red,
A burning bloom that seemed to breathe and beat
And waver only as flame with rapturous heat
Wavers ; and all the world therewith smelt sweet,
As incense kindling from the rose-red flame :
And when that full flush waned, and love became
Scarce fainter, though his fading horoscope
From certitude of sight receded, hope
Held yet her April-coloured light aloft
As though to lure back love, a lamp sublime and soft.
But soon that light paled as a leaf grows pale
And fluttered leaf-like in the gathering gale
And melted even as dew-flakes, whose brief sheen
The sun that gave despoils of glittering green ;
Till harder shone 'twixt hope and love grown cold
A sallow light like withering autumn's gold,
The pale strong flame of jealous thought, that glows
　　More deep than hope's green bloom or love's
　　　　enkindled rose :

As though the sunflower's faint fierce disk absorbed
The spirit and heart of starrier flowers disorbed.
　　That same full hour of twilight's doors unbarred
To let bright night behold in Joyous Gard
The glad grave eyes of lovers far away
Watch with sweet thoughts of death the death of day
Saw lonelier by the narrower opening sea
Sit fixed at watch Iseult of Brittany.
As darkness from deep valleys void and bleak
Climbs till it clothe with night the sunniest peak
Where only of all a mystic mountain-land
Day seems to cling yet with a trembling hand
And yielding heart reluctant to recede,
So, till her soul was clothed with night indeed,
Rose the slow cloud of envious will within
And hardening hate that held itself no sin,
Veiled heads of vision, eyes of evil gleam,
Dim thought on thought, and darkling dream on dream.
Far off she saw in spirit, and seeing abhorred,
The likeness wrought on darkness of her lord .
Shine, and the imperial semblance at his side
Whose shadow from her seat cast down the bride,
Whose power and ghostly presence thrust her forth :
Beside that unknown other sea far north
She saw them, clearer than in present sight
Rose on her eyes the starry shadow of night ;
And on her heart that heaved with gathering fate
Rose red with storm the starless shadow of hate ;
And eyes and heart made one saw surge and swell
The fires of sunset like the fires of hell.

As though God's wrath would burn up sin with shame,
The incensed red gold of deepening heaven grew
    flame :
The sweet green spaces of the soft low sky
Faded, as fields that withering wind leaves dry :
The sea's was like a doomsman's blasting breath
From lips afoam with ravenous lust of death.
A night like desolation, sombre-starred,
Above the great walled girth of Joyous Gard
Spread forth its wide sad strength of shadow and
    gloom
Wherein those twain were compassed round with doom :
Hell from beneath called on them, and she heard
Reverberate judgment in the wild wind's word
Cry, till the sole sound of their names that rang
Clove all the sea-mist with a clarion's clang,
And clouds to clouds and flames to clustering flames
Beat back the dark noise of the direful names.
Fear and strong exultation caught her breath,
And triumph like the bitterness of death,
And rapture like the rage of hate allayed
With ruin and ravin that its might hath made ;
And her heart swelled and strained itself to hear
What may be heard of no man's hungering ear,
And as a soil that cleaves in twain for drouth
Thirsted for judgment given of God's own mouth
Against them, till the strength of dark desire
Was in her as a flame of hell's own fire.
Nor seemed the wrath which held her spirit in stress
Aught else or worse than passionate holiness,

Nor the ardent hate which called on judgment's rod
More hateful than the righteousness of God.
' How long, till thou do justice, and my wrong
Stand expiate?   O long-suffering judge, how long?
Shalt thou not put him in mine hand one day
Whom I so loved, to spare not but to slay?
Shalt thou not cast her down for me to tread,
Me, on the pale pride of her humbled head?
Do I not well, being angry? doth not hell
Require them? yea, thou knowest that I do well.
Is not thy seal there set of bloodred light
For witness on the brows of day and night?
Who shall unseal it? what shall melt away
Thy signet from the doors of night and day?
No man, nor strength of any spirit above,
Nor prayer, nor ardours of adulterous love.
Thou art God, the strong lord over body and soul :
Hast thou not in the terrors of thy scroll
All names of all men written as with fire?
Thine only breath bids time and space respire :
And are not all things evil in them done
More clear in thine eyes than in ours the sun?
Hast thou not sight stretched wide enough to see
These that offend it, these at once and me?
Is thine arm shortened or thine hand struck down
As palsied? have thy brows not strength to frown?
Are thine eyes blind with film of withering age?
Burns not thine heart with righteousness of rage
Yet, and the royal rancour toward thy foes
Retributive of ruin?   Time should close,

Thou said'st, and earth fade as a leaf grows grey,
Ere one word said of thine should pass away.
Was this then not thy word, thou God most high,
That sin shall surely bring forth death and die,
Seeing how these twain live and have joy of life,
His harlot and the man that made me wife?
For is it I, perchance, I that have sinned?
Me, peradventure, should thy wasting wind
Smite, and thy sun blast, and thy storms devour
Me with keen fangs of lightning? should thy power
Put forth on me the weight of its awakening hour?
Shall I that bear this burden bear that weight
Of judgment? is my sin against thee great,
If all my heart against them burn with all its hate?
Thine, and not mine, should hate be? nay, but me
They have spoiled and scoffed at, who can touch not
  thee.
Me, me, the fullness of their joy drains dry,
Their fruitfulness makes barren : thou, not I,
Lord, is it, whom their wrongdoing clothes with shame,
That all who speak shoot tongues out at thy name
As all who hear mock mine?   Make me thy sword
At least, if even thou too be wronged, O Lord,
At all of these that wrong me : make mine hand
As lightning, or my tongue a fiery brand,
To burn or smite them with thy wrath : behold,
I have nought on earth save thee for hope or hold,
Fail me not thou : I have nought but this to crave,
Make me thy mean to give them to the grave,

Thy sign that all men seeing may speak thee just,
Thy word which turns the strengths of sin to dust,
Thy blast which burns up towers and thrones with fire.
Lord, is this gift, this grace that I require,
So great a gift, Lord, for thy grace to give
And bid me bear thy part retributive?
That I whom scorn makes mouths at, I might be
Thy witness if loud sin may mock at thee?
For lo, my life is as a barren ear
Plucked from the sheaf : dark days drive past me here
Downtrodden, while joy's reapers pile their sheaves,
A thing more vile than autumn's weariest leaves,
For these the sun filled once with sap of life.
O thou my lord that hadst me to thy wife,
Dost thou not fear at all, remembering me,
The love that bowed my whole soul down to thee?
Is this so wholly nought for man to dread,
Man, whose life walks between the quick and dead,
Naked, and warred about with wind and sea,
That one should love and hate as I do thee?
That one should live in all the world his foe
So mortal as the hate that loves him so?
Nought, is it nought, O husband, O my knight,
O strong man and indomitable in fight,
That one more weak than foam-bells on the sea
Should have in heart such thoughts as I of thee?
Thou art bound about with stately strengths for bands :
What strength shall keep thee from my strengthless
    hands?

Thou art girt about with goodly guards and great :
What fosse may fence thee round as deep as hate ?
Thou art wise : will wisdom teach thee fear of me ?
Thou art great of heart : shall this deliver thee ?
What wall so massive, or what tower so high,
Shall be thy surety that thou shouldst not die,
If that which comes against thee be but I ?
Who shall rise up of power to take thy part,
What skill find strength to save, what strength find art,
If that which wars against thee be my heart ?
Not iron, nor the might of force afield,
Nor edge of sword, nor sheltering weight of shield,
Nor all thy fame since all thy praise began,
Nor all the love and laud thou hast of man,
Nor, though his noiseless hours with wool be shod,
Shall God's love keep thee from the wrath of God.
O son of sorrows, hast thou said at heart,
Haply, God loves thee, God shall take thy part,
Who hath all these years endured thee, since thy birth
From sorrow's womb bade sin be born on earth ?
So long he hath cast his buckler over thee,
Shall he not surely guard thee even from me ?
Yea, but if yet he give thee while I live
Into mine hands as he shall surely give,
Ere death at last bring darkness on thy face,
Call then on him, call not on me for grace,
Cast not away one prayer, one suppliant breath,
On me that commune all this while with death.
For I that was not and that was thy wife
Desire not but one hour of all thy life

Wherein to triumph till that hour be past ;
But this mine hour I look for is thy last.'
    So mused she till the fire in sea and sky
Sank, and the northwest wind spake harsh on high,
And like the sea's heart waxed her heart that heard,
Strong, dark, and bitter, till the keen wind's word
Seemed of her own soul spoken, and the breath
All round her not of darkness, but of death.

VIII.

THE LAST PILGRIMAGE.

ENOUGH of ease, O Love, enough of light,
Enougn of rest before the shadow of night.
Strong Love, whom death finds feebler ; kingly Love,
Whom time discrowns in season, seeing thy dove
Spell-stricken by the serpent ; for thy sake
These that saw light see night's dawn only break,
Night's cup filled up with slumber, whence men think
The draught more dread than thine was dire to drink.
O Love, thy day sets darkling : hope and fear
Fall from thee standing stern as death stands here.
  For what have these to do with fear or hope
On whom the gates of outer darkness ope,
On whom the door of life's desire is barred ?
Past like a cloud, their days in Joyous Gard
Gleam like a cloud the westering sun stains red
Till all the blood of day's blithe heart be bled
And all night's heart requickened ; in their eyes
So flame and fade those far memorial skies,
So shines the moorland, so revives the sea,
Whereon they gazing mused of things to be

And wist not more of them than waters know
What wind with next day's change of tide shall blow.
Dark roll the deepening days whose waves divide
Unseasonably, with storm-struck change of tide,
Tristram from Iseult : nor may sorrow say
If better wind shall blow than yesterday
With next day risen or any day to come.
For ere the songs of summer's death fell dumb,
And autumn bade the imperial moorlands change
Their purples, and the bracken's bloom grow strange
As hope's green blossom touched with time's harsh
    rust,
Was all their joy of life shaken to dust,
And all its fire made ashes : by the strand
Where late they strayed and communed hand from
    hand
For the last time fell separate, eyes of eyes
Took for the last time leave, and saw the skies
Dark with their deep division.   The last time—
The last that ever love's rekindling rhyme
Should keep for them life's days and nights in tune
With refluence of the morning and the moon
Alternative in music, and make one
The secrets of the stardawn and the sun
For these twain souls ere darkness held them fast ;
The last before the labour marked for last
And toil of utmost knighthood, till the wage
Of rest might crown his crowning pilgrimage
Whereon forth faring must he take farewell,
With spear for staff and sword for scallop-shell

And scrip wherein close memory hoarded yet
Things holier held than death might well forget ;
The last time ere the travel were begun
Whose goal is unbeholden of the sun,
The last wherewith love's eyes might yet be lit,
Came, and they could but dream they knew not it.
    For Tristram parting from her wist at heart
How well she wist they might not choose but part,
And he pass forth a pilgrim, when there came
A sound of summons in the high king's name
For succour toward his vassal Triamour,
King in wild Wales, now spoiled of all his power,
As Tristram's father ere his fair son's birth,
By one the strongest of the sons of earth,
Urgan, an iron bulk of giant mould :
And Iseult in Tintagel as of old
Sat crowned with state and sorrow : for her lord
At Arthur's hand required her back restored,
And willingly compelled against her will
She yielded, saying within her own soul still
Some season yet of soft or stormier breath
Should haply give her life again or death:
For now nor quick nor dead nor bright nor dark
Were all her nights and days wherein King Mark
Held haggard watch upon her, and his eyes
Were cloudier than the gradual wintering skies
That closed about the wan wild land and sea.
And bitter toward him waxed her heart : but he
Was rent in twain betwixt harsh love and hate
With pain and passion half compassionate

That yearned and laboured to be quit of shame,
And could not : and his life grew smouldering flame,
And hers a cloud full-charged with storm and shower,
Though touched with trembling gleams of fire's bright
    flower
That flashed and faded on its fitful verge,
As hope would strive with darkness and emerge
And sink, a swimmer strangled by the swallowing
    surge.
  But Tristram by dense hills and deepening vales
Rode through the wild glad wastes of glorious Wales,
High-hearted with desire of happy fight
And strong in soul with merrier sense of might
Than since the fair first years that hailed him knight :
For all his will was toward the war, so long
Had love repressed and wrought his glory wrong,
So far the triumph and so fair the praise
Seemed now that kindled all his April days.
And here in bright blown autumn, while his life
Was summer's yet for strength toward love or strife,
Blithe waxed his hope toward battle, and high desire
To pluck once more as out of circling fire
Fame, the broad flower whose breath makes death
    more sweet
Than roses crushed by love's receding feet.
But all the lovely land wherein he went
The blast of ruin and ravenous war had rent ;
And black with fire the fields where homesteads were,
And foul with festering dead the high soft air,

And loud with wail of women many a stream
Whose own live song was like love's deepening dream,
Spake all against the spoiler : wherefore still
Wrath waxed with pity, quickening all his will,
In Tristram's heart for every league he rode
Through the aching land so broad a curse bestrode
With so supreme a shadow : till one dawn,
Above the green bloom of a gleaming lawn,
High on the strait steep windy bridge that spanned
A glen's deep mouth, he saw that shadow stand
Visible, sword on thigh and mace in hand
Vast as the mid bulk of a roof-tree's beam.
So, sheer above the wild wolf-haunted stream,
Dire as the face disfeatured of a dream,
Rose Urgan : and his eyes were night and flame ;
But like the fiery dawn were his that came
Against him, lit with more sublime desire
Than lifts toward heaven the leaping heart of fire :
And strong in vantage of his perilous place
The huge high presence, red as earth's first race,
Reared like a reed the might up of his mace,
And smote : but lightly Tristram swerved, and drove
Right in on him, whose void stroke only clove
Air, and fell wide, thundering athwart : and he
Sent forth a stormier cry than wind or sea
When midnight takes the tempest for her lord ;
And all the glen's throat seemed as hell's that roared ;
But high like heaven's light over hell shone Tristram's
    sword,

K

Falling, and bright as storm shows God's bare brand
Flashed as it shore sheer off the huge right hand
Whose strength was as the shadow of death on all that
    land.
And like the trunk of some grim tree sawn through
Reeled Urgan, as his left hand grasped and drew
A steel by sorcerers tempered : and anew
Raged the red wind of fluctuant fight, till all
The cliffs were thrilled as by the clangorous call
Of storm's blown trumpets from the core of night,
Charging : and even as with the storm-wind's might
On Tristram's helm that sword crashed : and the knight
Fell, and his arms clashed, and a wide cry brake
From those far off that heard it, for his sake
Soul-stricken : and that bulk of monstrous birth
Sent forth again a cry more dire for mirth :
But ere the sunbright arms were soiled of earth
They flashed again, re-risen : and swift and loud
Rang the strokes out as from a circling cloud,
So dense the dust wrought over them its drifted
    shroud.
Strong strokes, within the mist their battle made,
Each hailed on other through the shifting shade
That clung about them hurtling as the swift fight
    swayed :
And each between the jointed corslet saw
Break forth his foe's bright blood at each grim flaw
Steel made in hammered iron : till again
The fiend put forth his might more strong for pain
And cleft the great knight's glittering shield in twain,

Laughing for very wrath and thirst to kill,
A beast's broad laugh of blind and wolfish will,
And smote again ere Tristram's lips drew breath
Panting, and swept as by the sense of death,
That surely should have touched and sealed them fast
Save that the sheer stroke shrilled aside, and passed
Frustrate : but answering Tristram smote anew,
And thrust the brute breast as with lightning through
Clean with one cleaving stroke of perfect might :
And violently the vast bulk leapt upright,
And plunged over the bridge, and fell : and all
The cliffs reverberate from his monstrous fall
Rang : and the land by Tristram's grace was free.
So with high laud and honour thence went he,
And southward set his sail again, and passed
The lone land's ending, first beheld and last
Of eyes that look on England from the sea :
And his heart mourned within him, knowing how she
Whose heart with his was fatefully made fast
Sat now fast bound, as though some charm were cast
About her, such a brief space eastward thence,
And yet might soul not break the bonds of sense
And bring her to him in very life and breath
More than had this been even the sea of death
That washed between them, and its wide sweet light
The dim strait's darkness of the narrowing night
That shuts about men dying whose souls put forth
To pierce its passage through : but south and north
Alike for him were other than they were :
For all the northward coast shone smooth and fair,

And off its iron cliffs the keen-edged air
Blew summer, kindling from her mute bright mouth ;
But winter breathed out of the murmuring south,
Where, pale with wrathful watch on passing ships,
The lone wife lay in wait with wan dumb lips.
Yet, sailing where the shoreward ripple curled
Of the most wild sweet waves in all the world,
His soul took comfort even for joy to see
The strong deep joy of living sun and sea,
The large deep love of living sea and land,
As past the lonely lion-guarded strand
Where that huge warder lifts his couchant sides,
Asleep, above the sleepless lapse of tides,
The light sail swept, and past the unsounded caves
Unsearchable, wherein the pulse of waves
Throbs through perpetual darkness to and fro,
And the blind night swims heavily below
While heavily the strong noon broods above,
Even to the very bay whence very Love,
Strong daughter of the giant gods who wrought
Sun, earth, and sea out of their procreant thought,
Most meetly might have risen, and most divine
Beheld and heard things round her sound and shine
From floors of foam and gold to walls of serpentine.
For splendid as the limbs of that supreme
Incarnate beauty through men's visions gleam,
Whereof all fairest things are even but shadow or
    dream,
And lovely like as Love's own heavenliest face,

Gleams there and glows the presence and the grace
Even of the mother of all, in perfect pride of place.
For otherwhere beneath our world-wide sky
There may not be beheld of men that die
Aught else like this that dies not, nor may stress
Of ages that bow down men's works make less
The exultant awe that clothes with power its loveliness.
For who sets eye thereon soever knows
How since these rocks and waves first rolled and rose
The marvel of their many-coloured might
Hath borne this record sensible to sight,
The witness and the symbol of their own delight,   .
The gospel graven of life's most heavenly law,
Joy, brooding on its own still soul with awe,
A sense of godlike rest in godlike strife,
The sovereign conscience of the spirit of life.
Nor otherwhere on strand or mountain tower
Hath such fair beauty shining forth in flower
Put on the imperial robe of such imperious power.
For all the radiant rocks from depth to height
Burn with vast bloom of glories blossom-bright
As though the sun's own hand had thrilled them
    through with light
And stained them through with splendour : yet fiom
    thence
Such awe strikes rapture through the spirit of sense
From all the inaccessible sea-wall's girth,
That exultation, bright at heart as mirth,
Bows deeper down before the beauty of earth

Than fear may bow down ever : nor shall one
Who meets at Alpine dawn the mounting sun
On heights too high for many a wing to climb
Be touched with sense of aught seen more sublime
Than here smiles high and sweet in face of heaven
    and time.
For here the flower of fire, the soft hoar bloom
Of springtide olive-woods, the warm green gloom
Of clouded seas that swell and sound with dawn of
    doom,
The keen thwart lightning and the wan grey light
Of stormy sunrise crossed and vexed with night,
Flash, loom, and laugh with divers hues in one
From all the curved cliff's face, till day be done,
Against the sea's face and the gazing sun.
And whensoever a strong wave, high in hope,
Sweeps up some smooth slant breadth of stone aslope,
That glowed with duskier fire of hues less bright,
Swift as it sweeps back springs to sudden sight
The splendour of the moist rock's fervent light,
Fresh as from dew of birth when time was born
Out of the world-conceiving womb of morn.
All its quenched flames and darkling hues divine
Leap into lustrous life and laugh and shine
And darken into swift and dim decline
For one brief breath's space till the next wave run
Right up, and ripple down again, undone,
And leave it to be kissed and kindled of the sun.
And all these things, bright as they shone before
Man first set foot on earth or sail from shore,

Rose not less radiant than the sun sees now
When the autumn sea was cloven of Tristram's prow,
And strong in sorrow and hope and woful will
That hope might move not nor might sorrow kill
He held his way back toward the wild sad shore
Whence he should come to look on these no more,
Nor ever, save with sunless eyes shut fast,
Sail home to sleep in home-born earth at last.
　　And all these things fled fleet as light or breath
Past, and his heart waxed cold and dull as death,
Or swelled but as the tides of sorrow swell,
To sink with sullen sense of slow farewell.
So surely seemed the silence even to sigh
Assurance of inveterate prophecy,
'Thou shalt not come again home hither ere thou die.'
And the wind mourned and triumphed, and the sea
Wailed and took heart and trembled ; nor might he
Hear more of comfort in their speech, or see
More certitude in all the waste world's range
Than the only certitude of death and change.
And as the sense and semblance fluctuated
Of all things heard and seen alive or dead
That smote far off upon his ears or eyes
Or memory mixed with forecasts fain to rise
And fancies faint as ghostliest prophecies,
So seemed his own soul, changefully forlorn,
To shrink and triumph and mount up and mourn,
Yet all its fitful waters, clothed with night,
Lost heart not wholly, lacked not wholly light,
Seeing over life and death one star in sight

Where evening's gates as fair as morning's ope,
Whose name was memory, but whose flame was hope.
For all the tides of thought that rose and sank
Felt its fair strength wherefrom strong sorrow shrank
A mightier trust than time could change or cloy,
More strong than sorrow, more secure than joy.
So came he, nor content nor all unblest,
Back to the grey old land of Merlin's rest.

But ere six paces forth on shore he trod
Before him stood a knight with feet unshod,
And kneeling called upon him, as on God
Might sick men call for pity, praying aloud
With hands held up and head made bare and bowed;
' Tristram, for God's love and thine own dear fame,
I Tristram that am one with thee in name
And one in heart with all that praise thee—I,
Most woful man of all that may not die
For heartbreak and the heavier scourge of shame,
By all thy glory done our woful name
Beseech thee, called of all men gentlest knight,
Be now not slow to do my sorrows right.
I charge thee for thy fame's sake through this land,
I pray thee by thine own wife's fair white hand,
Have pity of me whose love is borne away
By one that makes of poor men's lives his prey,
A felon masked with knighthood : at his side
Seven brethren hath he night or day to ride
With seven knights more that wait on all his will :
And here at hand, ere yet one day fulfil
Its flight through light and darkness, shall they fare
Forth, and my bride among them, whom they bear

Through these wild lands his prisoner; and if now
I lose her, and my prayer be vain, and thou
Less fain to serve love's servants than of yore,
Then surely shall I see her face no more.
But if thou wilt, for love's sake of the bride
Who lay most loved of women at thy side,
Strike with me, straight then hence behoves us ride
And rest between the moorside and the sea
Where we may smite them passing : but for me
Poor stranger, me not worthy scarce to touch
Thy kind strong hand, how shouldst thou do so much ?
For now lone left this long time waits thy wife
And lacks her lord and light of wedded life
Whilst thou far off art famous : yet thy fame,
If thou take pity on me that bear thy name
Unworthily, but by that name implore
Thy grace, how shall not even thy fame grow more ?
But be thy will as God's among us done,
Who art far in fame above us as the sun :
Yet only of him have all men help and grace.'
     And all the lordly light of Tristram's face
Was softened as the sun's in kindly spring.
' Nay, then may God send me as evil a thing
When I give ear not to such prayers,' he said,
' And make my place among the nameless dead
When I put back one hour the time to smite
And do the unrighteous griefs of good men right.
Behold, I will not enter in nor rest
Here in mine own halls till this piteous quest
Find end ere noon to-morrow : but do thou,
Whose sister's face I may not look on now,

Go, Ganhardine, with tiding of the vow
That bids me turn aside for one day's strife
Or live dishonoured all my days of life,
And greet for me in brother's wise my wife,
And crave her pardon that for knighthood's sake
And womanhood's, whose bands may no man break
And keep the bands of bounden honour fast,
I seek not her till two nights yet be past
And this my quest accomplished, so God please
By me to give this young man's anguish ease
And on his wrongdoer's head his wrong requite.'
   And Tristram with that woful thankful knight
Rode by the seaside moorland wastes away
Between the quickening night and darkening day
Ere half the gathering stars had heart to shine.
And lightly toward his sister Ganhardine
Sped, where she sat and gazed alone afar
Above the grey sea for the sunset star,
And lightly kissed her hand and lightly spake
His tiding of that quest for knighthood's sake.
And the white-handed Iseult, bowing her head,
Gleamed on him with a glance athwart, and said ;
'As God's on earth and far above the sun,
So toward his handmaid be my lord's will done.'
And doubts too dim to question or divine
Touched as with shade the spirit of Ganhardine,
Hearing ; and scarce for half a doubtful breath
His bright light heart held half a thought of death
And knew not whence this darkling thought might be,
But surely not his sister's work : for she

Was ever sweet and good as summer air,
And soft as dew when all the night is fair,
And gracious as the golden maiden moon
When darkness craves her blessing : so full soon
His mind was light again as leaping waves,
Nor dreamed that hers was like a field of graves
Where no man's foot dares swerve to left or right,
Nor ear dares hearken, nor dares eye take sight
Of aught that moves and murmurs there at night.
   But by the sea-banks where at morn their foes
Might find them, lay those knightly name-fellows,
One sick with grief of heart and sleepless, one
With heart of hope triumphant as the sun
Dreaming asleep of love and fame and fight :
But sleep at last wrapped warm the wan young knight ;
And Tristram with the first pale windy light
Woke ere the sun spake summons, and his ear
Caught the sea's call that fired his heart to hear,
A noise of waking waters : for till dawn
The sea was silent as a mountain lawn
When the wind speaks not, and the pines are dumb,
And summer takes her fill ere autumn come
Of life more soft than slumber: but ere day
Rose, and the first beam smote the bounding bay,
Up sprang the strength of the dark East, and took
With its wide wings the waters as they shook,
And hurled them huddling on aheap, and cast
The full sea shoreward with a great glad blast,
Blown from the heart of morning : and with joy
Full-souled and perfect passion, as a boy

That leaps up light to wrestle with the sea
For pure heart's gladness and large ecstasy,
Up sprang the might of Tristram ; and his soul
Yearned for delight within him, and waxed whole
As a young child's with rapture of the hour
That brought his spirit and all the world to flower,
And all the bright blood in his veins beat time
To the wind's clarion and the water's chime
That called him and he followed it and stood
On the sand's verge before the grey great flood
Where the white hurtling heads of waves that met
Rose unsaluted of the sunrise yet.
And from his heart's root outward shot the sweet
Strong joy that thrilled him to the hands and feet,
Filling his limbs with pleasure and glad might,
And his soul drank the immeasurable delight
That earth drinks in with morning, and the free
Limitless love that lifts the stirring sea
When on her bare bright bosom as a bride
She takes the young sun, perfect in his pride,
Home to his place with passion : and the heart
Trembled for joy within the man whose part
Was here not least in living ; and his mind
Was rapt abroad beyond man's meaner kind
And pierced with love of all things and with mirth
Moved to make one with heaven and heavenlike earth
And with the light live water.   So awhile
He watched the dim sea with a deepening smile,
And felt the sound and savour and swift flight
Of waves that fled beneath the fading night

And died before the darkness, like a song
With harps between and trumpets blown along
Through the loud air of some triumphant day,
Sink through his spirit and purge all sense away
Save of the glorious gladness of his hour
And all the world about to break in flower
Before the sovereign laughter of the sun ;
And he, ere night's wide work lay all undone,
As earth from her bright body casts off night,
Cast off his raiment for a rapturous fight
And stood between the sea's edge and the sea
Naked, and godlike of his mould as he
Whose swift foot's sound shook all the towers of Troy;
So clothed with might, so girt upon with joy,
As, ere the knife had shorn to feed the fire
His glorious hair before the unkindled pyre
Whereon the half of his great heart was laid,
Stood, in the light of his live limbs arrayed,
Child of heroic earth and heavenly sea,
The flower of all men : scarce less bright than he,
If any of all men latter-born might stand,
Stood Tristram, silent, on the glimmering strand.
Not long : but with a cry of love that rang
As from a trumpet golden-mouthed, he sprang,
As toward a mother's where his head might rest
Her child rejoicing, toward the strong sea's breast
That none may gird nor measure : and his heart
Sent forth a shout that bade his lips not part,
But triumphed in him silent : no man's voice,
No song, no sound of clarions that rejoice,

Can set that glory forth which fills with fire
The body and soul that have their whole desire
Silent, and freer than birds or dreams are free
Take all their will of all the encountering sea.
And toward the foam he bent and forward smote,
Laughing, and launched his body like a boat
Full to the sea-breach, and against the tide
Struck strongly forth with amorous arms made wide
To take the bright breast of the wave to his
And on his lips the sharp sweet minute's kiss
Given of the wave's lip for a breath's space curled
And pure as at the daydawn of the world.
And round him all the bright rough shuddering sea
Kindled, as though the world were even as he,
Heart-stung with exultation of desire :
And all the life that moved him seemed to aspire,
As all the sea's life toward the sun : and still
Delight within him waxed with quickening will
More smooth and strong and perfect as a flame
That springs and spreads, till each glad limb became
A note of rapture in the tune of life,
Live music mild and keen as sleep and strife :
Till the sweet change that bids the sense grow sure
Of deeper depth and purity more pure
Wrapped him and lapped him round with clearer cold,
And all the rippling green grew royal gold
Between him and the far sun's rising rim.
And like the sun his heart rejoiced in him,
And brightened with a broadening flame of mirth :
And hardly seemed its life a part of earth,

But the life kindled of a fiery birth
And passion of a new-begotten son
Between the live sea and the living sun.
And mightier grew the joy to meet full-faced
Each wave, and mount with upward plunge, and taste
The rapture of its rolling strength, and cross
Its flickering crown of snows that flash and toss
Like plumes in battle's blithest charge, and thence
To match the next with yet more strenuous sense ;
Till on his eyes the light beat hard and bade
His face turn west and shoreward through the glad
Swift revel of the waters golden-clad,
And back with light reluctant heart he bore
Across the broad-backed rollers in to shore;
Strong-spirited for the chance and cheer of fight,
And donned his arms again, and felt the might
In all his limbs rejoice for strength, and praised
God for such life as that whereon he gazed,
And wist not surely its joy was even as fleet
As that which laughed and lapsed against his feet,
The bright thin grey foam-blossom, glad and hoar,
That flings its flower along the flowerless shore
On sand or shingle, and still with sweet strange snows,
As where one great white storm-dishevelled rose
May rain her wild leaves on a windy land,
Strews for long leagues the sounding slope of strand,
And flower on flower falls flashing, and anew
A fresh light leaps up whence the last flash flew,
And casts its brief glad gleam of life away
To fade not flowerwise but as drops the day

Storm·smitten, when at once the dark devours
Heaven and the sea and earth with all their flowers;
No star in heaven, on earth no rose to see,
But the white blown brief blossoms of the sea,
That make her green gloom starrier than the sky,
Dance yet before the tempest's tune, and die.
And all these things he glanced upon, and knew
How fair they shone, from earth's least flake of dew
To stretch of seas and imminence of skies,
Unwittingly, with unpresageful eyes,
For the last time.   The world's half heavenly face,
The music of the silence of the place,
The confluence and the refluence of the sea,
The wind's note ringing over wold and lea,
Smote once more through him keen as fire that smote,
Rang once more through him one reverberate note,
That faded as he turned again and went,
Fulfilled by strenuous joy with strong content,
To take his last delight of labour done
That yet should be beholden of the sun
Or ever give man comfort of his hand.

   Beside a wood's edge in the broken land
An hour at wait the twain together stood,
Till swift between the moorside and the wood
Flashed the spears forward of the coming train;
And seeing beside the strong chief spoiler's rein
His wan love riding prisoner in the crew,
Forth with a cry the young man leapt, and flew
Right on that felon sudden as a flame;
And hard at hand the mightier Tristram came,

Bright as the sun and terrible as fire :
And there had sword and spear their soul's desire,
And blood that quenched the spear's thirst as it poured
Slaked royally the hunger of the sword,
Till the fierce heart of steel could scarce fulfil
Its greed and ravin of insatiate will.
For three the fiery spear of Tristram drove
Down ere a point of theirs his harness clove
Or its own sheer mid shaft splintered in twain ;
And his heart bounded in him, and was fain
As fire or wind that takes its fill by night
Of tempest and of triumph : so the knight
Rejoiced and ranged among them, great of hand,
Till seven lay slain upon the heathery sand
Or in the dense breadth of the woodside fern.
Nor did his heart not mightier in him burn
Seeing at his hand that young knight fallen, and high
The red sword reared again that bade him die.
But on the slayer exulting like the flame
Whose foot foreshines the thunder Tristram came
Raging, for piteous wrath had made him fire ;
And as a lion's look his face was dire
That flashed against his foeman ere the sword
Lightened, and wrought the heart's will of its lord,
And clove through casque and crown the wrongdoer's
    head.
And right and left about their dark chief dead
Hurtled and hurled those felons to and fro,
Till as a storm-wind scatters leaves and snow

His right hand ravening scattered them ; but one
That fled with sidelong glance athwart the sun
Shot, and the shaft flew sure, and smote aright,
Full in the wound's print of his great first fight
When at his young strength's peril he made free
Cornwall, and slew beside its bordering sea
The fair land's foe, who yielding up his breath
Yet left him wounded nigh to dark slow death.
And hardly with long toil thence he won home
Between the grey moor and the glimmering foam,
And halting fared through his own gate, and fell,
Thirsting : for as the sleepless fire of hell
The fire within him of his wound again
Burned, and his face was dark as death for pain,
And blind the blithe light of his eyes : but they
Within that watched and wist not of the fray
Came forth and cried aloud on him for woe.
And scarce aloud his thanks fell faint and slow
As men reared up the strong man fallen and bore
Down the deep hall that looked along the shore,
And laid him soft abed, and sought in vain
If herb or hand of leech might heal his pain.
And the white-handed Iseult hearkening heard
All, and drew nigh, and spake no wifely word,
But gazed upon him doubtfully, with eyes
Clouded ; and he in kindly knightly wise
Spake with scant breath, and smiling : 'Surely this
Is penance for discourteous lips to kiss
And feel the brand burn through them, here to lie
And lack the strength here to do more than sigh

And hope not hence for pardon.' Then she bowed
Her head, still silent as a stooping cloud,
And laid her lips against his face; and he
Felt sink a shadow across him as the sea
Might feel a cloud stoop toward it : and his heart
Darkened as one that wastes by sorcerous art
And knows not whence it withers : and he turned
Back from her emerald eyes his own, and yearned
All night for eyes all golden : and the dark
Hung sleepless round him till the loud first lark
Rang record forth once more of darkness done,
And all things born took comfort from the sun.

IX.

THE SAILING OF THE SWAN.

FATE, that was born ere spirit and flesh were made,
The fire that fills man's life with light and shade ;
The power beyond all godhead which puts on
All forms of multitudinous unison,
A raiment of eternal change inwrought
With shapes and hues more subtly spun than thought,
Where all things old bear fruit of all things new
And one deep chord throbs all the music through,
The chord of change unchanging, shadow and light
Inseparable as reverberate day from night ;
Fate, that of all things save the soul of man
Is lord and God since body and soul began ;
Fate, that keeps all the tune of things in chime ;
Fate, that breathes power upon the lips of time ;
That smites and soothes with heavy and healing hand
All joys and sorrows born in life's dim land,
Till joy be found a shadow and sorrow a breath
And life no discord in the tune with death,
But all things fain alike to die and live
In pulse and lapse of tides alternative,

Through silence and through sound of peace and strife,
Till birth and death be one in sight of life ;
Fate, heard and seen of no man's eyes or ears,
To no man shown through light of smiles or tears,
And moved of no man's prayer to fold its wings ;
Fate, that is night and light on worldly things ;
Fate, that is fire to burn and sea to drown,
Strength to build up and thunder to cast down ;
Fate, shield and screen for each man's lifelong head,
And sword at last or dart that strikes it dead ;
Fate, higher than heaven and deeper than the grave,
That saves and spares not, spares and doth not save ;
Fate, that in gods' wise is not bought and sold
For prayer or price of penitence or gold ;
Whose law shall live when life bids earth farewell,
Whose justice hath for shadows heaven and hell ;
Whose judgment into no god's hand is given,
Nor is its doom not more than hell or heaven :
Fate, that is pure of love and clean of hate,
Being equal-eyed as nought may be but fate ;
Through many and weary days of foiled desire
Leads life to rest where tears no more take fire ;
Through many and weary dreams of quenched delight
Leads life through death past sense of day and night.
  Nor shall they feel or fear, whose date is done,
Aught that made once more dark the living sun
And bitterer in their breathing lips the breath
Than the dark dawn and bitter dust of death.
For all the light, with fragrance as of flowers,
That clothes the lithe live limbs of separate hours,

More sweet to savour and more clear to sight
Dawns on the soul death's undivided night.
No vigils has that perfect night to keep,
No fever-fits of vision shake that sleep.
Nor if they wake, and any place there be
Wherein the soul may feel her wings beat free
Through air too clear and still for sound or strife ;
If life were haply death, and death be life ;
If love with yet some lovelier laugh revive,
And song relume the light it bore alive,
And friendship, found of all earth's gifts most good,
Stand perfect in perpetual brotherhood ;
If aught indeed at all of all this be,
Though none might say nor any man might see,
Might he that sees the shade thereof not say
This dream were trustier than the truth of day.
Nor haply may not hope, with heart more clear,
Burn deathward, and the doubtful soul take cheer,
Seeing through the channelled darkness yearn a star
Whose eyebeams are not as the morning's are,
Transient, and subjugate of lordlier light,
But all unconquerable by noon or night,
Being kindled only of life's own inmost fire,
Truth, stablished and made sure by strong desire,
Fountain of all things living, source and seed,
Force that perforce transfigures dream to deed,
God that begets on time, the body of death,
Eternity : nor may man's darkening breath,
Albeit it stain, disfigure or destroy
The glass wherein the soul sees life and joy

Only, with strength renewed and spirit of youth,
And brighter than the sun's the body of Truth
Eternal, unimaginable of man,
Whose very face not Thought's own eyes may scan,
But see far off his radiant feet at least,
Trampling the head of Fear, the false high priest,
Whose broken chalice foams with blood no more,
And prostrate on that high priest's chancel floor,
Bruised, overthrown, blind, maimed, with bloodless rod,
The miscreation of his miscreant God.
That sovereign shadow cast of souls that dwell
In darkness and the prison-house of hell
Whose walls are built of deadly dread, and bound
The gates thereof with dreams as iron round,
And all the bars therein and stanchions wrought
Of shadow forged like steel and tempered thought
And words like swords and thunder-clouded creeds
And faiths more dire than sin's most direful deeds :
That shade accursed and worshipped, which hath made
The soul of man that brought it forth a shade
Black as the womb of darkness, void and vain,
A throne for fear, a pasturage for pain,
Impotent, abject, clothed upon with lies,
A foul blind fume of words and prayers that rise,
Aghast and harsh, abhorrent and abhorred,
Fierce as its God, blood-saturate as its Lord ;
With loves and mercies on its lips that hiss
Comfort, and kill compassion with a kiss,
And strike the world black with their blasting breath ;
That ghost whose core of life is very death

And all its light of heaven a shadow of hell,
Fades, falls, wanes, withers by none other spell
But theirs whose eyes and ears have seen and heard
Not the face naked, not the perfect word,
But the bright sound and feature felt from far
Of life which feeds the spirit and the star,
Thrills the live light of all the suns that roll,
And stirs the still sealed springs of every soul.
    Three dim days through, three slumberless nights
        long,
Perplexed at dawn, oppressed at evensong,
The strong man's soul now sealed indeed with pain,
And all its springs half dried with drought, had lain
Prisoner within the fleshly dungeon-dress
Sore chafed and wasted with its weariness.
And fain it would have found the star, and fain
Made this funereal prison-house of pain
A watch-tower whence its eyes might sweep, and see
If any place for any hope might be
Beyond the hells and heavens of sleep and strife,
Or any light at all of any life
Beyond the dense false darkness woven above,
And could not, lacking grace to look on love.
And in the third night's dying hour he spake,
Seeing scarce the seals that bound the dayspring
        break
And scarce the daystar burn above the sea :
'O Ganhardine, my brother true to me,
I charge thee by those nights and days we knew
No great while since in England, by the dew

That bathed those nights with blessing, and the fire
That thrilled those days as music thrills a lyre,
Do now for me perchance the last good deed
That ever love may crave or life may need
Ere love lay life in ashes : take to thee
My ship that shows aloft against the sea
Carved on her stem the semblance of a swan,
And ere the waves at even again wax wan
Pass, if it may be, to my lady's land,
And give this ring into her secret hand,
And bid her think how hard on death I lie,
And fain would look upon her face and die.
But as a merchant's laden be the bark
With royal ware for fraughtage, that King Mark
May take for toll thereof some costly thing ;
And when this gift finds grace before the king,
Choose forth a cup, and put therein my ring
Where sureliest only of one it may be seen,
And bid her handmaid bear it to the queen
For earnest of thine homage : then shall she
Fear, and take counsel privily with thee,
To know what errand there is thine from me
And what my need in secret of her sight.
But make thee two sails, one like sea-foam white
To spread for signal if thou bring her back,
And if she come not see the sail be black,
That I may know or ever thou take land
If these my lips may die upon her hand
Or hers may never more be mixed with mine.'
　　And his heart quailed for grief in Ganhardine,

Hearing ; and all his brother bade he swore
Surely to do, and straight fare forth from shore. ,
But the white-handed Iseult hearkening heard
All, and her heart waxed hot, and every word
Thereon seemed graven and printed in her thought
As lines with fire and molten iron wrought.
And hard within her heavy heart she cursed
Both, and her life was turned to fiery thirst,
And all her soul was hunger, and its breath
Of hope and life a blast of raging death.
For only in hope of evil was her life.
So bitter burned within the unchilded wife
A virgin lust for vengeance, and such hate
Wrought in her now the fervent work of fate.

   Then with a south-west wind the Swan set forth,
And over wintering waters bore to north,
And round the wild land's windy westward end
Up the blown channel bade her bright way bend
East on toward high Tintagel : where at dark
Landing, fair welcome found they of King Mark,
And Ganhardine with Brangwain as of old
Spake, and she took the cup of chiselled gold
Wherein lay secret Tristram's trothplight ring,
And bare it unbeholden of the king
Even to her lady's hand, which hardly took
A gift whereon a queen's eyes well might look,
With grace forlorn of weary gentleness.
But, seeing, her life leapt in her, keen to guess
The secret of the symbol : and her face
Flashed bright with blood whence all its grief-worn
      grace

Took fire and kindled to the quivering hair.
And in the dark soft hour of starriest air
Thrilled through with sense of midnight, when the
    world
Feels the wide wings of sleep about it furled,
Down stole the queen, deep-muffled to her wan
Mute restless lips, and came where yet the Swan
Swung fast at anchor : whence by starlight she
Hoised snowbright sails, and took the glimmering sea.
    But all the long night long more keen and sore
His wound's grief waxed in Tristram evermore,
And heavier always hung his heart asway
Between dim fear and clouded hope of day.
And still with face and heart at silent strife
Beside him watched the maiden called his wife,
Patient, and spake not save when scarce he spake,
Murmuring with sense distraught and spirit awake
Speech bitterer than the words thereof were sweet :
And hatred thrilled her to the hands and feet,
Listening : for alway back reiterate came
The passionate faint burden of her name.
Nor ever through the labouring lips astir
Came any word of any thought of her.
But the soul wandering struggled and clung hard
Only to dreams of joy in Joyous Gard
Or wildwood nights beside the Cornish strand,
Or Merlin's holier sleep here hard at hand
Wrapped round with deep soft spells in dim
    Broceliande.
And with such thirst as joy's drained wine-cup leaves

When fear to hope as hope to memory cleaves
His soul desired the dewy sense of leaves,
The soft green smell of thickets drenched with dawn,
The faint slot kindling on the fiery lawn
As day's first hour made keen the spirit again
That lured and spurred on quest his hound Hodain,
The breeze, the bloom, the splendour and the sound,
That stung like fire the hunter and the hound,
The pulse of wind, the passion of the sea,
The rapture of the woodland : then would he
Sigh, and as one that fain would all be dead
Heavily turn his heavy-laden head
Back, and close eyes for comfort, finding none.
And fain he would have died or seen the sun,
Being sick at heart of darkness : yet afresh
Began the long strong strife of spirit and flesh
And branching pangs of thought whose branches
     bear
The bloodred fruit whose core is black, despair.
And the wind slackened and again grew great,
Palpitant as men's pulses palpitate
Between the flowing and ebbing tides of fate
That wash their lifelong waifs of weal and woe
Through night and light and twilight to and fro.
Now as a pulse of hope its heartbeat throbbed,
Now like one stricken shrank and sank and sobbed,
Then, yearning as with child of death, put forth
A wail that filled the night up south and north
With woful sound of waters : and he said,
‘ So might the wind wail if the world were dead

And its wings wandered over nought but sea.
I would I knew she would not come to me,
For surely she will come not : then should I,
Once knowing I shall not look upon her, die.
I knew not life could so long breathe such breath
As I do.   Nay, what grief were this, if death,
The sole sure friend of whom the whole world saith
He lies not, nor hath ever this been said,
That death would heal not grief—if death were dead
And all ways closed whence grief might pass with life!'
    Then softly spake his watching virgin wife
Out of her heart, deep down below her breath :
' Fear not but death shall come—and after death
Judgment.'   And he that heard not answered her,
Saying—' Ah, but one there was, if truth not err,
For true men's trustful tongues have said it—one
Whom these mine eyes knew living while the sun
Looked yet upon him, and mine own ears heard   -
The deep sweet sound once of his godlike word—
Who sleeps and dies not, but with soft live breath
Takes always all the deep delight of death,
Through love's gift of a woman : but for me
Love's hand is not the hand of Nimue,
Love's word no still smooth murmur of the dove,
No kiss of peace for me the kiss of love.
Nor, whatsoe'er thy life's love ever give,
Dear, shall it ever bid me sleep or live ;
Nor from thy brows and lips and living breast
As his from Nimue's shall my soul take rest ;
Not rest but unrest hath our long love given—
Unrest on earth that wins not rest in heaven.

What rest may we take ever? what have we
Had ever more of peace than has the sea?
Has not our life been as a wind that blows
Through lonelier lands than rear the wild white rose
That each year sees requickened, but for us
Time once and twice hath here or there done thus
And left the next year following empty and bare?
What rose hath our last year's rose left for heir,
What wine our last year's vintage? and to me
More were one fleet forbidden sense of thee,
One perfume of thy present grace, one thought
Made truth one hour, ere all mine hours be nought,
One very word, breath, look, sign, touch of hand,
Than all the green leaves in Broceliande
Full of sweet sound, full of sweet wind and sun ;
O God, thou knowest I would no more but one,
I would no more but once more ere I die
Find thus much mercy. Nay, but then were I
Happier than he whom there thy grace hath found,
For thine it must be, this that wraps him round,
Thine only, albeit a fiend's force gave him birth,
Thine that has given him heritage on earth
Of slumber-sweet eternity to keep
Fast in soft hold of everliving sleep.
Happier were I, more sinful man, than he,
Whom one love-worthier then than Nimue
Should with a breath make blest among the dead.'
    And the wan wedded maiden answering said,
Soft as hate speaks within itself apart :
'Surely ye shall not, ye that rent mine heart,

Being one in sin, in punishment be twain.'
    And the great knight that heard not spake again
And sighed, but sweet thought of sweet things gone by
Kindled with fire of joy the very sigh
And touched it through with rapture : ' Ay, this were
How much more than the sun and sunbright air,
How much more than the springtide, how much more
Than sweet strong sea-wind quickening wave and
        shore
With one divine pulse of continuous breath,
If she might kiss me with the kiss of death,
And make the light of life by death's look dim !'
    And the white wedded virgin answered him,
Inwardly, wan with hurt no herb makes whole :
' Yea surely, ye whose sin hath slain my soul,
Surely your own souls shall have peace in death
And pass with benediction in their breath
And blessing given of mine their sin hath slain.'
    And Tristram with sore yearning spake again,
Saying : ' Yea, might this thing once be, how should I,
With all my soul made one thanksgiving, die,
And pass before what judgment-seat may be,
And cry, " Lord, now do all thou wilt with me,
Take all thy fill of justice, work thy will ;
Though all thy heart of wrath have all its fill,
My heart of suffering shall endure, and say,
For that thou gavest me living yesterday
I bless thee though thou curse me." Ay, and well
Might one cast down into the gulf of hell,

Remembering this, take heart and thank his fate—
That God, whose doom now scourges him with hate,
Once, in the wild and whirling world above,
Bade mercy kiss his dying lips with love.
But if this come not, then he doth me wrong.
For what hath love done, all this long life long,
That death should trample down his poor last prayer
Who prays not for forgiveness?   Though love were
Sin dark as hate, have we not here that sinned
Suffered? has that been less than wintry wind
Wherewith our love lies blasted?   O mine own,
O mine and no man's yet save mine alone,
Iseult! what ails thee that I lack so long
All of thee, all things thine for which I long?
For more than watersprings to shadeless sands,
More to me were the comfort of her hands
Touched once, and more than rays that set and rise
The glittering arrows of her glorious eyes,
More to my sense than fire to dead cold air
The wind and light and odour of her hair,
More to my soul than summer's to the south
The mute clear music of her amorous mouth,
And to my heart's heart more than heaven's great rest
The fullness of the fragrance of her breast.
Iseult, Iseult, what grace hath life to give
More than we twain have had of life, and live?
Iseult, Iseult, what grace may death not keep
As sweet for us to win of death, and sleep?
Come therefore, let us twain pass hence and try
If it be better not to live but die,

M

With love for lamp to light us out of life.'
    And on that word his wedded maiden wife,
Pale as the moon in star-forsaken skies
Ere the sun fill them, rose with set strange eyes
And gazed on him that saw not : and her heart
Heaved as a man's death-smitten with a dart
That smites him sleeping, warm and full of life :
So toward her lord that was not looked his wife,
His wife that was not : and her heart within
Burnt bitter like an aftertaste of sin
To one whose memory drinks and loathes the lee
Of shame or sorrow deeper than the sea :
And no fear touched him of her eyes above
And ears that hoarded each poor word whence love
Made sweet the broken music of his breath.
' Iseult, my life that wast and art my death,
My life in life that hast been, and that art
Death in my death, sole wound that cleaves mine heart,
Mine heart that else, how spent soe'er, were whole,
Breath of my spirit and anguish of my soul,
How can this be that hence thou canst not hear,
Being but by space divided ?   One is here,
But one of twain I looked at once to see ;
Shall death keep time and thou not keep with me ? '
    And the white married maiden laughed at heart,
Hearing, and scarce with lips at all apart
Spake, and as fire between them was her breath ;
' Yea, now thou liest not : yea, for I am death.'
    By this might eyes that watched without behold
Deep in the gulfs of aching air acold

The roses of the dawning heaven that strew
The low soft sun's way ere his power shine through
And burn them up with fire : but far to west
Had sunk the dead moon on the live sea's breast,
Slain as with bitter fear to see the sun :
And eastward was a strong bright wind begun
Between the clouds and waters : and he said,
Seeing hardly through dark dawn her doubtful head,
'Iseult ?' and like a death-bell faint and clear
The virgin voice rang answer—' I am here.'
And his heart sprang, and sank again : and she
Spake, saying, 'What would my knightly lord with me ?'
And Tristram : ' Hath my lady watched all night
Beside me, and I knew not?   God requite
Her love for comfort shown a man nigh dead.'

'Yea, God shall surely guerdon it,' she said,
' Who hath kept me all my days through to this hour.'

And Tristram : ' God alone hath grace and power
To pay such grace toward one unworthier shown
Than ever durst, save only of God alone,
Crave pardon yet and comfort, as I would
Crave now for charity if my heart were good,
But as a coward's it fails me, even for shame.'

Then seemed her face a pale funereal flame
That burns down slow by midnight, as she said :
'Speak, and albeit thy bidding spake me dead,
God's love renounce me if it were not done.'

And Tristram : ' When the sea-line takes the sun
That now should be not far off sight from far,
Look if there come not with the morning star

My ship bound hither from the northward back,
And if the sail be white thereof or black.'
　And knowing the soothfast sense of his desire
So sore the heart within her raged like fire
She could not wring forth of her lips a word,
But bowing made sign how humbly had she heard.
And the sign given made light his heart ; and she
Set her face hard against the yearning sea
Now all athirst with trembling trust of hope
To see the sudden gates of sunrise ope ;
But thirstier yearned the heart whose fiery gate
Lay wide that vengeance might come in to hate.
And Tristram lay at thankful rest, and thought
Now surely life nor death could grieve him aught,
Since past was now life's anguish as a breath,
And surely past the bitterness of death.
For seeing he had found at these her hands this grace,
It could not be but yet some breathing-space
Might leave him life to look again on love's own face.
'Since if for death's sake,' in his heart he said,
'Even she take pity upon me quick or dead,
How shall not even from God's hand be compassion
　　shed ?
For night bears dawn, how weak soe'er and wan,
And sweet ere death, men fable, sings the swan.
So seems the Swan my signal from the sea
To sound a song that sweetens death to me
Clasped round about with radiance from above
Of dawn, and closer clasped on earth by love.

Shall all things brighten, and this my sign be dark?'
  And high from heaven suddenly rang the lark,
Triumphant; and the far first refluent ray
Filled all the hollow darkness full with day.
And on the deep sky's verge a fluctuant light
Gleamed, grew, shone, strengthened into perfect sight,
As bowed and dipped and rose again the sail's clear
    white.
And swift and steadfast as a sea-mew's wing
It neared before the wind, as fain to bring
Comfort, and shorten yet its narrowing track.
And she that saw looked hardly toward him back,
Saying, 'Ay, the ship comes surely; but her sail is
    black.'
And fain he would have sprung upright, and seen,
And spoken: but strong death struck sheer between,
And darkness closed as iron round his head:
And smitten through the heart lay Tristram dead.
  And scarce the word had flown abroad, and wail
Risen, ere to shoreward came the snowbright sail,
And lightly forth leapt Ganhardine on land,
And led from ship with swift and reverent hand
Iseult: and round them up from all the crowd
Broke the great wail for Tristram out aloud.
And ere her ear might hear her heart had heard,
Nor sought she sign for witness of the word;
But came and stood above him newly dead,
And felt his death upon her: and her head
Bowed, as to reach the spring that slakes all drouth;
And their four lips became one silent mouth.

So came their hour on them that were in life
Tristram and Iseult : so from love and strife
The stroke of love's own hand felt last and best
Gave them deliverance to perpetual rest.
So, crownless of the wreaths that life had wound,
They slept, with flower of tenderer comfort crowned :
From bondage and the fear of time set free,
And all the yoke of space on earth and sea
Cast as a curb for ever : nor might now
Fear and desire bid soar their souls or bow,
Lift up their hearts or break them : doubt nor grief
More now might move them, dread nor disbelief
Touch them with shadowy cold or fiery sting,
Nor sleepless languor with its weary wing,
Nor harsh estrangement, born of time's vain breath,
Nor change, a darkness deeper far than death.
And round the sleep that fell around them then
Earth lies not wrapped, nor records wrought of men
Rise up for timeless token : but their sleep
Hath round it like a raiment all the deep ;
No change or gleam or gloom of sun and rain,
But all time long the might of all the main
Spread round them as round earth soft heaven is
     spread,
And peace more strong than death round all the dead.

For death is of an hour, and after death
Peace : nor for aught that fear or fancy saith,
Nor even for very love's own sake, shall strife
Perplex again that perfect peace with life.
And if, as men that mourn may deem or dream,
Rest haply here than there might sweeter seem,
And sleep, that lays one hand on all, more good
By some sweet grave's grace given of wold or wood
Or clear high glen or sunbright wind-worn down
Than where life thunders through the trampling town
With daylong feet and nightlong overhead,
What grave may cast such grace round any dead,
What so sublime sweet sepulchre may be
For all that life leaves mortal, as the sea?
And these, rapt forth perforce from earthly ground,
These twain the deep sea guards, and girdles round
Their sleep more deep than any sea's gulf lies,
Though changeless with the change in shifting skies,
Nor mutable with seasons : for the grave
That held them once, being weaker than a wave,
The waves long since have buried : though their tomb
Was royal that by ruth's relenting doom
Men gave them in Tintagel : for the word
Took wing which thrilled all piteous hearts that heard
The word wherethrough their lifelong lot stood shown,
And when the long sealed springs of fate were known,
The blind bright innocence of lips that quaffed
Love, and the marvel of the mastering draught,

And all the fraughtage of the fateful bark,
Loud like a child upon them wept King Mark,
Seeing round the sword's hilt which long since had
    fought
For Cornwall's love a scroll of writing wrought,
A scripture writ of Tristram's hand, wherein
Lay bare the sinless source of all their sin,
No choice of will, but chance and sorcerous art,
With prayer of him for pardon : and his heart
Was molten in him, wailing as he kissed
Each with the kiss of kinship—' Had I wist,
Ye had never sinned nor died thus, nor had I
Borne in this doom that bade you sin and die
So sore a part of sorrow.'   And the king
Built for their tomb a chapel bright like spring
With flower-soft wealth of branching tracery made
Fair as the frondage each fleet year sees fade,
That should not fall till many a year were done.
There slept they wedded under moon and sun
And change of stars : and through the casements came
Midnight and noon girt round with shadow and flame
To illume their grave or veil it : till at last
On these things too was doom as darkness cast :
For the strong sea hath swallowed wall and tower,
And where their limbs were laid in woful hour
For many a fathom gleams and moves and moans
The tide that sweeps above their coffined bones
In the wrecked chancel by the shivered shrine :
Nor where they sleep shall moon or sunlight shine

Nor man look down for ever : none shall say,
Here once, or here, Tristram and Iseult lay :
But peace they have that none may gain who live,
And rest about them that no love can give,
And over them, while death and life shall be,
The light and sound and darkness of the sea.

ATHENS:

AN ODE.

Eʀᴇ from under earth again like fire the violet
    kindle,   [*Str.* 1.
  Ere the holy buds and hoar on olive-branches
    bloom,
Ere the crescent of the last pale month of winter
    dwindle,
  Shrink, and fall as falls a dead leaf on the dead
    month's tomb,
Round the hills whose heights the first-born olive-
    blossom brightened,
  Round the city brow-bound once with violets like
    a bride,
Up from under earth again a light that long since
    lightened
  Breaks, whence all the world took comfort as all
    time takes pride.
Pride have all men in their fathers that were free
    before them,
  In the warriors that begat us free-born pride have
    we :

But the fathers of their spirits, how may men adore
    them,
    With what rapture may we praise, who bade our
        souls be free?
Sons of Athens born in spirit and truth are all born
    free men ;
    Most of all, we, nurtured where the north wind
        holds his reign :
Children all we sea-folk of the Salaminian seamen,
    Sons of them that beat back Persia they that beat
        back Spain.
Since the songs of Greece fell silent, none like ours
    have risen ;
    Since the sails of Greece fell slack, no ships have
        sailed like ours ;
How should we lament not, if her spirit sit in prison?
    How should we rejoice not, if her wreaths renew
        their flowers?
All the world is sweeter, if the Athenian violet
    quicken :
    All the world is brighter, if the Athenian sun
        return :
All things foul on earth wax fainter, by that sun's
    light stricken :
    All ill growths are withered, where those fragrant
        flower-lights burn.
All the wandering waves of seas with all their warring
    waters
    Roll the record on for ever of the sea-fight there,

When the capes were battle's lists, and all the straits
    were slaughter's,
    And the myriad Medes as foam-flakes on the
      scattering air.
Ours the lightning was that cleared the north and lit
    the nations,
    But the light that gave the whole world light of old
      was she :
Ours an age or twain, but hers are endless genera-
    tions :
    All the world is hers at heart, and most of all are
      we.

Ye that bear the name about you of her glory, [*Ant.* 1.
    Men that wear the sign of Greeks upon you
      sealed,
Yours is yet the choice to write yourselves in story
    Sons of them that fought the Marathonian field.
Slaves of no man were ye, said your warrior poet,
    Neither subject unto man as underlings :
Yours is now the season here wherein to show it,
    If the seed ye be of them that knew not kings.
If ye be not, swords nor words alike found brittle
    From the dust of death to raise you shall prevail :
Subject swords and dead men's words may stead you
    little,
    If their old king-hating heart within you fail.
If your spirit of old, and not your bonds, be broken,
    If the kingless heart be molten in your breasts,

By what signs and wonders, by what word or token,
  Shall ye drive the vultures from your eagles' nests?
All the gains of tyrants Freedom counts for losses ;
  Nought of all the work done holds she worth the
    work,
When the slaves whose faith is set on crowns and
    crosses
  Drive the Cossack bear against the tiger Turk.
Neither cross nor crown nor crescent shall ye bow to,
  Nought of Araby nor Jewry, priest nor king :
As your watchword was of old, so be it now too :
  As from lips long stilled, from yours let healing
    spring.
Through the fights of old, your battle-cry was healing,
  And the Saviour that ye called on was the Sun :
Dawn by dawn behold in heaven your God, revealing
  Light from darkness as when Marathon was won.
Gods were yours yet strange to Turk or Galilean,
  Light and Wisdom only then as gods adored :
Pallas was your shield, your comforter was Pæan,
  From your bright world's navel spake the Sun your
    Lord.

Though the names be lost, and changed the signs
    of Light and Wisdom be,   [*Ep.* 1.
By these only shall men conquer, by these only be set
    free :
When the whole world's eye was Athens, these were
    yours, and theirs were ye.

Light was given you of your wisdom, light ye gave the
world again :

As the sun whose godhead lightened on her soul was
Hellas then :

Yea, the least of all her children as the chosen of
other men.

Change your hearts not with your garments, nor your
faith with creeds that change :

Truth was yours, the truth which time and chance
transform not nor estrange :

Purer truth nor higher abides not in the reach of
time's whole range.

Gods are they in all men's memories and for all time's
periods,

They that hurled the host back seaward which had
scourged the sea with rods :

Gods for us are all your fathers, even the least of
these as gods.

In the dark of days the thought of them is with us,
strong to save,

They that had no lord, and made the Great King
lesser than a slave ;

They that rolled all Asia back on Asia, broken like a
wave.

No man's men were they, no master's and no God's
but these their own :

Gods not loved in vain nor served amiss, nor all yet
overthrown :

Love of country, Freedom, Wisdom, Light, and none
save these alone.

King by king came up against them, sire and son,
    and turned to flee :

Host on host roared westward, mightier each than
    each, if more might be :

Field to field made answer, clamorous like as wave to
    wave at sea.

Strife to strife responded, loud as rocks to clangorous
    rocks respond

Where the deep rings wreck to seamen held in tem-
    pest's thrall and bond,

Till when war's bright work was perfect peace as
    radiant rose beyond :

Peace made bright with fruit of battle, stronger made
    for storm gone down,

With the flower of song held heavenward for the
    violet of her crown

Woven about the fragrant forehead of the fostress
    maiden's town.

Gods arose alive on earth from under stroke of human
    hands :

As the hands that wrought them, these are dead, and
    mixed with time's dead sands :

But the godhead of supernal song, though these now
    stand not, stands.

Pallas is not, Phœbus breathes no more in breathing
    brass or gold :

Clytæmnestra towers, Cassandra wails, for ever:
    Time is bold,

But nor heart nor hand hath he to unwrite the scrip-
    tures writ of old.

Dead the great chryselephantine God, as dew last
    evening shed :
Dust of earth or foam of ocean is the symbol of his
    head :

Earth and ocean shall be shadows when Prometheus
    shall be dead.

Fame around her warriors living rang through Greece
    and lightened,   [*Str.* 2.
    Moving equal with their stature, stately with their
        strength :
Thebes and Lacedæmon at their breathing presence
    brightened,
    Sense or sound of them filled all the live land's
        breadth and length.
All the lesser tribes put on the pure Athenian fashion,
    One Hellenic heart was from the mountains to the
        sea :
Sparta's bitter self grew sweet with high half-human
    passion,
    And her dry thorns flushed aflower in strait Ther-
        mopylæ.
Fruitless yet the flowers had fallen, and all the deeds
    died fruitless,
    Save that tongues of after men, the children of her
        peace,
Took the tale up of her glories, transient else and
    rootless,
    And in ears and hearts of all men left the praise of
        Greece.

Fair the war-time was when still, as beacon answering
    beacon,
  Sea to land flashed fight, and thundered note of
    wrath or cheer ;
But the strength of noonday night hath power to
    waste and weaken,
  Nor may light be passed from hand to hand of
    year to year
If the dying deed be saved not, ere it die for ever,
  By the hands and lips of men more wise than years
    are strong ;
If the soul of man take heed not that the deed die
    never,
  Clothed about with purple and gold of story,
    crowned with song.
Still the burning heart of boy and man alike rejoices,
  Hearing words which made it seem of old for all
    who sang
That their heaven of heavens waxed happier when
    from free men's voices
  Well-beloved Harmodius and Aristogeiton rang.
Never fell such fragrance from the flower-month's
    rose-red kirtle
  As from chaplets on the bright friends' brows who
    slew their lord :
Greener grew the leaf and balmier blew the flower of
    myrtle
  When its blossom sheathed the sheer tyrannicidal
    sword.

None so glorious garland crowned the feast Panathe-
 næan
  As this wreath too frail to fetter fast the Cyprian
    dove :
None so fiery song sprang sunwards annual as the
 pæan
  Praising perfect love of friends and perfect country's
    love.

Higher than highest of all those heavens wherefrom
    the starry   [*Ant.* 2.
  Song of Homer shone above the rolling fight,
Gleams like spring's green bloom on boughs all gaunt
    and gnarry
  Soft live splendour as of flowers of foam in flight,
Glows a glory of mild-winged maidens upward mount-
    ing
  Sheer through air made shrill with strokes of smooth
    swift wings
Round the rocks beyond foot's reach, past eyesight's
    counting,
  Up the cleft where iron wind of winter rings
Round a God fast clenched in iron jaws of fetters,
  Him who culled for man the fruitful flower of fire,
Bared the darkling scriptures writ in dazzling letters,
  Taught the truth of dreams deceiving men's desire,
Gave their water-wandering chariot-seats of ocean
  Wings, and bade the rage of war-steeds champ the
    rein,

Showed the symbols of the wild birds' wheeling
    motion,
  Waged for man's sake war with God and all his
    train.
Earth, whose name was also Righteousness, a mother
Many-named and single-natured, gave him breath
Whence God's wrath could wring but this word and
    none other—
  He may smite me, yet he shall not do to death.
Him the tongue that sang triumphant while tormented
  Sang as loud the sevenfold storm that roared ere-
    while
Round the towers of Thebes till wrath might rest
    contented:
  Sang the flight from smooth soft-sanded banks of
    Nile,
When like mateless doves that fly from snare or
    tether
  Came the suppliants landwards trembling as they
    trod,
And the prayer took wing from all their tongues
    together—
  King of kings, most holy of holies, blessed God.
But what mouth may chant again, what heart may
    know it,
  All the rapture that all hearts of men put on
When of Salamis the time-transcending poet
  Sang, whose hand had chased the Mede at Marathon?

Darker dawned the song with stormier wings above
    the watch-fire spread   [*Ep.* 2.

Whence from Ida toward the hill of Hermes leapt the
    light that said

Troy was fallen, a torch funereal for the king's tri-
    umphal head.

Dire indeed the birth of Leda's womb that had God's
    self to sire

Bloomed, a flower of love that stung the soul with
    fangs that gnaw like fire :

But the twin-born human-fathered sister-flower bore
    fruit more dire.

Scarce the cry that called on airy heaven and all swift
    winds on wing,

Wells of river-heads, and countless laugh of waves
    past reckoning,

Earth which brought forth all, and the orbèd sun that
    looks on everything,

Scarce that cry fills yet men's hearts more full of
    heart-devouring dread

Than the murderous word said mocking, how the
    child whose blood he shed

Might clasp fast and kiss her father where the dead
    salute the dead.

But the latter note of anguish from the lips that
    mocked her lord,

When her son's hand bared against the breast that
    suckled him his sword,

How might man endure, O Æschylus, to hear it and
    record?

How might man endure, being mortal yet, O thou
  most highest, to hear?
How record, being born of woman? Surely not thy
  Furies near,
Surely this beheld, this only, blasted hearts to death
  with fear.
Not the hissing hair, nor flakes of blood that oozed
  from eyes of fire,
Nor the snort of savage sleep that snuffed the hunger-
  ing heart's desire
Where the hunted prey found hardly space and har-
  bour to respire ;
She whose likeness called them—'Sleep ye, ho?
  what need of you that sleep?'
(Ah, what need indeed, where she was, of all shapes
  that night may keep
Hidden dark as death and deeper than men's dreams
  of hell are deep?)
She the murderess of her husband, she the huntress
  of her son,
More than ye was she, the shadow that no God with-
  stands but one,
Wisdom equal-eyed and stronger and more splendid
  than the sun.
Yea, no God may stand betwixt us and the shadows
  of our deeds,
Nor the light of dreams that lighten darkness, nor the
  prayer that pleads,
But the wisdom equal-souled with heaven, the light
  alone that leads.

Light whose law bids home those childless children
    of eternal night,
Soothed and reconciled and mastered and transmuted
    in men's sight
Who behold their own souls, clothed with darkness
    once, now clothed with light.
King of kings and father crowned of all our fathers
    crowned of yore,
Lord of all the lords of song, whose head all heads
    bow down before,
Glory be to thee from all thy sons in all tongues ever-
    more.

Rose and vine and olive and deep ivy-bloom en-
    twining   [*Str.* 3.
  Close the goodliest grave that e'er they closeliest
    might entwine -
Keep the wind from wasting and the sun from too
    strong shining
  Where the sound and light of sweetest songs still
    float and shine.
Here the music seems to illume the shade, the light
    to whisper
  Song, the flowers to put not odours only forth, but
    words
Sweeter far than fragrance : here the wandering
    wreaths twine crisper
  Far, and louder far exults the note of all wild
    birds.

Thoughts that change us, joys that crown and sorrows
　　that enthrone us,
　Passions that enrobe us with a clearer air than ours,
Move and breathe as living things beheld round white
　　Colonus,
　Audibler than melodies and visibler than flowers.
Love, in fight unconquered, Love, with spoils of great
　　men laden,
　　Never sang so sweet from throat of woman or of
　　dove :
Love, whose bed by night is in the soft cheeks of a
　　maiden,
　　And his march is over seas, and low roofs lack not
　　Love ;
Nor may one of all that live, ephemeral or eternal,
　　Fly nor hide from Love ; but whoso clasps him
　　fast goes mad.
Never since the first-born year with flowers first-born
　　grew vernal
　　Such a song made listening hearts of lovers glad or
　　sad.
Never sounded note so radiant at the rayless portal
　　Opening wide on the all-concealing lowland of the
　　dead
As the music mingling, when her doomsday marked
　　her mortal,
　　From her own and old men's voices round the
　　bride's way shed,
Round the grave her bride-house, hewn for endless
　　habitation,

Where, shut out from sunshine, with no bridegroom
    by, she slept ;
But beloved of all her dark and fateful generation,
    But with all time's tears and praise besprinkled and
      bewept :
Well-beloved of outcast father and self-slaughtered
    mother,
    Born, yet unpolluted, of their blind incestuous
      bed ;
Best-beloved of him for whose dead sake she died,
    her brother,
    Hallowing by her own life's gift her own born
      brother's head :

Not with wine or oil nor any less libation   [*Ant.* 3.
    Hallowed, nor made sweet with humbler perfume's
      breath ;
Not with only these redeemed from desecration,
    But with blood and spirit of life poured forth to
      death ;
Blood unspotted, spirit unsullied, life devoted,
    Sister too supreme to make the bride's hope good,
Daughter too divine as woman to be noted,
    Spouse of only death in mateless maidenhood.
Yea, in her was all the prayer fulfilled, the saying
    All accomplished— *Would that fate would let me*
      wear
Hallowed innocence of words and all deeds, weighing
    Well the laws thereof, begot on holier air,

Far on high sublimely stablished, whereof only
  Heaven is father; nor did birth of mortal mould
Bring them forth, nor shall oblivion lull to lonely
  Slumber. Great in these is God, and grows not old.
Therefore even that inner darkness where she
    perished
  Surely seems as holy and lovely, seen aright,
As desirable and as dearly to be cherished,
  As the haunt closed in with laurels from the light,
Deep inwound with olive and wild vine inwoven,
  Where a godhead known and unknown makes men
    pale,
But the darkness of the twilight noon is cloven
  Still with shrill sweet moan of many a nightingale.
Closer clustering there they make sweet noise to-
    gether,
  Where the fearful gods look gentler than our fear,
And the grove thronged through with birds of holiest
    feather
  Grows nor pale nor dumb with sense of dark things
    near.
There her father, called upon with signs of wonder,
  Passed with tenderest words away by ways un-
    known,
Not by sea-storm stricken down, nor touched of
    thunder,
  To the dark benign deep underworld, alone.

Third of three that ruled in Athens, kings with
    sceptral song for staff, *[Ep.* 3.

Gladdest heart that God gave ever milk and wine of
    thought to quaff,

Clearest eye that lightened ever to the broad lip's
    lordliest laugh,

Praise be thine as theirs whose tragic brows the loftier
    leaf engirds

For the live and lyric lightning of thy honey-hearted
    words,

Soft like sunny dewy wings of clouds and bright as
    crying of birds;

Full of all sweet rays and notes that make of earth
    and air and sea

One great light and sound of laughter from one great
    God's heart, to be

Sign and semblance of the gladness of man's life
    where men breathe free.

With no Loxian sound obscure God uttered once, and
    all time heard,

All the soul of Athens, all the soul of England, in
    that word :

Rome arose the second child of freedom : northward
    rose the third.

Ere her Boreal dawn came kindling seas afoam and
    fields of snow,

Yet again, while Europe groaned and grovelled, shone
    like suns aglow

Doria splendid over Genoa, Venice bright with Dan-
    dolo.

Dead was Hellas, but Ausonia by the light of dead
    men's deeds
Rose and walked awhile alive, though mocked as
    whom the fen-fire leads
By the creed-wrought faith of faithless souls that
    mock their doubts with creeds.
Dead are these, and man is risen again : and haply
    now the Three
Yet coequal and triune may stand in story, marked as
    free
By the token of the washing of the waters of the sea.
Athens first of all earth's kindred many-tongued and
    many-kinned
Had the sea to friend and comfort, and for kinsman
    had the wind :
She that bare Columbus next: then she that made
    her spoil of Ind.
She that hears not what man's rage but only what the
    sea-wind saith :
She that turned Spain's ships to cloud-wrack at the
    blasting of her breath,
By her strengths of strong-souled children and of
    strong winds done to death.
North and south the Great King's galleons went in
    Persian wise : and here
She, with Æschylean music on her lips that laughed
    back fear,
In the face of Time's grey godhead shook the splen-
    dour of her spear.

Fair as Athens then with foot upon her foeman's
    front, and strong
Even as Athens for redemption of the world from
    sovereign wrong,
Like as Athens crowned she stood before the sun
    with crowning song.
All the world is theirs with whom is freedom : first of
    all the free,
Blest are they whom song has crowned and clothed
    with blessing : these as we,
These alone have part in spirit with the sun that
    crowns the sea.

April, 1881.

THE STATUE OF VICTOR HUGO.

1.

Since in Athens God stood plain for adoration,
  Since the sun beheld his likeness reared in stone,
Since the bronze or gold of human consecration
    Gave to Greece her guardian's form and feature
      shown,
Never hand of sculptor, never heart of nation,
  Found so glorious aim in all these ages flown
As is theirs who rear for all time's acclamation
  Here the likeness of our mightiest and their own.

2.

Theirs and ours and all men's living who behold him
  Crowned with garlands multiform and manifold;
Praise and thanksgiving of all mankind enfold him
  Who for all men casts abroad his gifts of gold.
With the gods of song have all men's tongues enrolled
      him,
    With the helpful gods have all men's hearts en-
      rolled:

Ours he is who love him, ours whose hearts' hearts
    hold him
Fast as his the trust that hearts like his may hold.

3.

He, the heart most high, the spirit on earth most
    blameless,
  Takes in charge all spirits, holds all hearts in trust :
As the sea-wind's on the sea his ways are tameless,
  As the laws that steer the world his works are just.
All most noble feel him nobler, all most shameless
  Feel his wrath and scorn make pale their pride and
    lust :
All most poor and lowliest, all whose wrongs were
    nameless,
  Feel his word of comfort raise them from the dust.

4.

Pride of place and lust of empire bloody-fruited
  Knew the blasting of his breath on leaf and fruit :
Now the hand that smote the death-tree now dis-
    rooted
  Plants the refuge-tree that has man's hope for root.
Ah, but we by whom his darkness was saluted,
  How shall now all we that see his day salute ?
How should love not seem by love's own speech con-
    futed,
  Song before the sovereign singer not be mute ?

5.

With what worship, by what blessing, in what measure,
  May we sing of him, salute him, or adore,
With what hymn for praise, what thanksgiving for
      pleasure,
  Who had given us more than heaven, and gives us
      more ?
Heaven's whole treasury, filled up full with night's
      whole treasure,
  Holds not so divine or deep a starry store
As the soul supreme that deals forth worlds at leisure
  Clothed with light and darkness, dense with flower
      and ore.

6.

Song had touched the bourn : fresh verses overflow it,
  Loud and radiant, waves on waves on waves that
      throng ;
Still the tide grows, and the sea-mark still below it
  Sinks and shifts and rises, changed and swept along.
Rose it like a rock ? the waters overthrow it,
  And another stands beyond them sheer and strong :
Goal by goal pays down its prize, and yields its poet
  Tribute claimed of triumph, palm achieved of song.

7.

Since his hand that holds the keys of fear and wonder
  Opened on the high priest's dreaming eyes a door

o

Whence the lights of heaven and hell above and
    under
  Shone, and smote the face that men bow down
    before,
Thrice again one singer's note had cloven in sunder
  Night, who blows again not one blast now but four,
And the fourfold heaven is kindled with his thunder,
  And the stars about his forehead are fourscore.

8.

From the deep soul's depths where alway love
    abounded
  First had risen a song with healing on its wings
Whence the dews of mercy raining balms unbounded
  Shed their last compassion even on sceptred things.[1]
Even on heads that like a curse the crown surrounded
  Fell his crowning pity, soft as cleansing springs ;
And the sweet last note his wrath relenting sounded
  Bade men's hearts be melted not for slaves but
    kings.

9.

Next, that faith might strengthen fear and love
    embolden,
  On the creeds of priests a scourge of sunbeams
    fell :
And its flash made bare the deeps of heaven, beholden
  Not of men that cry, Lord, Lord, from church or
    cell.[2]

---

[1] *La Pitié Suprême.* 1879.
[2] *Religions et Religion.* 1880.

Hope as young as dawn from night obscure and olden
  Rose again, such power abides in truth's one spell :
Night, if dawn it be that touches her, grows golden ;
  Tears, if such as angels weep, extinguish hell.

10.

Through the blind loud mills of barren blear-eyed
      learning
    Where in dust and darkness children's foreheads
      bow,
While men's labour, vain as wind or water turning
    Wheels and sails of dreams, makes life a leafless
      bough,
Fell the light of scorn and pity touched with yearning,
    Next, from words that shone as heaven's own kind-
      ling brow.[1]
Stars were these as watch-fires on the world's waste
      burning,
    Stars that fade not in the fourfold sunrise now.[2]

11.

Now the voice that faints not till all wrongs be wroken
    Sounds as might the sun's song from the morning's
      breast,
All the seals of silence sealed of night are broken,
    All the winds that bear the fourfold word are blest.

---

[1] *L'Ane.* 1880.
[2] *Les Quatre Vents de l'Esprit.* 1. *Le Livre satirique.*
11. *Le Livre dramatique.* 111. *Le Livre lyrique.* IV. *Le
Livre épique.* 1881.

All the keen fierce east flames forth one fiery token;
    All the north is loud with life that knows not rest,
All the south with song as though the stars had
        spoken ;
    All the judgment-fire of sunset scathes the west.

12.

Sound of pæan, roll of chanted panegyric,
    Though by Pindar's mouth song's trumpet spake
        forth praise,
March of warrior songs in Pythian mood or Pyrrhic,
    Though the blast were blown by lips of ancient
        days,
Ring not clearer than the clarion of satiric
    Song whose breath sweeps bare the plague-infected
        ways
Till the world be pure as heaven is for the lyric
    Sun to rise up clothed with radiant sounds as rays.

13.

Clear across the cloud-rack fluctuant and erratic
    As the strong star smiles that lets no mourner
        mourn,
Hymned alike from lips of Lesbian choirs or Attic
    Once at evensong and morning newly born,
Clear and sure above the changes of dramatic
    Tide and current, soft with love and keen with
        scorn,
Smiles the strong sweet soul of maidenhood, ecstatic
    And inviolate as the red glad mouth of morn.

14.

Pure and passionate as dawn, whose apparition
    Thrills with fire from heaven the wheels of hours
        that whirl,
Rose and passed her radiance in serene transition
    From his eyes who sought a grain and found a
        pearl.
But the food by cunning hope for vain fruition
    Lightly stolen away from keeping of a churl
Left the bitterness of death and hope's perdition
    On the lip that scorn was wont for shame to curl.[1]

15.

Over waves that darken round the wave-worn rover
    Rang his clarion higher than winds cried round
        the ship,
Rose a pageant of set suns and storms blown over,
    Hands that held life's guerdons fast or let them
        slip.
But no tongue may tell, no thanksgiving discover,
    Half the heaven of blessing, soft with clouds that
        drip,
Keen with beams that kindle, dear as love to lover,
    Opening by the spell's strength on his lyric lip.

[1] *Les Deux Trouvailles de Gallus.* 1. *Margarita, comédie.* 11. *Esca, drame.*

16.

By that spell the soul transfigured and dilated
    Puts forth wings that widen, breathes a brightening
        air,
Feeds on light and drinks of music, whence elated
    All her sense grows godlike, seeing all depths
        made bare,
All the mists wherein before she sat belated
    Shrink, till now the sunlight knows not if they
        were ;
All this earth transformed is Eden recreated,
    With the breath of heaven remurmuring in her
        hair.

17.

Sweeter far than aught of sweet that April nurses
    Deep in dew-dropt woodland folded fast and furled
Breathes the fragrant song whose burning dawn
        disperses
    Darkness, like the surge of armies backward hurled,
Even as though the touch of spring's own hand, that
        pierces
    Earth with life's delight, had hidden in the
        impearled
Golden bells and buds and petals of his verses
    All the breath of all the flowers in all the world.

18.

But the soul therein, the light that our souls follow,
    Fires and fills the song with more of prophet's
        pride,
More of life than all the gulfs of death may swallow,
    More of flame than all the might of night may hide.
Though the whole dark age were loud and void and
        hollow,
    Strength of trust were here, and help for all souls
        tried,
And a token from the flight of that strange swallow [1]
    Whose migration still is toward the wintry side.

19.

Never came such token for divine solution
    From the oraculous live darkness whence of yore
Ancient faith sought word of help and retribution,
    Truth to lighten doubt, a sign to go before.
Never so baptismal waters of ablution
    Bathed the brows of exile on so stern a shore,
Where the lightnings of the sea of revolution
    Flashed across them ere its thunders yet might
        roar.

[1] Je suis une hirondelle étrange, car j'émigre
    Du côté de l'hiver.
           Le Livre Lyrique, liii.

20.

By the lightning's light of present revelation
   Shown, with epic thunder as from skies that frown,
Clothed in darkness as of darkling expiation,
   Rose a vision of dead stars and suns gone down,
Whence of old fierce fire devoured the star-struck
      nation,
   Till its wrath and woe lit red the raging town,
Now made glorious with his statue's crowning station,
   Where may never gleam again a viler crown.

21.

King, with time for throne and all the years for pages,
   He shall reign though all thrones else be over-
      hurled,
Served of souls that have his living words for wages,
   Crowned of heaven each dawn that leaves his brows
      impearled ;
Girt about with robes unrent of storm that rages,
   Robes not wrought with hands, from no loom's
      weft unfurled ;
All the praise of all earth's tongues in all earth's ages,
   All the love of all men's hearts in all the world.

22.

Yet what hand shall carve the soul or cast the spirit,
   Mould the face of fame, bid glory's feature glow ?
Who bequeath for eyes of ages hence to inherit
   Him, the Master, whom love knows not if it know ?

Scarcely perfect praise of men man's work might
    merit,
  Scarcely bid such aim to perfect stature grow,
Were his hand the hand of Phidias who shall rear it,
  And his soul the very soul of Angelo.

23.

Michael, awful angel of the world's last session,
  Once on earth, like him, with fire of suffering tried,
Thine it were, if man's it were, without transgression,
  Thine alone, to take this toil upon thy pride.
Thine, whose heart was great against the world's
    oppression,
  Even as his whose word is lamp and staff and
    guide :
Advocate for man, untired of intercession,
  Pleads his voice for slaves whose lords his voice
    defied.

24.

Earth, with all the kings and thralls on earth, below it,
  Heaven alone, with all the worlds in heaven, above,
Let his likeness rise for suns and stars to know it,
  High for men to worship, plain for men to love :
Brow that braved the tides which fain would overflow
    it,
  Lip that gave the challenge, hand that flung the
    glove ;
Comforter and prophet, Paraclete and poet,
  Soul whose emblems are an eagle and a dove.

25.

Sun, that hast not seen a loftier head wax hoary,
　　Earth, which hast not shown the sun a nobler birth,
Time, that hast not on thy scroll defiled and gory
　　　One man's name writ brighter in its whole wide
　　　　　girth,
Witness, till the final years fulfil their story,
　　Till the stars break off the music of their mirth,
What among the sons of men was this man's glory,
　　What the vesture of his soul revealed on earth.

SONNETS

HOPE AND FEAR.

BENEATH the shadow of dawn's aerial cope,
   With eyes enkindled as the sun's own sphere,
   Hope from the front of youth in godlike cheer
Looks Godward, past the shades where blind men grope
Round the dark door that prayers nor dreams can ope,
   And makes for joy the very darkness dear
   That gives her wide wings play ; nor dreams that fear
At noon may rise and pierce the heart of hope.
Then, when the soul leaves off to dream and yearn,
May truth first purge her eyesight to discern
   What once being known leaves time no power to appal ;
Till youth at last, ere yet youth be not, learn
   The kind wise word that falls from years that fall—
   'Hope thou not much, and fear thou not at all.'

AFTER SUNSET.

'Si quis piorum Manibus locus.'

I.

STRAIGHT from the sun's grave in the deep clear west
   A sweet strong wind blows, glad of life : and I,
   Under the soft keen stardawn whence the sky
Takes life renewed, and all night's godlike breast
Palpitates, gradually revealed at rest
   By growth and change of ardours felt on high,
   Make onward, till the last flame fall and die
And all the world by night's broad hand lie blest.
Haply, meseems, as from that edge of death,
Whereon the day lies dark, a brightening breath
   Blows more of benediction than the morn,
So from the graves whereon grief gazing saith
   That half our heart of life there lies forlorn
   May light or breath at least of hope be born.

The wind was soft before the sunset fled :
   Now, while the cloud-enshrouded corpse of day
   Is lowered along a red funereal way
Down to the dark that knows not white from red,
A clear sheer breeze against the night makes head,
   Serene, but sure of life as ere a ray
   Springs, or the dusk of dawn knows red from grey,
Being as a soul that knows not quick from dead.
From far beyond the sunset, far above,
   Full toward the starry soundless east it blows
   Bright as a child's breath breathing on a rose,
Smooth to the sense as plume of any dove ;
   Till more and more as darkness grows and glows
Silence and night seem likest life and love.

If light of life outlive the set of sun
    That men call death and end of all things, then
    How should not that which life held best for men
And proved most precious, though it seem undone
By force of death and woful victory won,
    Be first and surest of revival, when
    Death shall bow down to life arisen again?
So shall the soul seen be the self-same one
That looked and spake with even such lips and eyes
As love shall doubt not then to recognise,
    And all bright thoughts and smiles of all time past
Revive, transfigured, but in spirit and sense
None other than we knew, for evidence
    That love's last mortal word was not his last.

A STUDY FROM MEMORY.

If that be yet a living soul which here
   Seemed brighter for the growth of numbered springs
   And clothed by Time and Pain with goodlier things
Each year it saw fulfilled a fresh fleet year,
Death can have changed not aught that made it dear ;
   Half humorous goodness, grave-eyed mirth on wings
   Bright-balanced, blither-voiced than quiring strings ;
Most radiant patience, crowned with conquering cheer ;
A spirit inviolable that smiled and sang
   By might of nature and heroic need
   More sweet and strong than loftiest dream or deed ;
A song that shone, a light whence music rang
   High as the sunniest heights of kindliest thought ;
   All these must be, or all she was be nought.

TO DR. JOHN BROWN.

BEYOND the north wind lay the land of old
  Where men dwelt blithe and blameless, clothed and fed
  With joy's bright raiment and with love's sweet bread,
The whitest flock of earth's maternal fold.
None there might wear about his brows enrolled
  A light of lovelier fame than rings your head,
  Whose lovesome love of children and the dead
All men give thanks for : I far off behold
A dear dead hand that links us, and a light
The blithest and benignest of the night,
  The night of death's sweet sleep, wherein may be
A star to show your spirit in present sight
  Some happier island in the Elysian sea
  Where Rab may lick the hand of Marjorie.

March 1882.

TO WILLIAM BELL SCOTT.

THE larks are loud above our leagues of whin
  Now the sun's perfume fills their glorious gold
  With odour like the colour : all the wold
Is only light and song and wind wherein
These twain are blent in one with shining din.
  And now your gift, a giver's kingly-souled,
  Dear old fast friend whose honours grow not old,
Bids memory's note as loud and sweet begin.
Though all but we from life be now gone forth
Of that bright household in our joyous north
Where I, scarce clear of boyhood just at end,
  First met your hand ; yet under life's clear dome,
Now seventy strenuous years have crowned my friend,
  Shines no less bright his full-sheaved harvest-home.

April 20, 1882.

A DEATH ON EASTER DAY.

THE strong spring sun rejoicingly may rise,
   Rise and make revel, as of old men said,
   Like dancing hearts of lovers newly wed :
A light more bright than ever bathed the skies
Departs for all time out of all men's eyes.
   The crowns that girt last night a living head
   Shine only now, though deathless, on the dead :
Art that mocks death, and Song that never dies.
Albeit the bright sweet mothlike wings be furled,
   Hope sees, past all division and defection,
      And higher than swims the mist of human breath,
The soul most radiant once in all the world
   Requickened to regenerate resurrection
      Out of the likeness of the shadow of death.

April 1882.

ON THE DEATHS OF THOMAS CARLYLE
AND GEORGE ELIOT.

Two souls diverse out of our human sight
    Pass, followed one with love and each with wonder :
    The stormy sophist with his mouth of thunder,
Clothed with loud words and mantled in the might
Of darkness and magnificence of night ;
    And one whose eye could smite the night in sunder,
    Searching if light or no light were thereunder,
And found in love of loving-kindness light.
Duty divine and Thought with eyes of fire
Still following Righteousness with deep desire
    Shone sole and stern before her and above,
Sure stars and sole to steer by ; but more sweet
Shone lower the loveliest lamp for earthly feet,
    The light of little children, and their love.

AFTER LOOKING INTO CARLYLE'S REMINISCENCES.

I.

THREE men lived yet when this dead man was young
   Whose names and words endure for ever : one
   Whose eyes grew dim with straining toward the sun,
And his wings weakened, and his angel's tongue
Lost half the sweetest song was ever sung,
   But like the strain half uttered earth hears none,
   Nor shall man hear till all men's songs are done :
One whose clear spirit like an eagle hung
Between the mountains hallowed by his love
And the sky stainless as his soul above :
   And one the sweetest heart that ever spake
The brightest words wherein sweet wisdom smiled.
These deathless names by this dead snake defiled
   Bid memory spit upon him for their sake.

II.

Sweet heart, forgive me for thine own sweet sake,
   Whose kind blithe soul such seas of sorrow swam,
   And for my love's sake, powerless as I am
For love to praise thee, or like thee to make
Music of mirth where hearts less pure would break,
   Less pure than thine, our life-unspotted Lamb.
   Things hatefullest thou hadst not heart to damn,
Nor wouldst have set thine heel on this dead snake.
Let worms consume its memory with its tongue,
The fang that stabbed fair Truth, the lip that stung
   Men's memories uncorroded with its breath.
Forgive me, that with bitter words like his
I mix the gentlest English name that is,
   The tenderest held of all that know not death.

A LAST LOOK.

Sick of self-love, Malvolio, like an owl
 That hoots the sun rerisen where starlight sank,
 With German garters crossed athwart thy frank
Stout Scottish legs, men watched thee snarl and scowl,
And boys responsive with reverberate howl
 Shrilled, hearing how to thee the springtime stank·
 And as thine own soul all the world smelt rank
And as thine own thoughts Liberty seemed foul.
Now, for all ill thoughts nursed and ill words given
Not all condemned, not utterly forgiven,
 Son of the storm and darkness, pass in peace.
Peace upon earth thou knewest not : now, being dead,
Rest, with nor curse nor blessing on thine head,
 Where high-strung hate and strenuous envy cease.

DICKENS.

CHIEF in thy generation born of men
   Whom English praise acclaimed as English-born,
   With eyes that matched the worldwide eyes of morn
For gleam of tears or laughter, tenderest then
When thoughts of children warmed their light, or when
   Reverence of age with love and labour worn,
   Or godlike pity fired with godlike scorn,
Shot through them flame that winged thy swift live pen :
Where stars and suns that we behold not burn,
   Higher even than here, though highest was here thy place,
   Love sees thy spirit laugh and speak and shine
With Shakespeare and the soft bright soul of Sterne
   And Fielding's kindliest might and Goldsmith's grace ;
   Scarce one more loved or worthier love than thine.

ON LAMB'S SPECIMENS OF DRAMATIC POETS.

I.

If all the flowers of all the fields on earth
   By wonder-working summer were made one,
   Its fragrance were not sweeter in the sun,
Its treasure-house of leaves were not more worth
Than those wherefrom thy light of musing mirth
   Shone, till each leaf whereon thy pen would run
   Breathed life, and all its breath was benison.
Beloved beyond all names of English birth,
More dear than mightier memories; gentlest name
That ever clothed itself with flower-sweet fame,
Or linked itself with loftiest names of old
   By right and might of loving; I, that am
Less than the least of those within thy fold,
   Give only thanks for them to thee, Charles Lamb.

II.

So many a year had borne its own bright bees
   And slain them since thy honey-bees were hived,
   John Day, in cells of flower-sweet verse contrived
So well with craft of moulding melodies,
Thy soul perchance in amaranth fields at ease
   Thought not to hear the sound on earth revived
   Of summer music from the spring derived
When thy song sucked the flower of flowering trees.
But thine was not the chance of every day :
   Time, after many a darkling hour, grew sunny,
     And light between the clouds ere sunset swam,
Laughing, and kissed their darkness all away,
   When, touched and tasted and approved, thy honey
     Took subtler sweetness from the lips of Lamb.

TO JOHN NICHOL.

I.

FRIEND of the dead, and friend of all my days
  Even since they cast off boyhood, I salute
  The song saluting friends whose songs are mute
With full burnt-offerings of clear-spirited praise.
That since our old young years our several ways
  Have led through fields diverse of flower and fruit
  Yet no cross wind has once relaxed the root
We set long since beneath the sundawn's rays,
The root of trust whence towered the trusty tree,
  Friendship—this only and duly might impel
    My song to salutation of your own ;
More even than praise of one unseen of me
  And loved—the starry spirit of Dobell,
    To mine by light and music only known.

II.

But more than this what moves me most of all
  To leave not all unworded and unsped
  The whole heart's greeting of my thanks unsaid
Scarce needs this sign, that from my tongue should fall
His name whom sorrow and reverent love recall,
  The sign to friends on earth of that dear head
  Alive, which now long since untimely dead
The wan grey waters covered for a pall.
Their trustless reaches dense with tangling stems
  Took never life more taintless of rebuke,
    More pure and perfect, more serene and kind,
Than when those clear eyes closed beneath the Thames,
  And made the now more hallowed name of Luke
    Memorial to us of morning left behind.

May 1881,

DYSTHANATOS.

Ad generem Cereris sine cæde et vulnere pauci
Descendunt reges, aut siccâ morte tyranni.

By no dry death another king goes down
   The way of kings.   Yet may no free man's voice,
   For stern compassion and deep awe, rejoice
That one sign more is given against the crown,
That one more head those dark red waters drown
   Which rise round thrones whose trembling equipoise
   Is propped on sand and bloodshed and such toys
As human hearts that shrink at human frown.
The name writ red on Polish earth, the star
That was to outshine our England's in the far
   East heaven of empire—where is one that saith
Proud words now, prophesying of this White Czar?
   'In bloodless pangs few kings yield up their breath,
   Few tyrants perish by no violent death.'

March 14, 1881.

EUONYMOS.

εὖ μὴν ᾗ τιμὴν ἐδίδου νικηφόρος ἀλκὴ
ἐκ νίκης ὄνομ' ἔσχε φόβου κέαρ αἰὲν ἄθικτος.

A YEAR ago red wrath and keen despair
   Spake, and the sole word from their darkness sent
   Laid low the lord not all omnipotent
Who stood most like a god of all that were
As gods for pride of power, till fire and air
   Made earth of all his godhead.   Lightning rent
   The heart of empire's lurid firmament,
And laid the mortal core of manhood bare.
But when the calm crowned head that all revere
For valour higher than that which casts out fear,
   Since fear came near it never, comes near death,
Blind murder cowers before it, knowing that here
   No braver soul drew bright and queenly breath
   Since England wept upon Elizabeth.

March 8, 1882.

ON THE RUSSIAN PERSECUTION OF
THE JEWS.

O son of man, by lying tongues adored,
  By slaughterous hands of slaves with feet red-shod
  In carnage deep as ever Christian trod
Profaned with prayer and sacrifice abhorred
And incense from the trembling tyrant's horde,
  Brute worshippers or wielders of the rod,
  Most murderous even of all that call thee God,
Most treacherous even that ever called thee Lord;
Face loved of little children long ago,
  Head hated of the priests and rulers then,
    If thou see this, or hear these hounds of thine
    Run ravening as the Gadarean swine,
Say, was not this thy Passion, to foreknow
  In death's worst hour the works of Christian men?

Jan. 23, 1882.

BISMARCK AT CANOSSA.

Not all disgraced, in that Italian town,
   The imperial German cowered beneath thine hand,
   Alone indeed imperial Hildebrand,
And felt thy foot and Rome's, and felt her frown
And thine, more strong and sovereign than his crown,
   Though iron forged its blood-encrusted band.
   But now the princely wielder of his land,
For hatred's sake toward freedom, so bows down,
No strength is in the foot to spurn : its tread
Can bruise not now the proud submitted head :
   But how much more abased, much lower brought low,
And more intolerably humiliated,
   The neck submissive of the prosperous foe,
   Than his whom scorn saw shuddering in the snow !

December 31, 1881.

QUIA NOMINOR LEO.

I.

WHAT part is left thee, lion? Ravenous beast,
   Which hadst the world for pasture, and for scope
   And compass of thine homicidal hope
The kingdom of the spirit of man, the feast
Of souls subdued from west to sunless east,
   From blackening north to bloodred south aslope,
   All servile; earth for footcloth of the pope,
And heaven for chancel-ceiling of the priest;
Thou that hadst earth by right of rack and rod,
Thou that hadst Rome because thy name was God,
   And by thy creed's gift heaven wherein to dwell;
Heaven laughs with all his light and might above
That earth has cast thee out of faith and love;
   Thy part is but the hollow dream of hell.

II.

The light of life has faded from thy cause,
   High priest of heaven and hell and purgatory :
   Thy lips are loud with strains of oldworld story,
But the red prey was rent out of thy paws
Long since : and they that dying brake down thy laws
   Have with the fires of death-enkindled glory
   Put out the flame that faltered on thy hoary
High altars, waning with the world's applause.
This Italy was Dante's : Bruno died
Here : Campanella, too sublime for pride,
   Endured thy God's worst here, and hence went home.
And what art thou, that time's full tide should shrink
For thy sake downward?   What art thou, to think
   Thy God shall give thee back for birthright Rome ?

January, 1882.

THE CHANNEL TUNNEL.

Not for less love, all glorious France, to thee,
  'Sweet enemy' called in days long since at end,
  Now found and hailed of England sweeter friend,
Bright sister of our freedom now, being free ;
Not for less love or faith in friendship we
  Whose love burnt ever toward thee reprehend
  The vile vain greed whose pursy dreams portend
Between our shores suppression of the sea.
Not by dull toil of blind mechanic art
Shall these be linked for no man's force to part
  Nor length of years and changes to divide,
But union only of trust and loving heart
  And perfect faith in freedom strong to abide
  And spirit at one with spirit on either side.

April 3, 1882.

SIR WILLIAM GOMM.

I.

AT threescore years and five aroused anew
　　To rule in India, forth a soldier went
　　On whose bright-fronted youth fierce war had spent
Its iron stress of storm, till glory grew
Full as the red sun waned on Waterloo.
　　Landing, he met the word from England sent
　′ Which bade him yield up rule : and he, content,
Resigned it, as a mightier warrior's due ;
And wrote as one rejoicing to record
That ' from the first ' his royal heart was lord
　　Of its own pride or pain ; that thought was none
Therein save this, that in her perilous strait
England, whose womb brings forth her sons so great,
　　Should choose to serve her first her mightiest son.

Glory beyond all flight of warlike fame
  Go with the warrior's memory who preferred
  To praise of men whereby men's hearts are stirred,
And acclamation of his own proud name
With blare of trumpet-blasts and sound and flame
  Of pageant honour, and the titular word
  That only wins men worship of the herd,
His country's sovereign good ; who overcame
Pride, wrath, and hope of all high chance on earth,
For this land's love that gave his great heart birth.
  O nursling of the sea-winds and the sea,
Immortal England, goddess ocean-born,
What shall thy children fear, what strengths not scorn,
  While children of such mould are born to thee ?

EUTHANATOS.

IN MEMORY OF MRS. THELLUSSON.

FORTH of our ways and woes,
Forth of the winds and snows,
A white soul soaring goes,
    Winged like a dove :
So sweet, so pure, so clear,
So heavenly tempered here,
Love need not hope or fear her changed above :

Ere dawned her day to die,
So heavenly, that on high
Change could not glorify
    Nor death refine her :
Pure gold of perfect love,
On earth like heaven's own dove,
She cannot wear, above, a smile diviner.

Her voice in heaven's own quire
Can sound no heavenlier lyre
Than here : no purer fire
    Her soul can soar :
No sweeter stars her eyes
In unimagined skies
Beyond our sight can rise than here before.

Hardly long years had shed
Their shadows on her head :
Hardly we think her dead,
　　Who hardly thought her
Old : hardly can believe
The grief our hearts receive
And wonder while they grieve, as wrong were wrought
　　　　her.

But though strong grief be strong
No word or thought of wrong
May stain the trembling song,
　　Wring the bruised heart,
That sounds or sighs its faint
Low note of love, nor taint
Grief for so sweet a saint, when such depart.

A saint whose perfect soul,
With perfect love for goal,
Faith hardly might control,
　　Creeds might not harden :
A flower more splendid far
Than the most radiant star
Seen here of all that are in God's own garden.

Surely the stars we see
Rise and relapse as we,
And change and set, may be
　　But shadows too :
But spirits that man's lot
Could neither mar nor spot
Like these false lights are not, being heavenly true.

Not like these dying lights
Of worlds whose glory smites
The passage of the nights
   Through heaven's blind prison :
Not like their souls who see,
If thought fly far and free,
No heavenlier heaven to be for souls rerisen.

A soul wherein love shone
Even like the sun, alone,
With fervour of its own
   And splendour fed,
Made by no creeds less kind
Toward souls by none confined,
Could Death's self quench or blind, Love's self were
     dead.

February 4, 1881.

FIRST AND LAST.

Upon the borderlands of being,
  Where life draws hardly breath
Between the lights and shadows fleeing
  Fast as a word one saith,
Two flowers rejoice our eyesight, seeing
  The dawns of birth and death.

Behind the babe his dawn is lying
  Half risen with notes of mirth
From all the winds about it flying
  Through new-born heaven and earth :
Before bright age his day for dying
  Dawns equal-eyed with birth.

Equal the dews of even and dawn,
  Equal the sun's eye seen
A hand's breadth risen and half withdrawn :
  But no bright hour between
Brings aught so bright by stream or lawn
  To noonday growths of green.

Which flower of life may smell the sweeter
  To love's insensual sense,
Which fragrance move with offering meeter
  His soothed omnipotence,
Being chosen as fairer or as fleeter,
  Borne hither or borne hence,

Love's foiled omniscience knows not : this
  Were more than all he knows
With all his lore of bale and bliss,
  The choice of rose and rose,
One red as lips that touch with his,
  One white as moonlit snows.

No hope is half so sweet and good,
  No dream of saint or sage
So fair as these are : no dark mood
  But these might best assuage ;
The sweet red rose of babyhood,
  The white sweet rose of age.

LINES ON THE DEATH OF EDWARD JOHN TRELAWNY.

Last high star of the years whose thunder
   Still men's listening remembrance hears,
   Last light left of our fathers' years,
Watched with honour and hailed with wonder
Thee too then have the years borne under,
   Thou too then hast regained thy peers.

Wings that warred with the winds of morning,
   Storm-winds rocking the red great dawn,
   Close at last, and a film is drawn
Over the eyes of the storm-bird, scorning
Now no longer the loud wind's warning,
   Waves that threaten or waves that fawn.

Peers were none of thee left us living,
   Peers of theirs we shall see no more.
   Eight years over the full fourscore
Knew thee : now shalt thou sleep, forgiving
All griefs past of the wild world's giving,
   Moored at last on the stormless shore.

Worldwide liberty's lifelong lover,
    Lover no less of the strength of song,
    Sea-king, swordsman, hater of wrong,
Over thy dust that the dust shall cover
Comes my song as a bird to hover,
    Borne of its will as of wings along.

Cherished of thee were this brief song's brothers
    Now that follows them, cherishing thee.
    Over the tides and the tideless sea
Soft as a smile of the earth our mother's
Flies it faster than all those others,
    First of the troop at thy tomb to be.

Memories of Greece and the mountain's hollow
    Guarded alone of thy loyal sword
    Hold thy name for our hearts in ward :
Yet more fain are our hearts to follow
One way now with the southward swallow
    Back to the grave of the man their lord.

Heart of hearts, art thou moved not, hearing
    Surely, if hearts of the dead may hear,
    Whose true heart it is now draws near?
Surely the sense of it thrills thee, cheering
Darkness and death with the news now nearing—·
    Shelley, Trelawny rejoins thee here.

ADIEUX À MARIE STUART.

I.

Queen, for whose house my fathers fought,
　　With hopes that rose and fell,
Red star of boyhood's fiery thought,
　　Farewell.

They gave their lives, and I, my queen,
　　Have given you of my life,
Seeing your brave star burn high between
　　Men's strife.

The strife that lightened round their spears
　　Long since fell still : so long
Hardly may hope to last in years
　　My song.

But still through strife of time and thought
　　Your light on me too fell :
Queen, in whose name we sang or fought,
　　Farewell.

II.

There beats no heart on either border
    Wherethrough the north blasts blow
But keeps your memory as a warder
    His beacon-fire aglow.

Long since it fired with love and wonder
    Mine, for whose April age
Blithe midsummer made banquet under
    The shade of Hermitage.

Soft sang the burn's blithe notes, that gather
    Strength to ring true :
And air and trees and sun and heather
    Remembered you.

Old border ghosts of fight or fairy
    Or love or teen,
These they forgot, remembering Mary
    The Queen.

III.

Queen once of Scots and ever of ours
    Whose sires brought forth for you
Their lives to strew your way like flowers,
    Adieu.

Dead is full many a dead man's name
    Who died for you this long
Time past : shall this too fare the same,
    My song ?

But surely, though it die or live,
    Your face was worth
All that a man may think to give
    On earth.

No darkness cast of years between
    Can darken you :
Man's love will never bid my queen
    Adieu.

IV.

Love hangs like light about your name
    As music round the shell :
No heart can take of you a tame
    Farewell.

Yet, when your very face was seen,
    Ill gifts were yours for giving :
Love gat strange guerdons of my queen
    When living.

O diamond heart unflawed and clear,
    The whole world's crowning jewel !
Was ever heart so deadly dear
    So cruel?

Yet none for you of all that bled
    Grudged once one drop that fell:
Not one to life reluctant said
    Farewell.

V.

Strange love they have given you, love disloyal,
    Who mock with praise your name,
To leave a head so rare and royal
    Too low for praise or blame.

You could not love nor hate, they tell us,
    You had nor sense nor sting :
In God's name, then, what plague befell us
    To fight for such a thing?

'Some faults the gods will give,' to fetter
    Man's highest intent :
But surely you were something better
    Than innocent !

No maid that strays with steps unwary
    Through snares unseen,
But one to live and die for ; Mary,
    The Queen.

VI.

Forgive them all their praise, who blot
    Your fame with praise of you :
Then love may say, and falter not
    Adieu.

R

Yet some you hardly would forgive
    Who did you much less wrong
Once : but resentment should not live
    Too long.

They never saw your lip's bright bow,
    Your swordbright eyes,
The bluest of heavenly things below
    The skies.

Clear eyes that love's self finds most like
    A swordblade's blue,
A swordblade's ever keen to strike,
    Adieu.

VII.

Though all things breathe or sound of fight
    That yet make up your spell,
To bid you were to bid the light
    Farewell.

Farewell the song says only, being
    A star whose race is run :
Farewell the soul says never, seeing
    The sun.

Yet, wellnigh as with flash of tears,
    The song must say but so
That took your praise up twenty years
    Ago.

More bright than stars or moons that vary,
   Sun kindling heaven and hell,
Here, after all these years, Queen Mary,
   Farewell.

HERSE.

WHEN grace is given us ever to behold
　　A child some sweet months old,
Love, laying across our lips his finger, saith,
　　Smiling, with bated breath,
Hush ! for the holiest thing that lives is here,
　　And heaven's own heart how near !
How dare we, that may gaze not on the sun,
　　Gaze on this verier one ?
Heart, hold thy peace ; eyes, be cast down for shame ;
　　Lips, breathe not yet its name.
In heaven they know what name to call it ; we,
　　How should we know ?　For, see !
The adorable sweet living marvellous
　　Strange light that lightens us
Who gaze, desertless of such glorious grace,
　　Full in a babe's warm face !
All roses that the morning rears are nought,
　　All stars not worth a thought,
Set this one star against them, or suppose
　　As rival this one rose.
What price could pay with earth's whole weight of gcld
　　One least flushed roseleaf's fold

Of all this dimpling store of smiles that shine
    From each warm curve and line,
Each charm of flower-sweet flesh, to reillume
    The dappled rose-red bloom
Of all its dainty body, honey-sweet
    Clenched hands and curled-up feet,
That on the roses of the dawn have trod
    As they came down from God,
And keep the flush and colour that the sky
    Takes when the sun comes nigh,
And keep the likeness of the smile their grace
    Evoked on God's own face
When, seeing this work of his most heavenly mood,
    He saw that it was good?
For all its warm sweet body seems one smile,
    And mere men's love too vile
To meet it, or with eyes that worship dims
    Read o'er the little limbs,
Read all the book of all their beauties o'er,
    Rejoice, revere, adore,
Bow down and worship each delight in turn,
    Laugh, wonder, yield, and yearn.
But when our trembling kisses dare, yet dread,
    Even to draw nigh its head,
And touch, and scarce with touch or breath surprise
    Its mild miraculous eyes
Out of their viewless vision—O, what then,
    What may be said of men?
What speech may name a new-born child? what word
    Earth ever spake or heard?

The best men's tongue that ever glory knew
 Called that a drop of dew
Which from the breathing creature's kindly womb
 Came forth in blameless bloom.
We have no word, as had those men most high,
 To call a baby by.
Rose, ruby, lily, pearl of stormless seas—
 A better word than these,
A better sign it was than flower or gem
 That love revealed to them :
They knew that whence comes light or quickening
  flame,
 Thence only this thing came,
And only might be likened of our love
 To somewhat born above,
Not even to sweetest things dropped else on earth,
 Only to dew's own birth.
Nor doubt we but their sense was heavenly true,
 Babe, when we gaze on you,
A dew-drop out of heaven whose colours are
 More bright than sun or star,
As now, ere watching love dare fear or hope,
 Lips, hands, and eyelids ope,
And all your life is mixed with earthly leaven.
 O child, what news from heaven ?

TWINS.

Affectionately inscribed to W. M. R. and L. R.

April, on whose wings
Ride all gracious things,
Like the star that brings
  All things good to man,
Ere his light, that yet
Makes the month shine, set,
And fair May forget
  Whence her birth began,

Brings, as heart would choose,
Sound of golden news,
Bright as kindling dews
  When the dawn begins ;
Tidings clear as mirth,
Sweet as air and earth
Now that hail the birth,
  Twice thus blest, of twins.

In the lovely land
Where with hand in hand
Lovers wedded stand
  Other joys before

Made your mixed life sweet:
Now, as Time sees meet,
Three glad blossoms greet
   Two glad blossoms more.

Fed with sun and dew,
While your joys were new,
First arose and grew
   One bright olive-shoot:
Then a fair and fine
Slip of warm-haired pine
Felt the sweet sun shine
   On its leaf and fruit.

And it wore for mark
Graven on the dark
Beauty of its bark
   That the noblest name
Worn in song of old
By the king whose bold
Hand had fast in hold
   All the flower of fame.

Then, with southern skies
Flattered in her eyes,
Which, in lovelier wise
   Yet, reflect their blue
Brightened more, being bright
Here with life's delight,
And with love's live light
   Glorified anew,

Came, as fair as came
One who bore her name
(She that broke as flame
　　From the swan-shell white),
Crowned with tender hair
Only, but more fair
Than all queens that were
　　Themes of oldworld fight,

Of your flowers the third
Bud, or new-fledged bird
In your hearts' nest heard
　　Murmuring like a dove
Bright as those that drew
Over waves where blew
No loud wind the blue
　　Heaven-hued car of love.

Not the glorious grace
Even of that one face
Potent to displace
　　All the towers of Troy
Surely shone more clear
Once with childlike cheer
Than this child's face here
　　Now with living joy.

After these again
Here in April's train
Breaks the bloom of twain
　　Blossoms in one birth

For a crown of May
On the front of day
When he takes his way
   Over heaven and earth.

Half a heavenly thing
Given from heaven to Spring
By the sun her king,
   Half a tender toy,
Seems a child of curl
Yet too soft to twirl ;
Seems the flower-sweet girl
   By the flower-bright boy.

All the kind gods' grace,
All their love, embrace
Ever either face,
   Ever brood above them :
All soft wings of hours
Screen them as with flowers
From all beams and showers :
   All life's seasons love them.

When the dews of sleep
Falling lightliest keep
Eyes too close to peep
   Forth and laugh off rest,
Joy from face to feet
Fill them, as is meet :
Life to them be sweet
   As their mother's breast.

When those dews are dry,
And in day's bright eye
Looking full they lie
   Bright as rose and pearl,
All returns of joy
Pure of time's alloy
Bless the rose-red boy,
   Guard the rose-white girl.

POSTSCRIPT.

Friends, if I could take
Half a note from Blake
Or but one verse make
   Of the Conqueror's mine,
Better than my best
Song above your nest
I would sing : the quest
   Now seems too divine.

April 28, 1881.

THE SALT OF THE EARTH.

If childhood were not in the world,
   But only men and women grown ;
No baby-locks in tendrils curled,
   No baby-blossoms blown ;

Though men were stronger, women fairer,
   And nearer all delights in reach,
And verse and music uttered rarer
   Tones of more godlike speech ;

Though the utmost life of life's best hours
   Found, as it cannot now find, words ;
Though desert sands were sweet as flowers
   And flowers could sing like birds,

But children never heard them, never
   They felt a child's foot leap and run :
This were a drearier star than ever
   Yet looked upon the sun.

SEVEN YEARS OLD.

I.

Seven white roses on one tree,
  Seven white loaves of blameless leaven,
Seven white sails on one soft sea,
Seven white swans on one lake's lee,
  Seven white flowerlike stars in heaven,
All are types unmeet to be
  For a birthday's crown of seven.

II.

Not the radiance of the roses,
  Not the blessing of the bread,
Not the breeze that ere day grows is
Fresh for sails and swans, and closes
  Wings above the sun's grave spread,
When the starshine on the snows is
  Sweet as sleep on sorrow shed,

III.

Nothing sweetest, nothing best,
  Holds so good and sweet a treasure

As the love wherewith once blest
Joy grows holy, grief takes rest,
   Life, half tired with hours to measure,
Fills his eyes and lips and breast
   With most light and breath of pleasure ;

IV.

As the rapture unpolluted,
   As the passion undefiled,
By whose force all pains heart-rooted
Are transfigured and transmuted,
   Recompensed and reconciled,
Through the imperial, undisputed,
   Present godhead of a child.

V.

Brown bright eyes and fair bright head,
   Worth a worthier crown than this is,
Worth a worthier song instead,
Sweet grave wise round mouth, full fed
   With the joy of love, whose bliss is
More than mortal wine and bread,
   Lips whose words are sweet as kisses,

VI.

Little hands so glad of giving,
   Little heart so glad of love,
Little soul so glad of living,

While the strong swift hours are weaving
  Light with darkness woven above,
Time for mirth and time for grieving,
  Plume of raven and plume of dove,

VII.

I can give you but a word
  Warm with love therein for leaven,
But a song that falls unheard
Yet on ears of sense unstirred
  Yet by song so far from heaven,
Whence you came the brightest bird,
  Seven years since, of seven times seven.

EIGHT YEARS OLD.

I.

Sun, whom the faltering snow-cloud fears,
  Rise, let the time of year be May,
Speak now the word that April hears,
  Let March have all his royal way ;
Bid all spring raise in winter's ears
  All tunes her children hear or play,
Because the crown of eight glad years
  On one bright head is set to-day.

II.

What matters cloud or sun to-day
  To him who wears the wreath of years
So many, and all like flowers at play
  With wind and sunshine, while his ears
Hear only song on every way ?
  More sweet than spring triumphant hears
Ring through the revel-rout of May
  Are these, the notes that winter fears.

III.

Strong-hearted winter knows and fears
    The music made of love at play,
Or haply loves the tune he hears
    From hearts fulfilled with flowering May,
Whose molten music thaws his ears
    Late frozen, deaf but yesterday
To sounds of dying and dawning years,
    Now quickened on his deathward way.

IV.

For deathward now lies winter's way
    Down the green vestibule of years
That each year brightens day by day
    With flower and shower till hope scarce fears
And fear grows wholly hope of May.
    But we—the music in our ears
Made of love's pulses as they play
    The heart alone that makes it hears.

V.

The heart it is that plays and hears
    High salutation of to-day.
Tongue falters, hand shrinks back, song fears
    Its own unworthiness to play
Fit music for those eight sweet years,
    Or sing their blithe accomplished way.
No song quite worth a young child's ears
    Broke ever even from birds in May.

S

VI.

There beats not in the heart of May,
  When summer hopes and springtide fears,
There falls not from the height of day,
  When sunlight speaks and silence hears,
So sweet a psalm as children play
  And sing, each hour of all their years,
Each moment of their lovely way,
  And know not how it thrills our ears.

VII.

Ah child, what are we, that our ears
  Should hear you singing on your way,
Should have this happiness?   The years
  Whose hurrying wings about us play
Are not like yours, whose flower-time fears
  Nought worse than sunlit showers in May,
Being sinless as the spring, that hears
  Her own heart praise her every day.

VIII.

Yet we too triumph in the day
  That bare, to entrance our eyes and ears,
To lighten daylight, and to play
  Such notes as darkness knows and fears,
The child whose face illumes our way,
  Whose voice lifts up the heart that hears,
Whose hand is as the hand of May
  To bring us flowers from eight full years.

February 4, 1882.

COMPARISONS.

Child, when they say that others
   Have been or are like you,
Babes fit to be your brothers,
   Sweet human drops of dew,
Bright fruit of mortal mothers,
   What should one say or do?

We know the thought is treason,
   We feel the dream absurd;
A claim rebuked of reason,
   That withers at a word:
For never shone the season
   That bore so blithe a bird.

Some smiles may seem as merry,
   Some glances gleam as wise,
From lips as like a cherry
   And scarce less gracious eyes;
Eyes browner than a berry,
   Lips red as morning's rise.

But never yet rang laughter
　　So sweet in gladdened ears
Through wall and floor and rafter
　　As all this household hears
And rings response thereafter
　　Till cloudiest weather clears.

When those your chosen of all men,
　　Whose honey never cloys,
Two lights whose smiles enthrall men,
　　Were called at your age boys,
Those mighty men, while small men,
　　Could make no merrier noise.

Our Shakespeare, surely, daffed not
　　More lightly pain aside
From radiant lips that quaffed not
　　Of forethought's tragic tide :
Our Dickens, doubtless, laughed not
　　More loud with life's first pride.

The dawn were not more cheerless
　　With neither light nor dew
Than we without the fearless
　　Clear laugh that thrills us through :
If ever child stood peerless,
　　Love knows that child is you

WHAT IS DEATH?

LOOKING on a page where stood
Graven of old on old-world wood
Death, and by the grave's edge grim,
Pale, the young man facing him,
Asked my well-beloved of me
Once what strange thing this might be,
    Gaunt and great of limb.

Death, I told him : and, surprise
Deepening more his wildwood eyes
(Like some sweet fleet thing's whose breath
Speaks all spring though nought it saith),
Up he turned his rosebright face
Glorious with its seven years' grace,
    Asking—What is death?

A CHILD'S PITY.

No sweeter thing than children's ways and wiles,
  Surely, we say, can gladden eyes and ears :
Yet sometime sweeter than their words or smiles
  Are even their tears.

To one for once a piteous tale was read,
  How, when the murderous mother crocodile
Was slain, her fierce brood famished, and lay dead,
  Starved, by the Nile.

In vast green reed-beds on the vast grey slime
  Those monsters motherless and helpless lay,
Perishing only for the parent's crime
  Whose seed were they.

Hours after, toward the dusk, our blithe small bird
  Of Paradise, who has our hearts in keeping,
Was heard or seen, but hardly seen or heard,
  For pity weeping.

He was so sorry, sitting still apart,
  For the poor little crocodiles, he said.
Six years had given him, for an angel's heart,
  A child's instead.

Feigned tears the false beasts shed for murderous
      ends,
  We know from travellers' tales of crocodiles :
But these tears wept upon them of my friend's
    Outshine his smiles.

What heavenliest angels of what heavenly city
  Could match the heavenly heart in children here?
The heart that hallowing all things with its pity
    Casts out all fear?

So lovely, so divine, so dear their laughter
  Seems to us, we know not what could be more
      dear :
But lovelier yet we see the sign thereafter
    Of such a tear.

With sense of love half laughing and half weeping
  We met your tears, our small sweet-spirited friend :
Let your love have us in its heavenly keeping
    To life's last end.

A CHILD'S LAUGHTER.

ALL the bells of heaven may ring,
All the birds of heaven may sing,
All the wells on earth may spring,
All the winds on earth may bring
  All sweet sounds together ;
Sweeter far than all things heard,
Hand of harper, tone of bird,
Sound of woods at sundawn stirred,
Welling water's winsome word,
  Wind in warm wan weather,

One thing yet there is, that none
Hearing ere its chime be done
Knows not well the sweetest one
Heard of man beneath the sun,
  Hoped in heaven hereafter ;
Soft and strong and loud and light,
Very sound of very light
Heard from morning's rosiest height,
When the soul of all delight
  Fills a child's clear laughter.

Golden bells of welcome rolled
Never forth such notes, nor told
Hours so blithe in tones so bold,
As the radiant mouth of gold
   Here that rings forth heaven.
If the golden-crested wren
Were a nightingale—why, then,
Something seen and heard of men
Might be half as sweet as when
   Laughs a child of seven.

A CHILD'S THANKS.

How low soe'er men rank us,
　　How high soe'er we win,
The children far above us
Dwell, and they deign to love us,
With lovelier love than ours,
And smiles more sweet than flowers ;
As though the sun should thank us
　　For letting light come in.

With too divine complaisance,
　　Whose grace misleads them thus,
Being gods, in heavenly blindness
They call our worship kindness,
Our pebble-gift a gem :
They think us good to them,
Whose glance, whose breath, whose presence,
　　Are gifts too good for us.

The poet high and hoary
　　Of meres that mountains bind
Felt his great heart more often
Yearn, and its proud strength soften

From stern to tenderer mood,
At thought of gratitude
Shown than of song or story
   He heard of hearts unkind.

But with what words for token
   And what adoring tears
Of reverence risen to passion,
In what glad prostrate fashion
Of spirit and soul subdued,
May man show gratitude
For thanks of children spoken
   That hover in his ears?

The angels laugh, your brothers,
   Child, hearing you thank me,
With eyes whence night grows sunny,
And touch of lips like honey,
And words like honey-dew:
But how shall I thank you?
For gifts above all others
   What guerdon-gift may be?

What wealth of words caressing,
   What choice of songs found best,
Would seem not as derision,
Found vain beside the vision
And glory from above
Shown in a child's heart's love?
His part in life is blessing;
   Ours, only to be blest.

A CHILD'S BATTLES.

τὸξ ἀρετὰν εὑρών.—PINDAR.

PRAISE of the knights of old
May sleep : their tale is told,
    And no man cares :
The praise which fires our lips is
A knight's whose fame eclipses
    All of theirs.

The ruddiest light in heaven
Blazed as his birth-star seven
    Long years ago :
All glory crown that old year
Which brought our stout small soldier
    With the snow !

Each baby born has one
Star, for his friends a sun,
    The first of stars :
And we, the more we scan it,
The more grow sure your planet,
    Child, was Mars.

For each one flower, perchance,
Blooms as his cognizance :
    The snowdrop chill,
The violet unbeholden,
For some : for you the golden
      Daffodil.

Erect, a fighting flower,
It breasts the breeziest hour
    That ever blew,
And bent or broke things brittle
Or frail, unlike a little
      Knight like you.

Its flower is firm and fresh
And stout like sturdiest flesh
    Of children : all
The strenuous blast that parches
Spring hurts it not till March is
      Near his fall.

If winds that prate and fret
Remark, rebuke, regret,
    Lament, or blame
The brave plant's martial passion,
It keeps its own free fashion
      All the same.

We that would fain seem wise
Assume grave mouths and eyes
    Whose looks reprove

Too much delight in battle :
But your great heart our prattle
    Cannot move.

We say, small children should
Be placid, mildly good
    And blandly meek :
Whereat the broad smile rushes
Full on your lips, and flushes
    All your cheek.

If all the stars that are
Laughed out, and every star
    Could here be heard,
Such peals of golden laughter
We should not hear, as after
    Such a word.

For all the storm saith, still,
Stout stands the daffodil :
    For all we say,
Howe'er he look demurely,
Our martialist will surely
    Have his way.

We may not bind with bands
Those large and liberal hands,
    Nor stay from fight,
Nor hold them back from giving :
No lean mean laws of living
    Bind a knight.

And always here of old
Such gentle hearts and bold
    Our land has bred :
How durst her eye rest else on
The glory shed from Nelson
      Quick and dead?

Shame were it, if but one
Such once were born her son,
    That one to have borne,
And brought him ne'er a brother :
His praise should bring his mother
      Shame and scorn.

A child high-souled as he
Whose manhood shook the sea
    Smiles haply here :
His face, where love lies basking,
With bright shut mouth seems asking,
      What is fear?

The sunshine-coloured fists
Beyond his dimpling wrists
    Were never closed
For saving or for sparing—
For only deeds of daring
      Predisposed.

Unclenched, the gracious hands
Let slip their gifts like sands
    Made rich with ore

That tongues of beggars ravish
From small stout hands so lavish
          Of their store.

Sweet hardy kindly hands
Like these were his that stands
          With heel on gorge
Seen trampling down the dragon
On sign or flask or flagon,
          Sweet Saint George.

Some tournament, perchance,
Of hands that couch no lance,
          Might mark this spot
Your lists, if here some pleasant
Small Guenevere were present,
          Launcelot.

My brave bright flower, you need
No foolish song, nor heed
          It more than spring
The sighs of winter stricken
Dead when your haunts requicken
          Here, my king.

Yet O, how hardly may
The wheels of singing stay
          That whirl along
Bright paths whence echo raises
The phantom of your praises,
          Child, my song !

Beyond all other things
That give my words fleet wings,
　　Fleet wings and strong,
You set their jesses ringing
Till hardly can I, singing,
　　Stint my song.

But all things better, friend,
And worse must find an end :
　　And, right or wrong,
'Tis time, lest rhyme should baffle,
I doubt, to put a snaffle
　　On my song.

And never may your ear
Aught harsher hear or fear,
　　Nor wolfish night
Nor dog-toothed winter snarling
Behind your steps, my darling
　　My delight !

For all the gifts you give
Me, dear, each day you live,
　　Of thanks above
All thanks that could be spoken
Take not my song in token,
　　Take my love.

A CHILD'S FUTURE.

WHAT will it please you, my darling, hereafter to be?
Fame upon land will you look for, or glory by sea?
Gallant your life will be always, and all of it free.

Free as the wind when the heart of the twilight is
stirred
Eastward, and sounds from the springs of the sunrise
are heard:
Free—and we know not another as infinite word.

Darkness or twilight or sunlight may compass us
round,
Hate may arise up against us, or hope may confound;
Love may forsake us; yet may not the spirit be
bound.

Free in oppression of grief as in ardour of joy
Still may the soul be, and each to her strength as a
toy:
Free in the glance of the man as the smile of the boy.

Freedom alone is the salt and the spirit that gives
Life, and without her is nothing that verily lives :
Death cannot slay her : she laughs upon death and
    forgives.

Brightest and hardiest of roses anear and afar
Glitters the blithe little face of you, round as a star :
Liberty bless you and keep you to be as you are.

England and liberty bless you and keep you to be
Worthy the name of their child and the sight of their
    sea :
Fear not at all ; for a slave, if he fears not, is free.

SONNETS

ON

ENGLISH DRAMATIC POETS

(1590–1650)

L.

CHRISTOPHER MARLOWE.

CROWNED, girdled, garbed and shod with light and fire,
 Son first-born of the morning, sovereign star !
 Soul nearest ours of all, that wert most far,
Most far off in the abysm of time, thy lyre
Hung highest above the dawn-enkindled quire
 Where all ye sang together, all that are,
 And all the starry songs behind thy car
Rang sequence, all our souls acclaim thee sire.

' If all the pens that ever poets held
 Had fed the feeling of their masters' thoughts,'
 And as with rush of hurtling chariots
The flight of all their spirits were impelled
 Toward one great end, thy glory—nay, not then,
 Not yet might'st thou be praised enough of men.

WILLIAM SHAKESPEARE.

Not if men's tongues and angels' all in one
   Spake, might the word be said that might speak Thee.
   Streams, winds, woods, flowers, fields, mountains,
      yea, the sea,
What power is in them all to praise the sun?
His praise is this,—he can be praised of none.
   Man, woman, child, praise God for him; but he
   Exults not to be worshipped, but to be.
He is; and, being, beholds his work well done.
All joy, all glory, all sorrow, all strength, all mirth,
Are his: without him, day were night on earth.
   Time knows not his from time's own period.
All lutes, all harps, all viols, all flutes, all lyres,
Fall dumb before him ere one string suspires.
   All stars are angels; but the sun is God.

III.

BEN JONSON.

BROAD-BASED, broad-fronted, bounteous, multiform,
  With many a valley impleached with ivy and vine,
  Wherein the springs of all the streams run wine,
And many a crag full-faced against the storm,
The mountain where thy Muse's feet made warm
  Those lawns that revelled with her dance divine
  Shines yet with fire as it was wont to shine
From tossing torches round the dance aswarm.

Nor less, high-stationed on the grey grave heights,
High-thoughted seers with heaven's heart-kindling lights
  Hold converse : and the herd of meaner things
Knows or by fiery scourge or fiery shaft
When wrath on thy broad brows has risen, and laughed,
  Darkening thy soul with shadow of thunderous wings.

IV.

BEAUMONT AND FLETCHER.

An hour ere sudden sunset fired the west,
   Arose two stars upon the pale deep east.
   The hall of heaven was clear for night's high feast,
Yet was not yet day's fiery heart at rest.
Love leapt up from his mother's burning breast
   To see those warm twin lights, as day decreased,
   Wax wider, till when all the sun had ceased
As suns they shone from evening's kindled crest.
Across them and between, a quickening fire,
Flamed Venus, laughing with appeased desire.
   Their dawn, scarce lovelier for the gleam of tears,
Filled half the hollow shell 'twixt heaven and earth
With sound like moonlight, mingling moan and mirth,
   Which rings and glitters down the darkling years.

PHILIP MASSINGER.

CLOUDS here and there arisen an hour past noon
    Chequered our English heaven with lengthening bars
    And shadow and sound of wheel-winged thunder-cars
Assembling strength to put forth tempest soon,
When the clear still warm concord of thy tune
    Rose under skies unscared by reddening Mars
    Yet, like a sound of silver speech of stars,
With full mild flame as of the mellowing moon.
Grave and great-hearted Massinger, thy face
High melancholy lights with loftier grace
    Than gilds the brows of revel : sad and wise,
The spirit of thought that moved thy deeper song,
Sorrow serene in soft calm scorn of wrong,
    Speaks patience yet from thy majestic eyes.

JOHN FORD.

HEW hard the marble from the mountain's heart
   Where hardest night holds fast in iron gloom
   Gems brighter than an April dawn in bloom,
That his Memnonian likeness thence may start
Revealed, whose hand with high funereal art
   Carved night, and chiselled shadow : be the tomb
   That speaks him famous graven with signs of doom
Intrenched inevitably in lines athwart,
As on some thunder-blasted Titan's brow
   His record of rebellion.   Not the day
     Shall strike forth music from so stern a chord,
Touching this marble : darkness, none knows how,
   And stars impenetrable of midnight, may.
     So locms the likeness of thy soul, John Ford.

VII.

JOHN WEBSTER.

THUNDER : the flesh quails, and the soul bows down.
  Night : east, west, south, and northward, very night.
  Star upon struggling star strives into sight,
Star after shuddering star the deep storms drown.
The very throne of night, her very crown,
  A man lays hand on, and usurps her right.
  Song from the highest of heaven's imperious height
Shoots, as a fire to smite some towering town.
Rage, anguish, harrowing fear, heart-crazing crime,
Make monstrous all the murderous face of Time
  Shown in the spheral orbit of a glass
Revolving.   Earth cries out from all her graves.
Frail, on frail rafts, across wide-wallowing waves,
  Shapes here and there of child and mother pass.

VIII.

THOMAS DECKER.

Out of the depths of darkling life where sin
  Laughs piteously that sorrow should not know
  Her own ill name, nor woe be counted woe ;
Where hate and craft and lust make drearier din
Than sounds through dreams that grief holds revel in ;
  What charm of joy-bells ringing, streams that flow,
  Winds that blow healing in each note they blow,
Is this that the outer darkness hears begin ?

O sweetest heart of all thy time save one,
Star seen for love's sake nearest to the sun,
  Hung lamplike o'er a dense and doleful city,
Not Shakespeare's very spirit, howe'er more great,
Than thine toward man was more compassionate,
  Nor gave Christ praise from lips more sweet with pity.

THOMAS MIDDLETON.

A WILD moon riding high from cloud to cloud,
   That sees and sees not, glimmering far beneath,
   Hell's children revel along the shuddering heath
With dirge-like mirth and raiment like a shroud:
A worse fair face than witchcraft's, passion-proud,
   With brows blood-flecked behind their bridal wreath
   And lips that bade the assassin's sword find sheath
Deep in the heart whereto love's heart was vowed:
A game of close contentious crafts and creeds
   Played till white England bring black Spain to shame :
A son's bright sword and brighter soul, whose deeds
   High conscience lights for mother's love and fame :
Pure gipsy flowers, and poisonous courtly weeds :
   Such tokens and such trophies crown thy name.

THOMAS HEYWOOD.

Tom, if they loved thee best who called thee Tom.
  What else may all men call thee, seeing thus bright
  Even yet the laughing and the weeping light
That still thy kind old eyes are kindled from?
Small care was thine to assail and overcome
  Time and his child Oblivion: yet of right
  Thy name has part with names of lordlier might
For English love and homely sense of home,
Whose fragrance keeps thy small sweet bayleaf young
  And gives it place aloft among thy peers
    Whence many a wreath once higher strong Time
      has hurled:
And this thy praise is sweet on Shakespeare's tongue—
  'O good old man, how well in thee appears
    The constant service of the antique world!'

XI.

GEORGE CHAPMAN.

HIGH priest of Homer, not elect in vain,
   Deep trumpets blow before thee, shawms behind
   Mix music with the rolling wheels that wind
Slow through the labouring triumph of thy train :
Fierce history, molten in thy forging brain,
   Takes form and fire and fashion from thy mind,
   Tormented and transmuted out of kind :
But howsoe'er thou shift thy strenuous strain,
Like Tailor [1] smooth, like Fisher [2] swollen, and now
   Grim Yarrington [3] scarce bloodier marked than thou,
   Then bluff as Mayne's [4] or broad-mouthed Barry's [5] glee ,
Proud still with hoar predominance of brow
   And beard like foam swept off the broad blown sea,
   Where'er thou go, men's reverence goes with thee.

[1] Author of *The Hog hath lost his Pearl.*
[2] Author of *Fuimus Troes, or the True Trojans.*
[3] Author of *Two Tragedies in One.*
[4] Author of *The City Match.*
[5] Author of *Ram-Alley, or Merry Tricks.*

JOHN MARSTON.

THE bitterness of death and bitterer scorn
    Breathes from the broad-leafed aloe-plant whence thou
    Wast fain to gather for thy bended brow
A chaplet by no gentler forehead worn.
Grief deep as hell, wrath hardly to be borne,
    Ploughed up thy soul till round the furrowing plough
    The strange black soil foamed, as a black beaked prow
Bids night-black waves foam where its track has torn.
Too faint the phrase for thee that only saith
Scorn bitterer than the bitterness of death
    Pervades the sullen splendour of thy soul,
Where hate and pain make war on force and fraud
And all the strengths of tyrants ; whence unflawed
    It keeps this noble heart of hatred whole.

XIII.

JOHN DAY.

Day was a full-blown flower in heaven, alive
  With murmuring joy of bees and birds aswarm,
  When in the skies of song yet flushed and warm
With music where all passion seems to strive
For utterance, all things bright and fierce to drive
  Struggling along the splendour of the storm,
  Day for an hour put off his fiery form,
And golden murmurs from a golden hive
Across the strong bright summer wind were heard,
  And laughter soft as smiles from girls at play
  And loud from lips of boys brow-bound with May.
Our mightiest age let fall its gentlest word,
When Song, in semblance of a sweet small bird,
  Lit fluttering on the light swift hand of Day.

JAMES SHIRLEY.

THE dusk of day's decline was hard on dark
    When evening trembled round thy glowworm lamp
    That shone across her shades and dewy damp
A small clear beacon whose benignant spark
Was gracious yet for loiterers' eyes to mark,
    Though changed the watchword of our English camp
    Since the outposts rang round Marlowe's lion ramp,
When thy steed's pace went ambling round Hyde Park.

And in the thickening twilight under thee
Walks Davenant, pensive in the paths where he,
The blithest throat that ever carolled love
    In music made of morning's merriest heart,
Glad Suckling, stumbled from his seat above
    And reeled on slippery roads of alien art.

XV.

THE TRIBE OF BENJAMIN.

Sons born of many a loyal Muse to Ben,
　All true-begotten, warm with wine or ale,
　Bright from the broad light of his presence, hail !
Prince Randolph, nighest his throne of all his men,
Being highest in spirit and heart who hailed him then
　King, nor might other spread so blithe a sail :
　Cartwright, a soul pent in with narrower pale,
Praised of thy sire for manful might of pen :
Marmion, whose verse keeps alway keen and fine
The perfume of their Apollonian wine
　Who shared with that stout sire of all and thee
The exuberant chalice of his echoing shrine :
　Is not your praise writ broad in gold which he
　Inscribed, that all who praise his name should see?

ANONYMOUS PLAYS:

'ARDEN OF FEVERSHAM.'

MOTHER whose womb brought forth our man of men,
   Mother of Shakespeare, whom all time acclaims
   Queen therefore, sovereign queen of English dames,
Throned higher than sat thy sonless empress then,
Was it thy son's young passion-guided pen
   Which drew, reflected from encircling flames,
   A figure marked by the earlier of thy names
Wife, and from all her wedded kinswomen
Marked by the sign of murderess?   Pale and great,
   Great in her grief and sin, but in her death
   And anguish of her penitential breath
Greater than all her sin or sin-born fate,
   She stands, the holocaust of dark desire,
   Clothed round with song for ever as with fire.

XVII.

ANONYMOUS PLAYS.

YE too, dim watchfires of some darkling hour,
  Whose fame forlorn time saves not nor proclaims
  For ever, but forgetfulness defames
And darkness and the shadow of death devour,
Lift up ye too your light, put forth your power,
  Let the far twilight feel your soft small flames
  And smile, albeit night name not even their names,
Ghost by ghost passing, flower blown down on flower :
That sweet-tongued shadow, like a star's that passed
Singing, and light was from its darkness cast
  To paint the face of Painting fair with praise : [1]
And that wherein forefigured smiles the pure
Fraternal face of Wordsworth's Elidure
  Between two child-faced masks of merrier days. [2]

---

[1] *Doctor Doäypol.*   [2] *Nobody and Somebody.*

XVIII.

ANONYMOUS PLAYS.

MORE yet and more, and yet we mark not all:
 The Warning fain to bid fair women heed
 Its hard brief note of deadly doom and deed;[1]
The verse that strewed too thick with flowers the hall
Whence Nero watched his fiery festival;[2]
 That iron page wherein men's eyes who read
 See, bruised and marred between two babes that bleed,
A mad red-handed husband's martyr fall;[3]
The scene which crossed and streaked with mirth the strife
Of Henry with his sons and witchlike wife;[4]
And that sweet pageant of the kindly fiend,
 Who, seeing three friends in spirit and heart made one,
Crowned with good hap the true-love wiles he screened
 In the pleached lanes of pleasant Edmonton.[5]

    [1] *A Warning for Fair Women.*
    [2] *The Tragedy of Nero.*
    [3] *A Yorkshire Tragedy.*
    [4] *Look about you.*
    [5] *The Merry Devil of Edmonton.*

XIX.

THE MANY.

I.

GREENE, garlanded with February's few flowers,
    Ere March came in with Marlowe's rapturous rage:
    Peele, from whose hand the sweet white locks of age
Took the mild chaplet woven of honoured hours :
Nash, laughing hard: Lodge, flushed from lyric bowers:
    And Lilly, a goldfinch in a twisted cage
    Fed by some gay great lady's pettish page
Till short sweet songs gush clear like short spring showers :
Kid, whose grim sport still gambolled over graves :
    And Chettle, in whose fresh funereal verse
    Weeps Marian yet on Robin's wildwood hearse :
Cooke, whose light boat of song one soft breath saves,
    Sighed from a maiden's amorous mouth averse :
Live likewise ye : Time takes not you for slaves.

THE MANY.

II.

Haughton, whose mirth gave woman all her will :
   Field, bright and loud with laughing flower and bird
   And keen alternate notes of laud and gird :
Barnes, darkening once with Borgia's deeds the quill
Which tuned the passion of Parthenophil :
   Blithe burly Porter, broad and bold of word :
   Wilkins, a voice with strenuous pity stirred :
Turk Mason: Brewer, whose tongue drops honey still
Rough Rowley, handling song with Esau's hand :
   Light Nabbes: lean Sharpham, rank and raw by turns,
   But fragrant with a forethought once of Burns :
Soft Davenport, sad-robed, but blithe and bland :
   Brome, gipsy-led across the woodland ferns :
Praise be with all, and place among our band.

XXI.

EPILOGUE.

OUR mother, which wast twice, as history saith,
   Found first among the nations : once, when she
   Who bore thine ensign saw the God in thee
Smite Spain, and bring forth Shakespeare : once, when death
Shrank, and Rome's bloodhounds cowered, at Milton's breath :
   More than thy place, then first among the free,
   More than that sovereign lordship of the sea
Bequeathed to Cromwell from Elizabeth,
More than thy fiery guiding-star, which Drake
Hailed, and the deep saw lit again for Blake,
   More than all deeds wrought of thy strong right hand,
This praise keeps most thy fame's memorial strong,
That thou wast head of all these streams of song,
   And time bows down to thee as Shakespeare's land.

A DARK MONTH.

'La maison sans enfants!'—Victor Hugo.

L

A MONTH without sight of the sun
   Rising or reigning or setting
Through days without use of the day,
Who calls it the month of May?
The sense of the name is undone
   And the sound of it fit for forgetting.

We shall not feel if the sun rise,
   We shall not care when it sets :
If a nightingale make night's air
As noontide, why should we care?
Till a light of delight that is done rise,
   Extinguishing grey regrets ;

Till a child's face lighten again
   On the twilight of older faces ;
Till a child's voice fall as the dew
On furrows with heat parched through
And all but hopeless of grain,
   Refreshing the desolate places—

Fall clear on the ears of us hearkening
   And hungering for food of the sound

And thirsting for joy of his voice :
Till the hearts in us hear and rejoice,
And the thoughts of them doubting and
    darkening
    Rejoice with a glad thing found.

When the heart of our gladness is gone,
    What comfort is left with us after?
When the light of our eyes is away,
What glory remains upon May,
What blessing of song is thereon
    If we drink not the light of his laughter?

No small sweet face with the daytime
    To welcome, warmer than noon !
No sweet small voice as a bird's
To bring us the day's first words !
Mid May for us here is not Maytime :
    No summer begins with June.

A whole dead month in the dark,
    A dawn in the mists that o'ercome her
Stifled and smothered and sad—
Swift speed to it, barren and bad !
And return to us, voice of the lark,
    And remain with us, sunlight of summer.

II.

ALAS, what right has the dawn to glimmer,
　　What right has the wind to do aught but
　　　　moan ?
All the day should be dimmer
　　Because we are left alone.

Yestermorn like a sunbeam present
　　Hither and thither a light step smiled,
And made each place for us pleasant
　　With the sense or the sight of a child.

But the leaves persist as before, and after
　　Our parting the dull day still bears flowers ;
And songs less bright than his laughter
　　Deride us from birds in the bowers.

Birds, and blossoms, and sunlight only,
　　As though such folly sufficed for spring !
As though the house were not lonely
　　For want of the child its king !

x

III.

ASLEEP and afar to-night my darling
  Lies, and heeds not the night,
If winds be stirring or storms be snarling ;
  For his sleep is its own sweet light.

I sit where he sat beside me quaffing
  The wine of story and song
Poured forth of immortal cups, and laughing
  When mirth in the draught grew strong.

I broke the gold of the words, to melt it
  For hands but seven years old,
And they caught the tale as a bird, and felt it
  More bright than visible gold.

And he drank down deep, with his eyes broad
      beaming,
  Here in this room where I am,
The golden vintage of Shakespeare, gleaming
  In the silver vessels of Lamb.

Here by my hearth where he was I listen
  For the shade of the sound of a word,
Athirst for the birdlike eyes to glisten,
  For the tongue to chirp like a bird.

At the blast of battle, how broad they brightened,
  Like fire in the spheres of stars,
And clung to the pictured page, and lightened
  As keen as the heart of Mars !

At the touch of laughter, how swift it twittered
  The shrillest music on earth ;
How the lithe limbs laughed and the whole child
    glittered
  With radiant riot of mirth !

Our Shakespeare now, as a man dumb-stricken,
  Stands silent there on the shelf :
And my thoughts, that had song in the heart of them,
    sicken,
  And relish not Shakespeare's self.

And my mood grows moodier than Hamlet's even,
  And man delights not me,
But only the face that morn and even
  My heart leapt only to see.

That my heart made merry within me seeing,
  And sang as his laugh kept time :
But song finds now no pleasure in being,
  And love no reason in rhyme.

IV.

MILD May-blossom and proud sweet bay-flower,
　What, for shame, would you have with us here?
It is not the month of the May-flower
　This, but the fall of the year.

Flowers open only their lips in derision,
　Leaves are as fingers that point in scorn :
The shows we see are a vision ;
　Spring is not verily born.

Yet boughs turn supple and buds grow sappy,
　As though the sun were indeed the sun :
And all our woods are happy
　With all their birds save one.

But spring is over, but summer is over,
　But autumn is over, and winter stands
With his feet sunk deep in the clover
　And cowslips cold in his hands.

His hoar grim head has a hawthorn bonnet,
　His gnarled gaunt hand has a gay green staff
With new-blown rose-blossom on it :
　But his laugh is a dead man's laugh.

The laugh of spring that the heart seeks after,
  The hand that the whole world yearns to kiss,
It rings not here in his laughter,
  The sign of it is not this.

There is not strength in it left to splinter
  Tall oaks, nor frost in his breath to sting :
Yet it is but a breath as of winter,
  And it is not the hand of spring.

V.

THIRTY-ONE pale maidens, clad
   All in mourning dresses,
Pass, with lips and eyes more sad
That it seems they should be glad,
Heads discrowned of crowns they had,
   Grey for golden tresses.

Grey their girdles too for green,
   And their veils dishevelled :
None would say, to see their mien,
That the least of these had been
Born no baser than a queen,
   Reared where flower-fays revelled.

Dreams that strive to seem awake,
   Ghosts that walk by daytime,
Weary winds the way they take,
Since, for one child's absent sake,
May knows well, whate'er things make
   Sport, it is not Maytime.

VI.

A HAND at the door taps light
As the hand of my heart's delight :
  It is but a full-grown hand,
Yet the stroke of it seems to start
Hope like a bird in my heart,
  Too feeble to soar or to stand.

To start light hope from her cover
Is to raise but a kite for a plover
  If her wings be not fledged to soar.
Desire, but in dreams, cannot ope
The door that was shut upon hope
  When love went out at the door.

Well were it if vision could keep
The lids of desire as in sleep
  Fast locked, and over his eyes
A dream with the dark soft key
In her hand might hover, and be
  Their keeper till morning rise ;

The morning that brings after many
Days fled with no light upon any
   The small face back which is gone ;
When the loved little hands once more
Shall struggle and strain at the door
   They beat their summons upon.

VII.

If a soul for but seven days were cast out of heaven
    and its mirth,
They would seem to her fears like as seventy years
    upon earth.

Even and morrow should seem to her sorrow as long
As the passage of numberless ages in slumberless
    song.

Dawn, roused by the lark, would be surely as dark in
    her sight
As her measureless measure of shadowless pleasure
    was bright.

Noon, gilt but with glory of gold, would be hoary
    and grey
In her eyes that had gazed on the depths, unamazed
    with the day.

Night hardly would seem to make darker her dream
    never done,
When it could but withhold what a man may behold
    of the sun.

For dreams would perplex, were the days that should
    vex her but seven,
The sight of her vision, made dark with division from
    heaven.

Till the light on my lonely way lighten that only now
    gleams,
I too am divided from heaven and derided of dreams.

VIII.

A TWILIGHT fire-fly may suggest
  How flames the fire that feeds the sun :
' A crooked figure may attest
  In little space a million.'

But this faint-figured verse, that dresses
  With flowers the bones of one bare month,
Of all it would say scarce expresses
  In crooked ways a millionth.

A fire-fly tenders to the father
  Of fires a tribute something worth :
My verse, a shard-borne beetle rather,
  Drones over scarce-illumined earth.

Some inches round me though it brighten
  With light of music-making thought,
The dark indeed it may not lighten,
  The silence moves not, hearing nought.

Only my heart is eased with hearing,
  Only mine eyes are soothed with seeing,
A face brought nigh, a footfall nearing,
  Till hopes take form and dreams have being.

IX.

As a poor man hungering stands with insatiate eyes
    and hands
        Void of bread
Right in sight of men that feast while his famine with
    no least
        Crumb is fed,

Here across the garden-wall can I hear strange chil-
    dren call,
        Watch them play,
From the windowed seat above, whence the goodlier
    child I love
        Is away.

Here the sights we saw together moved his fancy like
    a feather
        To and fro,
Now to wonder, and thereafter to the sunny storm of
    laughter
        Loud and low—

Sights engraven on storied pages where man's tale of
    seven swift ages
          All was told—
Seen of eyes yet bright from heaven—for the lips that
    laughed were seven
          Sweet years old.

X.

WHY should May remember
    March, if March forget
The days that began with December,
    The nights that a frost could fret?

All their griefs are done with
    Now the bright months bless
Fit souls to rejoice in the sun with,
    Fit heads for the wind's caress;

Souls of children quickening
    With the whole world's mirth,
Heads closelier than field-flowers thickening
    That crowd and illuminate earth,

Now that May's call musters
    Files of baby bands
To marshal in joyfuller clusters
    Than the flowers that encumber their hands.

Yet morose November
    Found them no less gay,
With nought to forget or remember
    Less bright than a branch of may.

All the seasons moving
　　Move their minds alike
Applauding, acclaiming, approving
　　All hours of the year that strike.

So my heart may fret not,
　　Wondering if my friend
Remember me not or forget not
　　Or ever the month find end.

Not that love sows lighter
　　Seed in children sown,
But that life being lit in them brighter
　　Moves fleeter than even our own.

May nor yet September
　　Binds their hearts, that yet
Remember, forget, and remember,
　　Forget, and recall, and forget.

XI.

As light on a lake's face moving
　　Between a cloud and a cloud
Till night reclaim it, reproving
　　The heart that exults too loud,

The heart that watching rejoices
　　When soft it swims into sight
Applauded of all the voices
　　And stars of the windy night,

So brief and unsure, but sweeter
　　Than ever a moondawn smiled,
Moves, measured of no tune's metre,
　　The song in the soul of a child ;

The song that the sweet soul singing
　　Half listens, and hardly hears,
Though sweeter than joy-bells ringing
　　And brighter than joy's own tears ;

The song that remembrance of pleasure
　　Begins, and forgetfulness ends
With a soft swift change in the measure
　　That rings in remembrance of friends

As the moon on the lake's face flashes,
    So haply may gleam at whiles
A dream through the dear deep lashes
    Whereunder a child's eye smiles,

And the least of us all that love him
    May take for a moment part
With angels around and above him,
    And I find place in his heart.

XII.

CHILD, were you kinless and lonely—
  Dear, were you kin to me—
My love were compassionate only
  Or such as it needs would be.

But eyes of father and mother
  Like sunlight shed on you shine :
What need you have heed of another
  Such new strange love as is mine ?

It is not meet if unruly
  Hands take of the children's bread
And cast it to dogs ; but truly
  The dogs after all would be fed.

On crumbs from the children's table
  That crumble, dropped from above,
My heart feeds, fed with unstable
  Loose waifs of a child's light love.

Though love in your heart were brittle
  As glass that breaks with a touch,
You haply would lend him a little
  Who surely would give you much.

XIII.

Here is a rough
  Rude sketch of my friend,
Faint-coloured enough
  And unworthily penned.

Fearlessly fair
  And triumphant he stands,
And holds unaware
  Friends' hearts in his hands ;

Stalwart and straight
  As an oak that should bring
Forth gallant and great
  Fresh roses in spring.

On the paths of his pleasure
  All graces that wait
What metre shall measure
  What rhyme shall relate

Each action, each motion,
  Each feature, each limb,
Demands a devotion
  In honour of him ;

Y 2

Head that the hand
    Of a god might have blest,
Laid lustrous and bland
    On the curve of its crest :

Mouth sweeter than cherries
    Keen eyes as of Mars
Browner than berries
    And brighter than stars.

Nor colour nor wordy
    Weak song can declare
The stature how sturdy,
    How stalwart his air.

As a king in his bright
    Presence-chamber may be,
So seems he in height—
    Twice higher than your knee.

As a warrior sedate
    With reserve of his power,
So seems he in state—
    As tall as a flower :

As a rose overtowering
    The ranks of the rest
That beneath it lie cowering,
    Less bright than their best.

And his hands are as sunny
　　As ruddy ripe corn
Or the browner-hued honey
　　From heather-bells borne.

When summer sits proudest,
　　Fulfilled with its mirth,
And rapture is loudest
　　In air and on earth,

The suns of all hours
　　That have ripened the roots
Bring forth not such flowers
　　And beget not such fruits.

And well though I know it,
　　As fain would I write,
Child, never a poet
　　Could praise you aright.

I bless you? the blessing
　　Were less than a jest
Too poor for expressing;
　　I come to be blest,

With humble and dutiful
　　Heart, from above :
Bless me, O my beautiful
　　Innocent love !

This rhyme in your praise
  With a smile was begun ;
But the goal of his ways
  Is uncovered to none,

Nor pervious till after
  The limit impend ;
It is not in laughter
  These rhymes of you end.

XIV.

Spring, and fall, and summer, and winter,
 Which may Earth love least of them all,
Whose arms embrace as their signs imprint her,
 Summer, or winter, or spring, or fall?

The clear-eyed spring with the wood-birds mating,
 The rose-red summer with eyes aglow,
The yellow fall with serene eyes waiting,
 The wild-eyed winter with hair all snow?

Spring's eyes are soft, but if frosts benumb her
 As winter's own will her shrewd breath sting :
Storms may rend the raiment of summer,
 And fall grow bitter as harsh-lipped spring.

One sign for summer and winter guides me,
 One for spring, and the like for fall :
Whichever from sight of my friend divides me,
 That is the worst ill season of all.

XV.

Worse than winter is spring
If I come not to sight of my king :
But then what a spring will it be
When my king takes homage of me !

I send his grace from afar
Homage, as though to a star ;
As a shepherd whose flock takes flight
May worship a star by night.

As a flock that a wolf is upon
My songs take flight and are gone :
No heart is in any to sing
Aught but the praise of my king.

Fain would I once and again
Sing deeds and passions of men :
But ever a child's head gleams
Between my work and my dreams.

Between my hand and my eyes
The lines of a small face rise,
And the lines I trace and retrace
Are none but those of the face.

XVI.

TILL the tale of all this flock of days alike
    All be done,
Weary days of waiting till the month's hand strike
    Thirty-one,
Till the clock's hand of the month break off, and end
    With the clock,
Till the last and whitest sheep at last be penned
    Of the flock,
I their shepherd keep the count of night and day
    With my song,
Though my song be, like this month which once was
    May,
      All too long.

XVII.

THE incarnate sun, a tall strong youth,
  On old Greek eyes in sculpture smiled:
But trulier had it given the truth
  To shape him like a child.

No face full-grown of all our dearest
  So lightens all our darkness, none
Most loved of all our hearts hold nearest
  So far outshines the sun,

As when with sly shy smiles that feign
  Doubt if the hour be clear, the time
Fit to break off my work again
  Or sport of prose or rhyme,

My friend peers in on me with merry
  Wise face, and though the sky stay dim
The very light of day, the very
  Sun's self comes in with him.

XVIII.

Out of sight,
  Out of mind !
Could the light
  Prove unkind?

Can the sun
  Quite forget
What was done
  Ere he set?

Does the moon
  When she wanes
Leave no tune
  That remains

In the void
  Shell of night
Overcloyed
  With her light?

Must the shore
  At low tide
Feel no more
  Hope or pride,

No intense
  Joy to be,
In the sense
  Of the sea—;

In the pulses
  Of her shocks
It repulses,
  When its rocks

Thrill and ring
  As with glee?
Has my king
  Cast off me,

Whom no bird
  Flying south
Brings one word
  From his mouth?

Not the ghost
  Of a word
Riding post
  Have I heard,

Since the day
  When my king
Took away
  With him spring,

And the cup
   Of each flower
Shrivelled up
   That same hour,

With no light
   Left behind.
Out of sight,
   Out of mind !

XIX.

Because I adore you
   And fall
On the knees of my spirit before you—
   After all,

You need not insult,
   My king,
With neglect, though your spirit exult
   In the spring,

Even me, though not worth,
   God knows,
One word of you sent me in mirth,
   Or one rose

Out of all in your garden
   That grow
Where the frost and the wind never harden
   Flakes of snow,

Nor ever is rain
   At all,
But the roses rejoice to remain
   Fair and tall—

The roses of love,
  More sweet
Than blossoms that rain from above
  Round our feet,

When under high bowers
  We pass,
Where the west wind freckles with flowers
  All the grass.

But a child's thoughts bear
  More bright
Sweet visions by day, and more fair
  Dreams by night,

Than summer's whole treasure
  Can be :
What am I that his thought should take pleasure,
  Then, in me ?

I am only my love's
  True lover,
With a nestful of songs, like doves
  Under cover,

That I bring in my cap
  Fresh caught,
To be laid on my small king's lap—
  Worth just nought.

Yet it haply may hap
  That he,
When the mirth in his veins is as sap
  In a tree,

Will remember me too
  Some day
Ere the transit be thoroughly through
  Of this May—

Or perchance, if such grace
  May be,
Some night when I dream of his face,
  Dream of me.

Or if this be too high
  A hope
For me to prefigure in my
  Horoscope,

He may dream of the place
  Where we
Basked once in the light of his face,
  Who now see

Nought brighter, not one
  Thing bright,
Than the stars and the moon and the sun,
  Day nor night.

XX.

DAY by darkling day,
Overpassing, bears away
Somewhat of the burden of this weary May.

Night by numbered night,
Waning, brings more near in sight
Hope that grows to vision of my heart's delight.

Nearer seems to burn
In the dawn's rekindling urn
Flame of fragrant incense, hailing his return.

Louder seems each bird
In the brightening branches heard
Still to speak some ever more delightful word.

All the mists that swim
Round the dawns that grow less dim
Still wax brighter and more bright with hope of him.

z

All the suns that rise
Bring that day more near our eyes
When the sight of him shall clear our clouded skies.

All the winds that roam
Fruitful fields or fruitless foam
Blow the bright hour near that brings his bright
face home.

XXI.

I HEAR of two far hence
   In a garden met,
And the fragrance blown from thence
   Fades not yet.

The one is seven years old,
   And my friend is he :
But the years of the other have told
   Eighty-three.

To hear these twain converse
   Or to see them greet
Were sweeter than softest verse
   May be sweet.

The hoar old gardener there
   With an eye more mild
Perchance than his mild white hair
   Meets the child.

I had rather hear the words
   That the twain exchange
Than the songs of all the birds
   There that range,

Call, chirp, and twitter there
  Through the garden-beds
Where the sun alike sees fair
  Those two heads,

And which may holier be
  Held in heaven of those
Or more worth heart's thanks to see
  No man knows.

XXII.

Of such is the kingdom of heaven.
  No glory that ever was shed
From the crowning star of the seven
  That crown the north world's head,

No word that ever was spoken
  Of human or godlike tongue,
Gave ever such godlike token
  Since human harps were strung.

No sign that ever was given
  To faithful or faithless eyes
Showed ever beyond clouds riven
  So clear a Paradise.

Earth's creeds may be seventy times seven
  And blood have defiled each creed :
If of such be the kingdom of heaven,
  It must be heaven indeed.

XXIII.

THE wind on the downs is bright
  As though from the sea :
And morning and night
  Take comfort again with me.

He is nearer to-day,
  Each night to each morning saith,
Whose return shall revive dead May
  With the balm of his breath.

The sunset says to the moon,
  He is nearer to-night
Whose coming in June
  Is looked for more than the light.

Bird answers to bird,
  Hour passes the sign on to hour,
And for joy of the bright news heard
  Flower murmurs to flower.

The ways that were glad of his feet
  In the woods that he knew
Grow softer to meet
  The sense of his footfall anew.

He is near now as day,
  Says hope to the new-born light :
He is near now as June is to May,
  Says love to the night.

XXIV.

Good things I keep to console me
  For lack of the best of all,
A child to command and control· me,
  Bid come and remain at his calL

Sun, wind, and woodland and highland,
  Give all that ever they gave :
But my world is a cultureless island,
  My spirit a masterless slave.

And friends are about me, and better
  At summons of no man stand :
But I pine for the touch of a fetter,
  The curb of a strong king's hand.

Each hour of the day in her season
  Is mine to be served as I will :
And for no more exquisite reason ,
  Are all served idly and ilL

By slavery my sense is corrupted,
  My soul not fit to be free :
I would fain be controlled, interrupted,
  Compelled as a thrall may be.

For fault of spur and of bridle
  I tire of my stall to death :
My sail flaps joyless and idle
  For want of a small child's breath.

XXV.

Whiter and whiter
  The dark lines grow,
And broader opens and brighter
  The sense of the text below.

Nightfall and morrow
  Bring nigher the boy
Whom wanting we want not sorrow,
  Whom having we want no joy.

Clearer and clearer
  The sweet sense grows
Of the word which hath summer for hearer,
  The word on the lips of the rose.

Duskily dwindles
  Each deathlike day,
Till June rearising rekindles
  The depth of the darkness of May.

XXVI.

'In his bright radiance and collateral light
Must I be comforted, not in his sphere.'

STARS in heaven are many,
    Suns in heaven but one :
Nor for man may any
    Star supplant the sun.

Many a child as joyous
    As our far-off king
Meets as though to annoy us
    In the paths of spring.

Sure as spring gives warning,
    All things dance in tune :
Sun on Easter morning,
    Cloud and windy moon,

Stars between the tossing
    Boughs of tuneful trees,
Sails of ships recrossing
    Leagues of dancing seas ;

Best, in all this playtime,
   Best of all in tune,
Girls more glad than Maytime,
   Boys more bright than June ;

Mixed with all those dances,
   Far through field and street
Sing their silent glances,
   Ring their radiant feet.

Flowers wherewith May crowned us
   Fall ere June be crowned :
Children blossom round us
   All the whole year round.

Is the garland worthless
   For one rose the less,
And the feast made mirthless ?
   Love, at least, says yes.

Strange it were, with many
   Stars enkindling air,
Should but one find any
   Welcome : strange it were,

Had one star alone won
   Praise for light from far :
Nay, love needs his own one
   Bright particular star.

Hope and recollection
　Only lead him right
In its bright reflection
　And collateral light.

Find as yet we may not
　Comfort in its sphere :
Yet these days will weigh not
　When it warms us here ;

When full-orbed it rises,
　Now divined afar :
None in all the skies is
　Half so good a star ;

None that seers importune
　Till a sign be won :
Star of our good fortune,
　Rise and reign, our sun !

XXVII.

I PASS by the small room now forlorn
  Where once each night as I passed I knew
A child's bright sleep from even to morn
  Made sweet the whole night through.

As a soundless shell, as a songless nest,
  Seems now the room that was radiant then
And fragrant with his happier rest
  Than that of slumbering men.

The day therein is less than the day,
  The night is indeed night now therein :
Heavier the dark seems there to weigh,
  And slower the dawns begin.

As a nest fulfilled with birds, as a shell
  Fulfilled with breath of a god's own hymn,
Again shall be this bare blank cell,
  Made sweet again with him.

XXVIII.

Spring darkens before us,
  A flame going down,
With chant from the chorus
  Of days without crown—
Cloud, rain, and sonorous
  Soft wind on the down.

She is wearier not of us
  Than we of the dream
That spring was to love us
  And joy was to gleam
Through the shadows above us
  That shift as they stream.

Half dark and half hoary,
  Float far on the loud
Mild wind, as a glory
  Half pale and half proud
From the twilight of story,
  Her tresses of cloud ;

Like phantoms that glimmer
　Of glories of old
With ever yet dimmer
　Pale circlets of gold
As darkness grows grimmer
　And memory more cold.

Like hope growing clearer
　With wane of the moon,
Shines toward us the nearer
　Gold frontlet of June,
And a face with it dearer
　Than midsummer noon.

XXIX.

You send me your love in a letter,
  I send you my love in a song :
Ah child, your gift is the better,
  Mine does you but wrong.

No fame, were the best less brittle,
  No praise, were it wide as earth,
Is worth so much as a little
  Child's love may be worth.

We see the children above us
  As they might angels above :
Come back to us, child, if you love us,
  And bring us your love.

XXX.

No time for books or for letters :
　　What time should there be ?
No room for tasks and their fetters:
　　Full room to be free.

The wind and the sun and the Maytime
　　Had never a guest
More worthy the most that his playtime
　　Could give of its best.

If rain should come on, peradventure,
　　(But sunshine forbid !)
Vain hope in us haply might venture
　　To dream as it did.

But never may come, of all comers
　　Least welcome, the rain,
To mix with his servant the summer's
　　Rose-garlanded train !

He would write, but his hours are as busy
   As bees in the sun,
And the jubilant whirl of their dizzy
   Dance never is done.

The message is more than a letter,
   Let love understand,
And the thought of his joys even better
   Than sight of his hand.

XXXI.

WIND, high-souled, full-hearted
    South-west wind of the spring !
Ere April and earth had parted,
    Skies, bright with thy forward wing,
Grew dark in an hour with the shadow behind it, that
        bade not a bird dare sing.

Wind whose feet are sunny,
    Wind whose wings are cloud,
With lips more sweet than honey
    Still, speak they low or loud,
Rejoice now again in the strength of thine heart: let
        the depth of thy soul wax proud.

We hear thee singing or sighing,
    Just not given to sight,
All but visibly flying
    Between the clouds and the light,
And the light in our hearts is enkindled, the shadow
        therein of the clouds put to flight.

From the gift of thine hands we gather
　　The core of the flowers therein,
　Keen glad heart of heather,
　　Hot sweet heart of whin,
Twin breaths in thy godlike breath close blended of
　　wild spring's wildest of kin.

　All but visibly beating
　　We feel thy wings in the far
　Clear waste, and the plumes of them fleeting,
　　Soft as swan's plumes are,
And strong as a wild swan's pinions, and swift as the
　　flash of the flight of a star.

　As the flight of a planet enkindled
　　Seems thy far soft flight
　Now May's reign has dwindled
　　And the crescent of June takes light
And the presence of summer is here, and the hope of
　　a welcomer presence in sight.

　Wind, sweet-souled, great-hearted
　　Southwest wind on the wold !
　From us is a glory departed
　　That now shall return as of old,
Borne back on thy wings as an eagle's expanding, and
　　crowned with the sundawn's gold.

There is not a flower but rejoices,
 There is not a leaf but has heard:
All the fields find voices,
 All the woods are stirred:
There is not a nest but is brighter because of the
  coming of one bright bird.

Out of dawn and morning,
 Noon and afternoon,
The sun to the world gives warning
 Of news that brightens the moon ;
And the stars all night exult with us, hearing of joy
  that shall come with June.

SUNRISE.

IF the wind and the sunlight of April and August had
    mingled the past and hereafter
In a single adorable season whose life were a rapture
    of love and of laughter,
And the blithest of singers were back with a song ; if
    again from his tomb as from prison,
If again from the night or the twilight of ages Aristo-
    phanes had arisen,
With the gold-feathered wings of a bird that were also
    a god upon earth at his shoulders,
And the gold-flowing laugh of the manhood of old at
    his lips, for a joy to beholders,
He alone unrebuked of presumption were able to set
    to some adequate measure
The delight of our eyes in the dawn that restores
    them the sun of their sense and the pleasure.
For the days of the darkness of spirit are over for all
    of us here, and the season
When desire was a longing, and absence a thorn, and
    rejoicing a word without reason.

For the roof overhead of the pines is astir with delight
    as of jubilant voices,
And the floor underfoot of the bracken and heather
    alive as a heart that rejoices.
For the house that was childless awhile, and the light
    of it darkened, the pulse of it dwindled,
Rings radiant again with a child's bright feet, with the
    light of his face is rekindled.
And the ways of the meadows that knew him, the
    sweep of the down that the sky's belt closes,
Grow gladder at heart than the soft wind made them
    whose feet were but fragrant with roses,
Though the fall of the year be upon us, who trusted
    in June and by June were defrauded,
And the summer that brought us not back the desire
    of our eyes be gone hence unapplauded.
For July came joyless among us, and August went
    out from us arid and sterile,
And the hope of our hearts, as it seemed, was no
    more than a flower that the seasons imperil,
And the joy of our hearts, as it seemed, than a thought
    which regret had not heart to remember,
Till four dark months overpast were atoned for, and
    summer began in September.
Hark, April again as a bird in the house with a child's
    voice hither and thither :
See, May in the garden again with a child's face
    cheering the woods ere they wither.
June laughs in the light of his eyes, and July on the
    sunbright cheeks of him slumbers,

And August glows in a smile more sweet than the
    cadence of gold-mouthed numbers.
In the morning the sight of him brightens the sun,
    and the noon with delight in him flushes,
And the silence of nightfall is music about him as
    soft as the sleep that it hushes.
We awake with a sense of a sunrise that is not a gift
    of the sundawn's giving,
And a voice that salutes us is sweeter than all sounds
    else in the world of the living,
And a presence that warms us is brighter than all in
    the world of our visions beholden,
Though the dreams of our sleep were as those that
    the light of a world without grief makes golden.
For the best that the best of us ever devised as a
    likeness of heaven and its glory,
What was it of old, or what is it and will be for ever,
    in song or in story,
Or in shape or in colour of carven or painted resem-
    blance, adored of all ages,
But a vision recorded of children alive in the pictures
    of old or the pages?
Where children are not, heaven is not, and heaven if
    they come not again shall be never:
But the face and the voice of a child are assurance of
    heaven and its promise for ever.

Spottiswoode & Co., Printers, New-street Square, London

B B

AN ALPHABETICAL CATALOGUE
OF BOOKS IN FICTION AND
GENERAL LITERATURE
PUBLISHED BY
CHATTO & WINDUS
111 ST. MARTIN'S LANE
CHARING CROSS
LONDON, W.C.
[NOV. 1900.]

About (Edmond).—The Fellah: An Egyptian Novel. Translated by Sir RANDAL ROBERTS. Post 8vo, illustrated boards, 2s.

Adams (W. Davenport), Works by.
A Dictionary of the Drama: being a comprehensive Guide to the Plays, Playwrights, Players, and Playhouses of the United Kingdom and America, from the Earliest Times to the Present Day. Crown 8vo, half-bound, 12s. 6d. [Preparing.
Quips and Quiddities. Selected by W. DAVENPORT ADAMS. Post 8vo, cloth limp, 2s. 6t.

Agony Column (The) of 'The Times,' from 1800 to 1870. Edited with an Introduction, by ALICE CLAY. Post 8vo, cloth limp, 2s. 6d.

Alexander (Mrs.), Novels by. Post 8vo, illustrated boards, 2s. each.
Maid, Wife, or Widow? | Blind Fate.
Crown 8vo, cloth, 3s. 6d. each; post 8vo, picture boards, 2s. each.
Valerie's Fate. | A Life Interest. | Mona's Choice. | By Woman's Wit.
Crown 8vo, cloth 3s. 6d. each.
The Cost of her Pride. | Barbara, Lady's Maid and Peeress. | A Fight with Fate.
A Golden Autumn. | Mrs. Crichton's Creditor. | The Step-mother.
A Missing Hero. Crown 8vo, cloth, gilt top, 6s. [Jan.

Allen (F. M.).—Green as Grass. Crown 8vo, cloth, 3s. 6d.

Allen (Grant), Works by. Crown 8vo, cloth, 6s. each.
The Evolutionist at Large. | Moorland Idylls.
Post-Prandial Philosophy. Crown 8vo, art linen, 3s. 6d.
Crown 8vo, cloth extra, 3s. 6d. each; post 8vo, illustrated boards, 2s. each.
Babylon. 12 Illustrations. | The Devil's Die. | The Duchess of Powysland.
Strange Stories. Frontis. | This Mortal Coil. | Blood Royal.
The Beckoning Hand. | The Tents of Shem. Frontis. | Ivan Greet's Masterpiece.
For Maimie's Sake. | The Great Taboo. | The Scallywag. 24 Illusts.
Philistia. | Dumaresq's Daughter. | At Market Value.
In all Shades. | Under Sealed Orders. |
Dr. Palliser's Patient. Fcap. 8vo, cloth boards, 1s. 6d.

Anderson (Mary).—Othello's Occupation. Crown 8vo, cloth, 3s. 6d.

Arnold (Edwin Lester), Stories by.
The Wonderful Adventures of Phra the Phœnician. Crown 8vo, cloth extra, with 12 Illustrations by H. M. PAGET, 3s. 6d.; post 8vo, illustrated boards, 2s.
The Constable of St. Nicholas. With Frontispiece by S. L. WOOD. Crown 8vo, cloth, 3s. 6d.

Artemus Ward's Works. With Portrait and Facsimile. Crown 8vo, cloth extra, 3s. 6d.—Also a POPULAR EDITION post 8vo, picture boards, 2s.

Ashton (John), Works by. Crown 8vo, cloth extra, 7s. 6d. each.
History of the Chap-Books of the 18th Century. With 334 Illustrations.
Humour, Wit, and Satire of the Seventeenth Century. With 82 Illustrations.
English Caricature and Satire on Napoleon the First. With 115 Illustrations.
Modern Street Ballads. With 57 Illustrations.
Social Life in the Reign of Queen Anne. With 85 Illustrations. Crown 8vo, cloth, 3s. 6d.
Crown 8vo, cloth, gilt top, 6s. each.
Social Life under the Regency. With 90 Illustrations.
Florizel's Folly: The Story of GEORGE IV. With Photogravure Frontispiece and 12 Illustrations.

Bacteria, Yeast Fungi, and Allied Species, A Synopsis of. By W. B. GROVE B.A. With 87 Illustrations. Crown 8vo, cloth extra, 3s. 6d.

Bardsley (Rev. C. Wareing, M.A.), Works by.
English Surnames : Their Sources and Significations. Crown 8vo, cloth, 7s. 6d.
Curiosities of Puritan Nomenclature. Crown 8vo, cloth, 3s. 6d.

Baring Gould (Sabine, Author of 'John Herring,' &c.), Novels by.
Crown 8vo, cloth extra, 3s. 6d. each ; post 8vo, illustrated boards, 2s. each.
Red Spider. | **Eve.**

Barr (Robert: Luke Sharp), Stories by. Cr. 8vo, cl., 3s. 6d. each.
In a Steamer Chair. With Frontispiece and Vignette by DEMAIN HAMMOND.
From Whose Bourne, &c. With 47 Illustrations by HAL HURST and others.
Revenge ! With 12 Illustrations by LANCELOT SPEED and others.
A Woman Intervenes. With 8 Illustrations by HAL HURST.
The Unchanging East : Notes on a Visit to the Farther Edge of the Mediterranean. With a Frontispiece. Crown 8vo, cloth, gilt top, 6s.

Barrett (Frank), Novels by.
Post 8vo, illustrated boards, 2s. each ; cloth, 2s. 6d. each.

The Sin of Olga Zassoulich.	**John Ford : and His Helpmate.**
Between Life and Death.	**A Recoiling Vengeance.**
Folly Morrison. | **Honest Davie.**	**Lieut. Barnabas.** | **Found Guilty.**
Little Lady Linton.	**For Love and Honour.**
A Prodigal's Progress.	

Crown 8vo, cloth, 3s. 6d. each ; post 8vo, picture boards, 2s each ; cloth limp, 2s. 6d. each.
Fettered for Life. | **The Woman of the Iron Bracelets.** | **The Harding Scandal.**
A Missing Witness. With 8 Illustrations by W. H. MARGETSON.
Crown 8vo, cloth, 3s. 6d. each.
Under a Strange Mask. With 19 Illusts. by E. F. BREWTNALL. | **Was She Justified ?**

Barrett (Joan).—Monte Carlo Stories. Fcap. 8vo, cloth, 1s. 6d.

Beaconsfield, Lord. By T. P. O'CONNOR, M.P. Cr. 8vo, cloth, 5s.

Besant (Sir Walter) and James Rice, Novels by.
Crown 8vo, cloth extra, 3s. 6d. each ; post 8vo, illustrated boards, 2s. each ; cloth limp, 2s. 6d. each.

Ready-Money Mortiboy.	**The Golden Butterfly.**	**The Seamy Side.**
My Little Girl.	**The Monks of Thelema.**	**The Case of Mr. Lucraft.**
With Harp and Crown.	**By Celia's Arbour.**	**'Twas in Trafalgar's Bay.**
This Son of Vulcan.	**The Chaplain of the Fleet.**	**The Ten Years' Tenant.**

** There are also LIBRARY EDITIONS of all the above, excepting Ready-Money Mortiboy and **The Golden Butterfly,** handsomely set in new type on a large crown 8vo page, and bound in cloth extra, 6s. each ; and POPULAR EDITIONS of **The Golden Butterfly** and of **All Sorts and Conditions of Men,** medium 8vo, cloth, 6d. each

Besant (Sir Walter), Novels by.
Crown 8vo, cloth extra, 3s. 6d. each ; post 8vo, illustrated boards, 2s. each ; cloth limp, 2s. 6d. each.
All Sorts and Conditions of Men. With 12 Illustrations by FRED. BARNARD.
The Captains' Room, &c. With Frontispiece by E. J. WHEELER.
All in a Garden Fair. With 6 Illustrations by HARRY FURNISS.
Dorothy Forster. With Frontispiece by CHARLES GREEN.
Uncle Jack, and other Stories. | **Children of Gibeon.**
The World Went Very Well Then. With 12 Illustrations by A. FORESTIER.
Herr Paulus : His Rise, his Greatness, and his Fall. | **The Bell of St. Paul's.**
For Faith and Freedom. With Illustrations by A. FORESTIER and F. WADDY.
To Call Her Mine, &c. With 9 Illustrations by A. FORESTIER.
The Holy Rose, &c. With Frontispiece by F. BARNARD.
Armorel of Lyonesse : A Romance of To-day. With 12 Illustrations by F. BARNARD.
St. Katherine's by the Tower. With 12 Illustrations by C. GREEN.
Verbena Camellia Stephanotis, &c. With a Frontispiece by GORDON BROWNE.
The Ivory Gate. | **The Rebel Queen.**
Beyond the Dreams of Avarice. With 12 Illustrations by W. H. HYDE.
In Deacon's Orders, &c. With Frontispiece by A. FORESTIER. | **The Revolt of Man.**
The Master Craftsman. | **The City of Refuge.**
Crown 8vo, cloth, 3s. 6d. each.
A Fountain Sealed. With a Frontispiece. | **The Changeling.**
Crown 8vo, cloth, gilt top, 6s. each.
The Orange Girl. With 8 Illustrations by F. PEGRAM. | **The Fourth Generation.**
The Charm, and other Drawing-room Plays. By Sir WALTER BESANT and WALTER H. POLLOCK
With 50 Illustrations by CHRIS HAMMOND and JULE GOODMAN. Crown 8vo, cloth, gilt edges, 6s. or blue cloth, to range with the Uniform Edition of Sir WALTER BESANT'S Novels, 3s. 6d.
Fifty Years Ago. With 144 Illustrations. Crown 8vo, cloth, 3s. 6d.
The Eulogy of Richard Jefferies. With Portrait. Crown 8vo, cloth, 6s.
London. With 125 Illustrations. Demy 8vo, cloth, 7s. 6d.
Westminster. With Etched Frontispiece by F. S. WALKER, R.E., and 130 Illustrations by WILLIAM PATTEN and others. Demy 8vo, cloth, 7s. 6d.
South London. With Etched Frontispiece by F. S. WALKER, R.E., and 118 Illustrations. Demy 8vo, cloth, gilt top, 18s.
East London. With 55 Illustrations by PHIL MAY, L. RAVEN HILL, and JOSEPH PENNELL. Demy 8vo, cloth, 18s. [Shortly.
Jerusalem : The City of Herod and Saladin. By WALTER BESANT and E. H. PALMER. Fourth Edition. With a new Chapter, a Map, and 11 Illustrations. Small demy 8vo, cloth, 7s. 6d.
Sir Richard Whittington. With Frontispiece. Crown 8vo, art linen, 3s. 6d.
Gaspard de Goligny. With a Portrait. Crown 8vo, art linen, 3s. 6d.

Bechstein (Ludwig).—As Pretty as Seven, and other German Stories. With Additional Tales by the Brothers GRIMM, and 98 Illustrations by RICHTER. Square 8vo, cloth extra, 6s. 6d.; gilt edges, 7s. 6d.

Bellew (Frank).—The Art of Amusing: A Collection of Graceful Arts, Games, Tricks, Puzzles, and Charades. With 300 Illustrations. Crown 8vo, cloth extra, 4s. 6d.

Bennett (W. C., LL.D.).—Songs for Sailors. Post 8vo, cl. limp, 2s.

Bewick (Thomas) and his Pupils. By AUSTIN DOBSON. With 95 Illustrations. Square 8vo, cloth extra, 3s. 6d.

Bierce (Ambrose).—In the Midst of Life: Tales of Soldiers and Civilians. Crown 8vo, cloth extra, 3s. 6d.; post 8vo, illustrated boards, 2s.

Bill Nye's Comic History of the United States. With 146 Illustrations by F. OPPER. Crown 8vo, cloth extra, 3s. 6d.

Bindloss (Harold).—Ainslie's Ju-Ju: A Romance of the Hinterland. Crown 8vo, cloth, 3s. 6d.

Blackburn's (Henry) Art Handbooks.

Academy Notes, 1900.
Academy Notes, 1875-79. Complete in One Vol., with 600 Illustrations. Cloth, 6s.
Academy Notes, 1880-84. Complete in One Vol., with 700 Illustrations. Cloth, 6s.
Academy Notes, 1890-94. Complete in One Vol., with 800 Illustrations. Cloth, 7s. 6d.
Academy Notes, 1895-99. Complete in One Vol., with 800 Illustrations. Cloth, 7s. 6d.
Grosvenor Notes, Vol. I., 1877-82. With 300 Illustrations. Demy 8vo, cloth 6s.

Grosvenor Notes, Vol. II., 1883-87. With 300 Illustrations. Demy 8vo, cloth, 6s.
Grosvenor Notes, Vol. III., 1888-90. With 230 Illustrations. Demy 8vo cloth, 3s. 6d.
The New Gallery, 1888-1892. With 250 Illustrations. Demy 8vo, cloth, 6s.
English Pictures at the National Gallery. With 114 Illustrations. 1s.
Old Masters at the National Gallery. With 128 Illustrations. 1s. 6d.
Illustrated Catalogue to the National Gallery. With 242 Illusts. Demy 8vo, cloth, 3s

Illustrated Catalogue of the Paris Salon, 1900. With 400 Illustrations. Demy 8vo, 3s.

Bodkin (M. McD., Q.C.).—Dora Myrl, the Lady Detective. Crown 8vo, cloth, 3s. 6d.

Bourget (Paul).—A Living Lie. Translated by JOHN DE VILLIERS. With special Preface for the English Edition. Crown 8vo, cloth, 3s. 6d.

Bourne (H. R. Fox), Books by.
English Merchants: Memoirs in Illustration of the Progress of British Commerce. With 32 Illustrations. Crown 8vo, cloth, 3s. 6d.
English Newspapers: Chapters in the History of Journalism. Two Vols., demy 8vo, cloth, 25s.
The Other Side of the Emin Pasha Relief Expedition. Crown 8vo, cloth, 6s.

Boyle (Frederick), Works by. Post 8vo, illustrated bds., 2s. each.
Chronicles of No-Man's Land. | **Camp Notes.** | **Savage Life.**

Brand (John).—Observations on Popular Antiquities; chiefly illustrating the Origin of our Vulgar Customs, Ceremonies, and Superstitions. With the Additions of Sir HENRY ELLIS. Crown 8vo, cloth, 3s. 6d.

Brayshaw (J. Dodsworth).—Slum Silhouettes: Stories of London Life. Crown 8vo, cloth, 3s. 6d.

Brewer (Rev. Dr.), Works by.
The Reader's Handbook of Famous Names in Fiction, Allusions, References, Proverbs, Plots, Stories, and Poems. Together with an ENGLISH AND AMERICAN BIBLIOGRAPHY, and a LIST OF THE AUTHORS AND DATES OF DRAMAS AND OPERAS. A New Edition, Revised and Enlarged. Crown 8vo, cloth, 7s. 6d.
A Dictionary of Miracles: Imitative, Realistic, and Dogmatic. Crown 8vo, cloth, 3s. 6d.

Brewster (Sir David), Works by. Post 8vo, cloth, 4s. 6d. each.
More Worlds than One: Creed of the Philosopher and Hope of the Christian. With Plates.
The Martyrs of Science: GALILEO, TYCHO BRAHE, and KEPLER. With Portraits.
Letters on Natural Magic. With numerous Illustrations.

Brillat-Savarin.—Gastronomy as a Fine Art. Translated by R. E. ANDERSON, M.A. Post 8vo, half-bound, 2s.

Bryden (H. A.).—An Exiled Scot: A Romance. With a Frontispiece, by J. S. CROMPTON, R.I. Crown 8vo, cloth, 6s.

Brydges (Harold).—Uncle Sam at Home. With 91 Illustrations. Post 8vo, illustrated boards, 2s.; cloth limp, 2s. 6d.

Buchanan (Robert), Novels, &c., by.

Crown 8vo, cloth extra, 3s. 6d. each; post 8vo, illustrated boards, 2s. each.

The Shadow of the Sword. | Love Me for Ever. With Frontispiece.
A Child of Nature. With Frontispiece. | Annan Water. | Foxglove Manor.
God and the Man. With 11 Illustrations by | The New Abelard. | Rachel Dene.
Lady Kilpatrick. [FRED. BARNARD]. | Matt: A Story of a Caravan. With Frontispiece.
The Martyrdom of Madeline. With | The Master of the Mine. With Frontispiece.
Frontispiece by A. W. COOPER. | The Heir of Linne. | Woman and the Man.

Red and White Heather. Crown 8vo, cloth extra, 3s. 6d.

The Wandering Jew: a Christmas Carol. Crown 8vo, cloth, 6s.

The Charlatan. By ROBERT BUCHANAN and HENRY MURRAY. Crown 8vo, cloth, with a Frontispiece by T. H. ROBINSON, 3s. 6d.; post 8vo, picture boards, 2s.
Andromeda: An Idyll of the Great River. Crown 8vo, cloth, gilt top, 6s.

Burton (Robert).—The Anatomy of Melancholy. With Transla-
tions of the Quotations. Demy 8vo, cloth extra, 7s. 6d.
Melancholy Anatomised: An Abridgment of BURTON'S ANATOMY. Post 8vo, half-cl., 2s. 6d.

Caine (Hall), Novels by. Crown 8vo, cloth extra, 3s. 6d. each.; post
8vo, illustrated boards, 2s. each; cloth limp, 2s. 6d. each.
The Shadow of a Crime. | A Son of Hagar. | The Deemster.
Also LIBRARY EDITIONS of **The Deemster** and **The Shadow of a Crime**, set in new type, crown 8vo, and bound uniform with **The Christian**, 6s. each; and CHEAP POPULAR EDITIONS of **The Deemster, The Shadow of a Crime,** and **A Son of Hagar**, medium 8vo, portrait-cover, 6d. each.

Cameron (Commander V. Lovett).—The Cruise of the 'Black
Prince' Privateer. Post 8vo, picture boards, 2s.

Canada (Greater): The Past, Present, and Future of the Canadian
North-West. By E. B. OSBORN, B.A. With a Map. Crown 8vo, cloth, 3s. 6d.

Captain Coignet, Soldier of the Empire: An Autobiography.
Edited by LOREDAN LARCHEY. Translated by Mrs. CAREY. With 100 Illustrations. Crown 8vo, cloth, 3s. 6d.

Carlyle (Thomas).—On the Choice of Books. Post 8vo, cl., 1s. 6d.
Correspondence of Thomas Carlyle and R. W. Emerson, 1834-1872. Edited by C. E. NORTON. With Portraits. Two Vols., crown 8vo, cloth, 24s.

Carruth (Hayden).—The Adventures of Jones. With 17 Illustra-
tions. Fcap. 8vo, cloth, 2s.

Chambers (Robert W.), Stories of Paris Life by.
The King in Yellow. Crown 8vo, cloth, 3s. 6d.; fcap. 8vo, cloth limp, 2s. 6d.
In the Quarter. Fcap. 8vo, cloth, 2s. 6d.

Chapman's (George), Works. Vol. I., Plays Complete, including the
Doubtful Ones.—Vol. II., Poems and Minor Translations, with Essay by A. C. SWINBURNE.—Vol. III., Translations of the Iliad and Odyssey. Three Vols., crown 8vo, cloth, 3s. 6d. each.

Chapple (J. Mitchell).—The Minor Chord: The Story of a Prima
Donna. Crown 8vo, cloth, 3s. 6d.

Chaucer for Children: A Golden Key. By Mrs. H. R. HAWEIS. With
8 Coloured Plates and 30 Woodcuts. Crown 4to, cloth extra, 3s. 6d.
Chaucer for Schools. With the Story of his Times and his Work. By Mrs. H. R. HAWEIS. A New Edition, revised. With a Frontispiece. Demy 8vo, cloth, 2s. 6d.

Chess, The Laws and Practice of. With an Analysis of the Open-
ings. By HOWARD STAUNTON. Edited by R. B. WORMALD. Crown 8vo, cloth, 5s.
The Minor Tactics of Chess: A Treatise on the Deployment of the Forces in obedience to Strategic Principle. By F. K. YOUNG and E. C. HOWELL. Long fcap. 8vo, cloth, 2s. 6d.
The Hastings Chess Tournament. Containing the Authorised Account of the 230 Games played Aug.-Sept., 1895. With Annotations by PILLSBURY, LASKER, TARRASCH, STEINITZ, SCHIFFERS, TEICHMANN, BARDELEBEN, BLACKBURNE, GUNSBERG, TINSLEY, MASON, and ALBIN; Biographical Sketches of the Chess Masters, and 22 Portraits. Edited by H. F. CHESHIRE. Cheaper Edition. Crown 8vo, cloth, 5s.

Clare (Austin), Stories by.
For the Love of a Lass. Post 8vo, illustrated boards, 2s.; cloth, 2s. 6d.
By the Rise of the River: Tales and Sketches in South Tynedale. Crown 8vo, cloth, 3s. 6d.

Clive (Mrs. Archer), Novels by. Post 8vo, illust. boards, 2s. each.
Paul Ferroll. | Why Paul Ferroll Killed his Wife.

Clodd (Edward, F.R.A.S.).—Myths and Dreams. Cr. 8vo, 3s. 6d.

Coates (Anné).—Rie's Diary. Crown 8vo, cloth, 3s. 6d.

Cobban (J. Maclaren), Novels by.
The Cure of Souls. Post 8vo, Illustrated boards, 2s.
The Red Sultan. Crown 8vo, cloth extra, 3s. 6d. ; post 8vo, illustrated boards, 2s.
The Burden of Isabel. Crown 8vo, cloth extra, 3s. 6d.

Coleridge (M. E.).—The Seven Sleepers of Ephesus. Fcap. 8vo, leatherette, 1s. ; cloth, 1s. 6d.

Collins (C. Allston).—The Bar Sinister. Post 8vo, boards, 2s.

Collins (John Churton, M.A.), Books by.
Illustrations of Tennyson. Crown 8vo, cloth extra, 6s.
Jonathan Swift. A Biographical and Critical Study. Crown 8vo, cloth extra, 8s.

Collins (Mortimer and Frances), Novels by.
Crown 8vo, cloth extra, 3s. 6d. each; post 8vo, illustrated boards, 2s. each.
From Midnight to Midnight. | Blacksmith and Scholar.
You Play me False. | The Village Comedy.

Post 8vo, illustrated boards, 2s. each.
Transmigration. | Sweet Anne Page. | Frances.
A Fight with Fortune. | Sweet and Twenty. |

Collins (Wilkie), Novels by.
Crown 8vo, cloth extra, many Illustrated, 3s. 6d. each ; post 8vo, picture boards, 2s. each ;
cloth limp, 2s. 6d. each.

Antonina.	My Miscellanies.	Jezebel's Daughter.
Basil.	Armadale.	The Black Robe.
Hide and Seek.	Poor Miss Finch.	Heart and Science.
The Woman in White.	Miss or Mrs.?	'I Say No.'
The Moonstone.	The New Magdalen.	A Rogue's Life.
Man and Wife.	The Frozen Deep.	The Evil Genius.
After Dark.	The Law and the Lady.	Little Novels.
The Dead Secret.	The Two Destinies.	The Legacy of Cain.
The Queen of Hearts.	The Haunted Hotel.	Blind Love.
No Name.	The Fallen Leaves.	

POPULAR EDITIONS. Medium 8vo, 6d. each.
The Woman in White. | The Moonstone. | Antonina. | The Dead Secret.
The New Magdalen.

Colman's (George) Humorous Works: 'Broad Grins,' 'My Nightgown and Slippers,' &c. With Life and Frontispiece. Crown 8vo, cloth extra, 3s. 6d.

Colquhoun (M. J.).—Every Inch a Soldier. Crown 8vo, cloth, 3s. 6d. ; post 8vo, illustrated boards, 2s.

Colt-breaking, Hints on. By W. M. HUTCHISON. Cr. 8vo, cl., 3s. 6d.

Compton (Herbert). — The Inimitable Mrs. Massingham: a Romance of Botany Bay. Crown 8vo, cloth, gilt top, 6s.

Convalescent Cookery. By CATHERINE RYAN. Cr. 8vo, 1s. ; cl., 1s. 6d.

Cooper (Edward H.).—Geoffory Hamilton. Cr. 8vo, cloth, 3s. 6d.

Cornish (J. F.).—Sour Grapes: A Novel. Cr. 8vo, cloth, gilt top, 6s.

Cornwall.—Popular Romances of the West of England; or, The Drolls, Traditions, and Superstitions of Old Cornwall. Collected by ROBERT HUNT, F.R.S. With two Steel Plates by GEORGE CRUIKSHANK. Crown 8vo, cloth, 7s. 6d.

Cotes (V. Cecil).—Two Girls on a Barge. With 44 Illustrations by F. H. TOWNSEND. Crown 8vo, cloth extra, 3s. 6d.; post 8vo, cloth, 2s. 6d.

Craddock (C. Egbert), Stories by.
The Prophet of the Great Smoky Mountains. Post 8vo, Illustrated boards, 2s.
His Vanished Star. Crown 8vo, cloth extra, 3s. 6d.

Cram (Ralph Adams).—Black Spirits and White. Fcap. 8vo, cloth, 1s. 6d.

Crellin (H. N.), Books by.
Romances of the Old Seraglio. With 28 Illustrations by S. L. WOOD. Crown 8vo, cloth, 3s. 6d.
Tales of the Caliph. Crown 8vo, cloth, 2s.
The Nazarenes: A Drama. Crown 8vo, 1s.

Crim (Matt.).—Adventures of a Fair Rebel. Crown 8vo, cloth
extra, with a Frontispiece by DAN. BEARD, 3s. 6d.; post 8vo, illustrated boards, 2s.

Crockett (S. R.) and others. — Tales of Our Coast. By S. R.
CROCKETT, GILBERT PARKER, HAROLD FREDERIC, 'Q.,' and W. CLARK RUSSELL With 2
Illustrations by FRANK BRANGWYN. Crown 8vo, cloth, 3s. 6d.

Croker (Mrs. B. M.), Novels by. Crown 8vo, cloth extra, 3s. 6d.
each; post 8vo, illustrated boards, 2s. each; cloth limp, 2s. 6d. each.

Pretty Miss Neville.	Interference.	Village Tales & Jungle
Proper Pride.	A Family Likeness.	Tragedies.
A Bird of Passage.	'To Let.'	The Real Lady Hilda.
Diana Barrington.	A Third Person.	Married or Single?
Two Masters.	Mr. Jervis.	

Crown 8vo, cloth extra, 3s. 6d. each.

Some One Else.	Miss Balmaine's Past.	Beyond the Pale.
In the Kingdom of Kerry.	Jason, &c.	Infatuation.

Terence. With 6 Illustrations by SIDNEY PAGET. Crown 8vo, cloth, gilt top, 6s.

Cruikshank's Comic Almanack. Complete in TWO SERIES: The
FIRST, from 1835 to 1843; the SECOND, from 1844 to 1853. A Gathering of the Best Humour of
THACKERAY, HOOD, MAYHEW, ALBERT SMITH, A'BECKETT, ROBERT BROUGH, &c. With
numerous Steel Engravings and Woodcuts by GEORGE CRUIKSHANK, HINE, LANDELLS, &c.
Two Vols., crown 8vo, cloth gilt, 7s. 6d. each.
The Life of George Cruikshank. By BLANCHARD JERROLD. With 84 Illustrations and a
Bibliography. Crown 8vo, cloth extra, 3s. 6d.

Cumming (C. F. Gordon), Works by. Demy 8vo, cl. ex., 8s. 6d. ea.
In the Hebrides. With an Autotype Frontispiece and 23 Illustrations.
In the Himalayas and on the Indian Plains. With 42 Illustrations.
Two Happy Years in Ceylon. With 29 Illustrations.

Via Cornwall to Egypt. With a Photogravure Frontispiece. Demy 8vo, cloth, 7s. 6d.

Cussans (John E.).—A Handbook of Heraldry; with Instructions
for Tracing Pedigrees and Deciphering Ancient MSS., &c. Fourth Edition, revised, with 408 Woodcuts
and 2 Coloured Plates. Crown 8vo, cloth extra, 6s.

Cyples (William).—Hearts of Gold. Crown 8vo, cloth, 3s. 6d.

Daudet (Alphonse).—The Evangelist; or, Port Salvation. Crown
8vo, cloth extra, 3s. 6d.; post 8vo, illustrated boards, 2s.

Davenant (Francis, M.A.).—Hints for Parents on the Choice of
a Profession for their Sons when Starting in Life. Crown 8vo, cloth, 1s. 6d.

Davidson (Hugh Coleman).—Mr. Sadler's Daughters. With a
Frontispiece by STANLEY WOOD. Crown 8vo, cloth extra, 3s. 6d.

Davies (Dr. N. E. Yorke-), Works by. Cr. 8vo, 1s. ea.; cl., 1s. 6d. ea.
One Thousand Medical Maxims and Surgical Hints.
Nursery Hints: A Mother's Guide in Health and Disease.
Foods for the Fat: The Dietetic Cure of Corpulency and of Gout.

Aids to Long Life. Crown 8vo, 2s.; cloth limp, 2s. 6d.

Davies' (Sir John) Complete Poetical Works. Collected and Edited,
with Introduction and Notes, by Rev. A. B. GROSART, D.D. Two Vols., crown 8vo, cloth, 3s. 6d. each.

Dawson (Erasmus, M.B.).—The Fountain of Youth. Crown 8vo,
cloth extra, with Two Illustrations by HUME NISBET, 3s. 6d.

De Guerin (Maurice), The Journal of. Edited by G. S. TREBUTIEN.
With a Memoir by SAINTE-BEUVE. Translated from the 20th French Edition by JESSIE P. FROTH-
INGHAM. Fcap. 8vo, half-bound, 2s. 6d.

De Maistre (Xavier).—A Journey Round my Room. Translated
by HENRY ATTWELL. Post 8vo, cloth limp, 2s. 6d.

De Mille (James).—A Castle in Spain. Crown 8vo, cloth extra, with
a Frontispiece, 3s. 6d.

Derby (The) : The Blue Ribbon of the Turf. With Brief Accounts
of THE OAKS. By LOUIS HENRY CURZON. Crown 8vo, cloth limp, 2s. 6d.

Derwent (Leith), Novels by. Crown 8vo, cloth, 3s. 6d. each.
Our Lady of Tears. | Circe's Lovers.

Dewar (T. R.).—A Ramble Round the Globe. With 220 Illustra-
tions. Crown 8vo, cloth extra, 7s. 6d.

De Windt (Harry), Books by.
Through the Gold-Fields of Alaska to Bering Straits. With Map and 33 full-page Illustrations. Cheaper Issue. Demy 8vo, cloth, 6s.
True Tales of Travel and Adventure. Crown 8vo, cloth, 3s. 6d.

Dickens (Charles), About England with. By ALFRED RIMMER.
With 57 Illustrations by C. A. VANDERHOOF and the AUTHOR. Square 8vo, cloth, 3s. 6d.

Dictionaries.
The Reader's Handbook of Famous Names in Fiction, Allusions, References, Proverbs, Plots, Stories, and Poems. Together with an ENGLISH AND AMERICAN BIBLIOGRAPHY. and a LIST OF THE AUTHORS AND DATES OF DRAMAS AND OPERAS. By Rev. E. C. BREWER, LL.D A New Edition, Revised and Enlarged. Crown 8vo, cloth, 7s. 6d.
A Dictionary of Miracles: Imitative, Realistic, and Dogmatic. By the Rev. E. C. BREWER, LL.D. Crown 8vo, cloth, 3s. 6d.
Familiar Short Sayings of Great Men. With Historical and Explanatory Notes by SAMUEL A. BENT, A.M. Crown 8vo, cloth extra, 7s. 6d.
The Slang Dictionary: Etymological, Historical, and Anecdotal. Crown 8vo, cloth, 6s. 6d.
Words, Facts, and Phrases: A Dictionary of Curious, Quaint, and Out-of-the-Way Matters. By ELIEZER EDWARDS. Crown 8vo, cloth extra, 3s. 6d.

Dilke (Rt. Hon. Sir Charles, Bart., M.P.).—The British Empire.
Crown 8vo, buckram, 3s. 6d.

Dobson (Austin), Works by.
Thomas Bewick and his Pupils. With 95 Illustrations. Square 8vo, cloth, 3s. 6d.
Four Frenchwomen. With Four Portraits. Crown 8vo, buckram, gilt top, 6s.
Eighteenth Century Vignettes. IN THREE SERIES. Crown 8vo, buckram, 6s. each.
A Paladin of Philanthropy, and other Papers. With 2 Illustrations. Crown 8vo, buckram, 6s.

Dobson (W. T.).—Poetical Ingenuities and Eccentricities. Post
8vo, cloth limp, 2s. 6d.

Donovan (Dick), Detective Stories by.
Post 8vo, illustrated boards, 2s. each ; cloth limp, 2s. 6d. each.

The Man-Hunter. | **Wanted!**	**A Detective's Triumphs.**
Caught at Last. | **Tracked to Doom.**	**In the Grip of the Law.**
Tracked and Taken.	**From Information Received.**
Who Poisoned Hetty Duncan?	**Link by Link.** | **Dark Deeds.**
Suspicion Aroused.	**Riddles Read.**

Crown 8vo, cloth extra, 3s. 6d. each ; post 8vo, illustrated boards, 2s. each ; cloth, 2s. 6d. each.
The Man from Manchester. With 23 Illustrations.
The Mystery of Jamaica Terrace. | **The Chronicles of Michael Danevitch.**
Crown 8vo, cloth, 3s. 6d. each.
The Records of Vincent Trill, of the Detective Service. | **Tales of Terror.**
The Adventures of Tyler Tatlock, Private Detective.

Dowling (Richard).—Old Corcoran's Money. Crown 8vo, cl., 3s. 6d.

Doyle (A. Conan).—The Firm of Girdlestone. Cr. 8vo, cl., 3s. 6d.

Dramatists, The Old. Cr. 8vo, cl. ex., with Portraits, 3s. 6d. per Vol.
Ben Jonson's Works. With Notes, Critical and Explanatory, and a Biographical Memoir by WILLIAM GIFFORD. Edited by Colonel CUNNINGHAM. Three Vols.
Chapman's Works. Three Vols. Vol. I. contains the Plays complete ; Vol. II., Poems and Minor Translations, with an Essay by A. C. SWINBURNE ; Vol. III., Translations of the Iliad and Odyssey.
Marlowe's Works. Edited, with Notes, by Colonel CUNNINGHAM. One Vol.
Massinger's Plays. From GIFFORD'S Text. Edited by Colonel CUNNINGHAM. One Vol.

Dudgeon (R. E., M.D.).—The Prolongation of Life. Crown 8vo,
buckram, 3s. 6d.

Duncan (Sara Jeannette: Mrs. EVERARD COTES), Works by.
Crown 8vo, cloth extra, 7s. 6d. each.
A Social Departure. With 111 Illustrations by F. H. TOWNSEND.
An American Girl in London. With 80 Illustrations by F. H. TOWNSEND.
The Simple Adventures of a Memsahib. With 37 Illustrations by F. H. TOWNSEND.
Crown 8vo, cloth extra, 3s. 6d. each.
A Daughter of To-Day. | **Vernon's Aunt.** With 47 Illustrations by HAL HURST.

Dutt (Romesh C.).—England and India: A Record of Progress
during One Hundred Years. Crown 8vo, cloth, 2s.

Early English Poets. Edited, with Introductions and Annotations,
by Rev. A. B. GROSART, D.D. Crown 8vo, cloth boards, 3s. 6d. per Volume.
Fletcher's (Giles) Complete Poems. One Vol.
Davies' (Sir John) Complete Poetical Works. Two Vols.
Herrick's (Robert) Complete Collected Poems. Three Vols.
Sidney's (Sir Philip) Complete Poetical Works. Three Vols.

Edgcumbe (Sir E. R. Pearce).—Zephyrus: A Holiday in Brazil
and on the River Plate. With 41 Illustrations. Crown 8vo, cloth extra, 5s.

Edwardes (Mrs. Annie), Novels by. Post 8vo, illust. bds., 2s. each.
Archie Lovell. | **A Point of Honour.**
A Plaster Saint. Crown 8vo, cloth, 3s. 6d.

Edwards (Eliezer).—Words, Facts, and Phrasemonger. Post 8vo, of Curious, Quaint, and Out-of-the-Way Matters. Cheaper Edition. Cro

Egan (Pierce).—Life in London. With an Introduction. Crown 8vo,
CAMDEN HOTTEN, and a Coloured Frontispiece. Small demy 8vo, cloth, 3s. 6d.

Egerton (Rev. J. C., M.A.).—Sussex Folk and Sussex Ways.
With Introduction by Rev. Dr. H. WACE, and Four Illustrations. Crown 8vo, cloth extra, 5s.

Eggleston (Edward).—Roxy: A Novel. Post 8vo, illust. boards, 2s.

Englishman (An) in Paris. Notes and Recollections during the
Reign of Louis Philippe and the Empire. Crown 8vo, cloth, 3s. 6d.

Englishman's House, The: A Practical Guide for Selecting or Build-
ing a House. By C. J. RICHARDSON. Coloured Frontispiece and 534 Illusts. Cr. 8vo, cloth, 3s. 6d.

Ewald (Alex. Charles, F.S.A.), Works by.
The Life and Times of Prince Charles Stuart, Count of Albany (THE YOUNG PRETEN-
DER). With a Portrait. Crown 8vo, cloth extra, 7s. 6d.
Stories from the State Papers. With Autotype Frontispiece. Crown 8vo, cloth, 6s.

Eyes, Our: How to Preserve Them. By JOHN BROWNING. Cr. 8vo, 1s.

Familiar Short Sayings of Great Men. By SAMUEL ARTHUR BENT,
A.M. Fifth Edition, Revised and Enlarged. Crown 8vo, cloth extra, 7s. 6d.

Faraday (Michael), Works by. Post 8vo, cloth extra, 4s. 6d. each.
The Chemical History of a Candle: Lectures delivered before a Juvenile Audience. Edited
by WILLIAM CROOKES, F.C.S. With numerous Illustrations.
On the Various Forces of Nature, and their Relations to each other. Edited by
WILLIAM CROOKES, F.C.S. With Illustrations.

Farrer (J. Anson).—War: Three Essays. Crown 8vo, cloth, 1s. 6d.

Fenn (G. Manville), Novels by.
Crown 8vo, cloth extra, 3s. 6d. each ; post 8vo, illustrated boards, 2s. each.
The New Mistress. | Witness to the Deed. | The Tiger Lily. | The White Virgin.

Crown 8vo, cloth 3s. 6d. each.

A Woman Worth Winning.	**Double Cunning.**	**The Story of Antony Grace**
Cursed by a Fortune.	**A Fluttered Dovecote.**	**The Man with a Shadow.**
The Case of Ailsa Gray.	**King of the Castle.**	**One Maid's Mischief.**
Commodore Junk.	**The Master of the Cere-**	**This Man's Wife.**
Black Blood.	**monies.**	**In Jeopardy.**

Crown 8vo, cloth, gilt top, 6s. each.
A Crimson Crime.
The Bag of Diamonds, and Three Bits of Paste.

Feuerheerd (H.).—The Gentleman's Cellar ; or, The Butler and
Cellarman's Guide. Fcap. 8vo, cloth, 1s.

Fiction, A Catalogue of, with Descriptive Notices and Reviews of
over NINE HUNDRED NOVELS, will be sent free by Messrs. CHATTO & WINDUS upon application.

Fin-Bec.—The Cupboard Papers: Observations on the Art of Living
and Dining. Post 8vo, cloth limp, 2s. 6d.

Firework-Making, The Complete Art of ; or, The Pyrotechnist's
Treasury. By THOMAS KENTISH. With 267 Illustrations. Crown 8vo, cloth, 3s. 6d.

First Book, My. By WALTER BESANT, JAMES PAYN, W. CLARK RUS-
SELL, GRANT ALLEN, HALL CAINE, GEORGE R. SIMS, RUDYARD KIPLING, A. CONAN DOYLE,
M. E. BRADDON, F. W. ROBINSON, H. RIDER HAGGARD, R. M. BALLANTYNE, I. ZANGWILL,
MORLEY ROBERTS, D. CHRISTIE MURRAY, MARY CORELLI, J. K. JEROME, JOHN STRANGE
WINTER, BRET HARTE, 'Q.,' ROBERT BUCHANAN, and R. L. STEVENSON. With a Prefatory Story
by JEROME K. JEROME, and 185 Illustrations. A New Edition. Small demy 8vo, art linen, 3s. 6d.

Fitzgerald (Percy), Works by.
Little Essays: Passages from the Letters of CHARLES LAMB. Post 8vo, cloth, 2s. 6d.
Fatal Zero. Crown 8vo, cloth extra, 3s. 6d. ; post 8vo, illustrated boards, 2s.

Post 8vo, illustrated boards, 2s. each.

Bella Donna.	**The Lady of Brantome.**	**The Second Mrs. Tillotson.**
Polly.	**Never Forgotten.**	**Seventy-five Brooke Street.**

Sir Henry Irving: Twenty Years at the Lyceum. With Portrait. Crown 8vo, cloth, 1s. 6d.

Flammarion (Camille), Works by.
Popular Astronomy: A General Description of the Heavens. Translated by J. ELLARD GORE,
F.R.A.S. With Three Plates and 288 Illustrations. Medium 8vo, cloth, 10s. 6d.
Urania: A Romance. With 87 Illustrations. Crown 8vo, cloth extra, 5s.

Fletcher's (Giles, B.D.) Complete Poems: Christ's Victorie in
Heaven, Christ's Victorie on Earth, Christ's Triumph over Death, and Minor Poems. With Notes by
Rev. A. B. GROSART, D.D. Crown 8vo, cloth boards, 3s. 6d.

—The Life of Napoleon III. With Photo-
CHATTO & WIND... thirty-six full-page Illustrations. Cheaper Issue. Demy 8vo, cloth, 6s.

Har.....on (R. E.), Novels by.
Crown 8vo, cloth extra, 3s. 6d. each; post 8vo, illustrated boards, 2s. each.
One by One. | **A Real Queen.** | **A Dog and his Shadow.**
Ropes of Sand. Illustrated.

Post 8vo, illustrated boards, 2s. each.
Queen Cophetua. | **Olympia.** | **Romances of the Law.** | **King or Knave?**
Jack Doyle's Daughter. Crown 8vo, cloth, 3s. 6d.

Frederic (Harold), Novels by. Post 8vo, cloth extra, 3s. 6d. each;
illustrated boards, 2s. each.
Seth's Brother's Wife. | **The Lawton Girl.**

French Literature, A History of. By HENRY VAN LAUN. Three
Vols., demy 8vo, cloth boards, 22s. 6d.

Fry's (Herbert) Royal Guide to the London Charities. Edited
by JOHN LANE. Published Annually. Crown 8vo, cloth, 1s. 6d.

Gardening Books. Post 8vo, 1s. each; cloth limp. 1s. 6d. each.
A Year's Work in Garden and Greenhouse. By GEORGE GLENNY.
Household Horticulture. By TOM and JANE JERROLD. Illustrated.
The Garden that Paid the Rent. By TOM JERROLD.

Gardner (Mrs. Alan).—Rifle and Spear with the Rajpoots: Being
the Narrative of a Winter's Travel and Sport in Northern India. With numerous Illustrations by the
Author and F. H. TOWNSEND. Demy 4to, half-bound, 21s.

Gaulot (Paul).—The Red Shirts: A Tale of "The Terror." Trans-
lated by JOHN DE VILLIERS. With a Frontispiece by STANLEY WOOD. Crown 8vo, cloth, 3s. 6d.

Gentleman's Magazine, The. 1s. Monthly. Contains Stories,
Articles upon Literature, Science, Biography, and Art, and **'Table Talk'** by SYLVANUS URBAN.
⁎ Bound Volumes for recent years kept in stock, 8s. 6d. each. Cases for binding, 2s. each.

Gentleman's Annual, The. Published Annually in November. 1s.
That for 1900 is entitled **The Strange Experiences of Mr. Verschoyle, told by Himself,**
and Edited by T. W. SPEIGHT.

German Popular Stories. Collected by the Brothers GRIMM and
Translated by EDGAR TAYLOR. With Introduction by JOHN RUSKIN, and 22 Steel Plates after
GEORGE CRUIKSHANK. Square 8vo, cloth, 6s. 6d.; gilt edges, 7s. 6d.

Gibbon (Chas.), Novels by. Cr. 8vo, cl., 3s. 6d. ea.; post 8vo, bds., 2s. ea.
Robin Gray. With Frontispiece. | **Loving a Dream.** | **The Braes of Yarrow.**
The Golden Shaft. With Frontispiece. | **Of High Degree.**

Post 8vo, illustrated boards, 2s. each.
The Flower of the Forest. | **A Hard Knot.** | **By Mead and Stream.**
The Dead Heart. | **Queen of the Meadow.** | **Fancy Free.**
For Lack of Gold. | **In Pastures Green.** | **In Honour Bound.**
What Will the World Say? | **In Love and War.** | **Heart's Delight.**
For the King. | **A Heart's Problem.** | **Blood-Money.**

Gibney (Somerville).—Sentenced! Crown 8vo, cloth, 1s. 6d.

Gilbert (W. S.), Original Plays by. In Three Series, 2s. 6d. each.
The FIRST SERIES contains: The Wicked World—Pygmalion and Galatea—Charity—The Princess—
The Palace of Truth—Trial by Jury.
The SECOND SERIES: Broken Hearts—Engaged—Sweethearts—Gretchen—Dan'l Druce—Tom Cobb
—H.M.S. 'Pinafore'—The Sorcerer—The Pirates of Penzance.
The THIRD SERIES: Comedy and Tragedy—Foggerty's Fairy—Rosencrantz and Guildenstern—
Patience—Princess Ida—The Mikado—Ruddigore—The Yeomen of the Guard—The Gondoliers—
The Mountebanks—Utopia.

Eight Original Comic Operas written by W. S. GILBERT. In Two Series. Demy 8vo, cloth,
2s. 6d. each. The FIRST containing: The Sorcerer—H.M.S. 'Pinafore'—The Pirates of Penzance—
Iolanthe—Patience—Princess Ida—The Mikado—Trial by Jury.
The SECOND SERIES containing: The Gondoliers—The Grand Duke—The Yeomen of the Guard—
His Excellency—Utopia, Limited—Ruddigore—The Mountebanks—Haste to the Wedding.
The Gilbert and Sullivan Birthday Book: Quotations for Every Day in the Year, selected
from Plays by W. S. GILBERT set to Music by Sir A. SULLIVAN. Compiled by ALEX. WATSON.
Royal 16mo, Japanese leather, 2s. 6d.

Gilbert (William).— James Duke, Costermonger. Post 8vo, illustrated boards, 2s.

Gissing (Algernon).—A Secret of the North Sea. Crown 8vo, cloth, gilt top, 6s.

Glanville (Ernest), Novels by.
Crown 8vo, cloth extra, 3s. 6d. each ; post 8vo, illustrated boards, 2s. each.
The Lost Heiress: A Tale of Love, Battle, and Adventure. With Two Illustrations by H. NISBET.
The Fossicker: A Romance of Mashonaland. With Two Illustrations by HUME NISBET.
A Fair Colonist. With a Frontispiece by STANLEY WOOD.
The Golden Rock. With a Frontispiece by STANLEY WOOD. Crown 8vo, cloth extra, 3s. 6d.
Kloof Yarns. Crown 8vo cloth, 1s. 6d.
Tales from the Veld. With Twelve Illustrations by M. NISBET. Crown 8vo, cloth, 3s. 6d.
Max Thornton: A Boys' Story of the War. With Six full-page Illustrations. Small demy 8vo,
cloth, gilt edges, 5s. [Shortly.

Glenny (George).—A Year's Work in Garden and Greenhouse:
Practical Advice as to the Management of the Flower, Fruit, and Frame Garden. Post 8vo, 1s. ; cloth, 1s. 6d.

Godwin (William).—Lives of the Necromancers. Post 8vo, cl., 2s.

Golden Treasury of Thought, The : A Dictionary of Quotations
from the Best Authors. By THEODORE TAYLOR. Crown 8vo, cloth, 3s. 6d.

Goodman (E. J.).—The Fate of Herbert Wayne. Cr. 8vo, 3s. 6d.

Greeks and Romans, The Life of the, described from Antique
Monuments. By ERNST GUHL and W. KONER. Edited by Dr. F. HUEFFER. With 545 Illustrations. Large crown 8vo, cloth extra, 7s. 6d.

Greville (Henry).—Nikanor. Translated by ELIZA E. CHASE. Post 8vo, illustrated boards, 2s.

Grey (Sir George).—The Romance of a Proconsul: Being the
Personal Life and Memoirs of Sir GEORGE GREY, K.C.B. By JAMES MILNE. With Portrait. SECOND EDITION. Crown 8vo, buckram, 6s.

Griffith (Cecil).—Corinthia Marazion : A Novel. Crown 8vo, cloth extra, 3s. 6d.

Gunter (A. Clavering, Author of 'Mr. Barnes of New York').—
A Florida Enchantment. Crown 8vo, cloth, 3s. 6d.

Habberton (John, Author of 'Helen's Babies'), **Novels by.**
Post 8vo, cloth limp, 2s. 6d. each.
Brueton's Bayou. | **Country Luck.**

Hair, The : Its Treatment in Health, Weakness, and Disease. Trans-
lated from the German of Dr. J. PINCUS. Crown 8vo, 1s. ; cloth, 1s. 6d.

Hake (Dr. Thomas Gordon), Poems by. Cr. 8vo, cl. ex., 6s. each.
New Symbols. | **Legends of the Morrow.** | **The Serpent Play.**
Maiden Ecstasy. Small 4to, cloth extra, 8s.

Halifax (C.).—Dr. Rumsey's Patient. By Mrs. L. T. MEADE and
CLIFFORD HALIFAX, M.D. Crown 8vo, cloth, 3s. 6d.

Hall (Mrs. S. C.).—Sketches of Irish Character. With numerous
Illustrations on Steel and Wood by MACLISE, GILBERT, HARVEY, and GEORGE CRUIKSHANK. Small demy 8vo, cloth extra, 7s. 6d.

Hall (Owen), Novels by. Crown 8vo, cloth, 3s. 6d. each.
The Track of a Storm. | **Jetsam.**
Eureka. Crown 8vo, cloth, gilt top, 6s.

Halliday (Andrew).—Every-day Papers. Post 8vo, boards, 2s.

Hamilton (Cosmo).—Stories by. Crown 8vo, cloth gilt, 3s. 6d. each.
The Glamour of the Impossible. | **Through a Keyhole.**

Handwriting, The Philosophy of. With over 100 Facsimiles and
Explanatory Text. By DON FELIX DE SALAMANCA. Post 8vo, half-cloth, 2s. 6d.

Hanky-Panky : Easy and Difficult Tricks, White Magic, Sleight of
Hand, &c. Edited by W. H. CREMER. With 200 Illustrations. Crown 8vo, cloth extra, 4s. 6d.

Hardy (Iza Duffus).—The Lesser Evil. Crown 8vo, cloth, 6s. [Shortly.

Hardy (Thomas).—Under the Greenwood Tree. Post 8vo, cloth
extra, 3s. 6d. ; Illustrated boards, 2s. ; cloth limp, 2s. 6d.

Harte's (Bret) Collected Works. Revised by the Author, LIBRARY
EDITION, in Ten Volumes, crown 8vo, cloth extra, 6r. each.

Vol.   I. COMPLETE POETICAL AND DRAMATIC WORKS. With Steel-plate Portrait.
"   II. THE LUCK OF ROARING CAMP—BOHEMIAN PAPERS—AMERICAN LEGEND.
"   III. TALES OF THE ARGONAUTS—EASTERN SKETCHES.
"   IV. GABRIEL CONROY. | Vol. V. STORIES—CONDENSED NOVELS, &c.
"   VI. TALES OF THE PACIFIC SLOPE.
"   VII. TALES OF THE PACIFIC SLOPE—II. With Portrait by JOHN PETTIE, R.A.
"   VIII. TALES OF THE PINE AND THE CYPRESS.
"   IX. BUCKEYE AND CHAPPAREL.
"   X. TALES OF TRAIL AND TOWN, &c.

Bret Harte's Choice Works, in Prose and Verse. With Portrait of the Author and 40 Illustrations. Crown 8vo, cloth, 3s. 6d.
Bret Harte's Poetical Works. Printed on hand-made paper. Crown 8vo, buckram, 4s. 6d.
Some Later Verses. Crown 8vo, linen gilt, 5s.

Crown 8vo, cloth extra, 3s. 6d. each ; post 8vo, picture boards, 2s. each.
Gabriel Conroy.
A Waif of the Plains. With 60 Illustrations by STANLEY L. WOOD.
A Ward of the Golden Gate. With 59 Illustrations by STANLEY L. WOOD.

Crown 8vo, cloth extra, 3s. 6d. each.
A Sappho of Green Springs, &c. With Two Illustrations by HUME NISBET.
Colonel Starbottle's Client, and Some Other People. With a Frontispiece.
Susy : A Novel. With Frontispiece and Vignette by J. A. CHRISTIE.
Sally Dows, &c. With 47 Illustrations by W. D. ALMOND and others.
A Protegee of Jack Hamlin's, &c. With 26 Illustrations by W. SMALL and others.
The Bell-Ringer of Angel's, &c. With 39 Illustrations by DUDLEY HARDY and others
Clarence : A Story of the American War. With Eight Illustrations by A. JULE GOODMAN.
Barker's Luck, &c. With 39 Illustrations by A. FORESTIER, PAUL HARDY, &c.
Devil's Ford, &c. With a Frontispiece by W. H. OVEREND.
The Crusade of the "Excelsior." With a Frontispiece by J. BERNARD PARTRIDGE.
Three Partners ; or, The Big Strike on Heavy Tree Hill. With 8 Illustrations by J. GULICH.
Tales of Trail and Town. With Frontispiece by G. P. JACOMB-HOOD.

Post 8vo, illustrated boards, 2s. each.
An Heiress of Red Dog, &c. | **The Luck of Roaring Camp,** &c.
Californian Stories.

Post 8vo, illustrated boards, 2s. each ; cloth, 2s. 6d. each.
Flip. | **Maruja.** | **A Phyllis of the Sierras.**

Haweis (Mrs. H. R.), Books by.
The Art of Beauty. With Coloured Frontispiece and 91 Illustrations. Square 8vo, cloth bds., 6s.
The Art of Decoration. With Coloured Frontispiece and 74 Illustrations. Sq. 8vo, cloth bds., 6s.
The Art of Dress. With 32 Illustrations. Post 8vo, 1s. ; cloth, 1s. 6d.
Chaucer for Schools. With the Story of his Times and his Work. A New Edition, revised. With a Frontispiece. Demy 8vo, cloth, 2s. 6d.
Chaucer for Children. With 38 Illustrations (8 Coloured). Crown 4to, cloth extra, 3s. 6d.

Haweis (Rev. H. R., M.A.).—American Humorists: WASHINGTON
IRVING, OLIVER WENDELL HOLMES, JAMES RUSSELL LOWELL, ARTEMUS WARD, MARK TWAIN, and BRET HARTE. Crown 8vo, cloth, 6s.

Hawthorne (Julian), Novels by.
Crown 8vo, cloth extra, 3s. 6d. each ; post 8vo, illustrated boards, 2s. each.
Garth. | **Ellice Quentin.** | **Beatrix Randolph.** With Four Illusts.
Sebastian Strome. | | **David Poindexter's Disappearance.**
Fortune's Fool. | **Dust.** Four Illusts. | **The Spectre of the Camera.**

Post 8vo, illustrated boards, 2s. each.
Miss Cadogna. | **Love—or a Name.**

Heckethorn (C. W.), Books by.
London Souvenirs. | **London Memories : Social, Historical, and Topographical.**

Helps (Sir Arthur), Books by. Post 8vo, cloth limp, 2s. 6d. each.
Animals and their Masters. | **Social Pressure.**

Ivan de Biron : A Novel. Crown 8vo, cloth extra, 3s. 6d. ; post 8vo, illustrated boards, 2s.

Henderson (Isaac). — Agatha Page: A Novel. Cr. 8vo, cl., 3s. 6d.

Henty (G. A.), Novels by.
Rujub, the Juggler. With Eight Illustrations by STANLEY L. WOOD. Small demy 8vo, cloth, gilt edges, 5s. ; post 8vo, illustrated boards, 2s.
Colonel Thorndyke's Secret. With a Frontispiece by STANLEY L. WOOD. Small demy 8vo, cloth, gilt edges, 5s.

Crown 8vo, cloth, 3s. 6d. each.
The Queen's Cup. | **Dorothy's Double.**

Herman (Henry).—A Leading Lady. Post 8vo, cloth, 2s. 6d.

Hertzka (Dr. Theodor).—Freeland: A Social Anticipation. Translated by ARTHUR RANSOM. Crown 8vo, cloth extra, 6s.

Hesse-Wartegg (Chevalier Ernst von).— Tunis: The Land and the People. With 22 Illustrations. Crown 8vo, cloth extra, 3s. 6d.

Hill (Headon).—Zambra the Detective. Crown 8vo, cloth, 3s. 6d.; post 8vo, picture boards, 2s.

Hill (John), Works by.
Treason-Felony. Post 8vo, boards, 2s. | The Common Ancestor. Cr. 8vo, cloth, 3s. 6d.

Hoey (Mrs. Cashel).—The Lover's Creed. Post 8vo, boards, 2s.

Holiday, Where to go for a. By E. P. SHOLL, Sir H. MAXWELL, Bart., M.P., JOHN WATSON, JANE BARLOW, MARY LOVETT CAMERON, JUSTIN H. McCARTHY, PAUL LANGE, J. W. GRAHAM, J. H. SALTER, PHŒBE ALLEN, S. J. BECKETT, L. RIVERS VINE, and C. F. GORDON CUMMING. Crown 8vo, cloth, 1s. 6d.

Hollingshead (John).—According to My Lights. With a Portrait. Crown 8vo, cloth, gilt top, 6s.

Holmes (Oliver Wendell), Works by.
The Autocrat of the Breakfast-Table. Illustrated by J. GORDON THOMSON. Post 8vo, cloth limp, 2s. 6d. Another Edition, post 8vo, cloth, 2s.
The Autocrat of the Breakfast-Table and The Professor at the Breakfast-Table. In One Vol. Post 8vo, half-bound, 2s.

Hood's (Thomas) Choice Works in Prose and Verse. With Life of the Author, Portrait, and 200 Illustrations. Crown 8vo, cloth, 3s. 6d.
Hood's Whims and Oddities. With 85 Illustrations. Post 8vo, half-bound, 2s.

Hook's (Theodore) Choice Humorous Works; including his Ludicrous Adventures, Bons Mots, Puns, and Hoaxes. With Life of the Author, Portraits, Facsimiles and Illustrations. Crown 8vo, cloth extra, 7s. 6d.

Hooper (Mrs. Geo.).—The House of Raby. Post 8vo, boards, 2s.

Hopkins (Tighe), Novels by. Crown 8vo, cloth, 6s. each.
Nell Haffenden. With 8 Illustrations by C. GREGORY. | For Freedom.

Crown 8vo, cloth, 3s. 6d. each.
'Twixt Love and Duty. With a Frontispiece. | The Incomplete Adventurer.
The Nugents of Carriconna.

Horne (R. Hengist). — Orion: An Epic Poem. With Photograph Portrait by SUMMERS. Tenth Edition. Crown 8vo, cloth extra, 7s.

Hugo (Victor).—The Outlaw of Iceland (Han d'Islande). Translated by Sir GILBERT CAMPBELL. Crown 8vo, cloth, 3s. 6d.

Hume (Fergus).—The Lady from Nowhere. Crown 8vo, cloth, 3s. 6d.

Hungerford (Mrs., Author of ' Molly Bawn '), Novels by.
Post 8vo, illustrated boards, 2s. each : cloth limp, 2s. 6d. each.
Marvel. | A Modern Circe. | Lady Patty.
In Durance Vile. | An Unsatisfactory Lover.

Crown 8vo, cloth extra, 3s. 6d. each; post 8vo, illustrated boards, 2s. each : cloth limp, 2s. 6d. each.
A Maiden All Forlorn. | Lady Verner's Flight. | The Three Graces.
April's Lady. | The Red-House Mystery. | Nora Creina.
Peter's Wife. | The Professor's Experiment. | A Mental Struggle.

Crown 8vo, cloth extra, 3s. 6d. each.
An Anxious Moment. | A Point of Conscience.
The Coming of Chloe. | Lovice.

Hunt's (Leigh) Essays: A Tale for a Chimney Corner, &c. Edited by EDMUND OLLIER. Post 8vo, half-bound, 2s.

Hunt (Mrs. Alfred), Novels by.
Crown 8vo, cloth extra, 3s. 6d. each ; post 8vo, illustrated boards, 2s. each.
The Leaden Casket. | Self-Condemned. | That Other Person.

Thornicroft's Model. Post 8vo, boards, 2s. | Mrs. Juliet. Crown 8vo, cloth extra, 3s. 6d.

Hutchison (W. M.).—Hints on Colt-breaking. With 25 Illustrations. Crown 8vo, cloth extra, 3s. 6d.

Hydrophobia: An Account of M. PASTEUR'S System ; The Technique of his Method, and Statistics. By RENAUD SUZOR, M.B. Crown 8vo, cloth extra, 6s.

Hyne (C. J. Cutcliffe).— Honour of Thieves. Cr. 8vo, cloth, 3s. 6d.

Impressions (The) of Aureole. Post 8vo, blush-rose paper and cloth, 2s. 6d.

Indoor Paupers. By ONE OF THEM. Crown 8vo, 1s. ; cloth, 1s. 6d.

Innkeeper's Handbook (The) and Licensed Victualler's Manual. By J. TREVOR-DAVIES. A New Edition. Crown 8vo, cloth, 2s.

Irish Wit and Humour, Songs of. Collected and Edited by A. PERCEVAL GRAVES. Post 8vo, cloth limp, 2s. 6d.

Irving (Sir Henry): A Record of over Twenty Years at the Lyceum. By PERCY FITZGERALD. With Portrait. Crown 8vo, cloth, 1s. 6d.

James (C. T. C.). — A Romance of the Queen's Hounds. Post 8vo, cloth limp, 1s. 6d.

Jameson (William).—My Dead Self. Post 8vo, cloth, 2s. 6d.

Japp (Alex. H., LL.D.).—Dramatic Pictures, &c. Cr. 8vo, cloth, 5s.

Jay (Harriett), Novels by. Post 8vo, illustrated boards, 2s. each.
The Dark Colleen. | The Queen of Connaught.

Jefferies (Richard), Books by. Post 8vo, cloth limp, 2s. 6d. each.
Nature near London. | The Life of the Fields. | The Open Air.
*** Also the HAND-MADE PAPER EDITION, crown 8vo, buckram, gilt top, 6s. each.

The Eulogy of Richard Jefferies. By Sir WALTER BESANT. With a Photograph Portrait.
Crown 8vo, cloth extra, 6s.

Jennings (Henry J.), Works by.
Curiosities of Criticism. Post 8vo, cloth limp, 2s. 6d.
Lord Tennyson: A Biographical Sketch. With Portrait. Post 8vo, cloth, 1s. 6d.

Jerome (Jerome K.), Books by.
Stageland. With 64 Illustrations by J. BERNARD-PARTRIDGE. Fcap. 4to, picture cover, 1s.
John Ingerfield, &c. With 9 Illusts. by A. S. BOYD and JOHN GULICH. Fcap. 8vo, pic. cov. 1s. 6d.
The Prude's Progress: A Comedy by J. K. JEROME and EDEN PHILLPOTTS. Cr. 8vo, 1s. 6d.

Jerrold (Douglas).—The Barber's Chair; and The Hedgehog Letters. Post 8vo, printed on laid paper and half-bound, 2s.

Jerrold (Tom), Works by. Post 8vo, 1s. ea. ; cloth limp, 1s. 6d. each.
The Garden that Paid the Rent.
Household Horticulture: A Gossip about Flowers. Illustrated.

Jesse (Edward).—Scenes and Occupations of a Country Life. Post 8vo, cloth limp, 2s.

Jones (William, F.S.A.), Works by. Cr. 8vo, cl. extra, 3s. 6d. each.
Finger-Ring Lore: Historical, Legendary, and Anecdotal. With Hundreds of Illustrations.
Credulities, Past and Present. Including the Sea and Seamen, Miners, Talismans, Word and
 Letter Divination, Exorcising and Blessing of Animals, Birds, Eggs, Luck, &c. With Frontispiece.
Crowns and Coronations: A History of Regalia. With 91 Illustrations.

Jonson's (Ben) Works. With Notes Critical and Explanatory, and a Biographical Memoir by WILLIAM GIFFORD. Edited by Colonel CUNNINGHAM. Three Vols. crown 8vo, cloth extra, 3s. 6d. each.

Josephus, The Complete Works of. Translated by WHISTON. Containing 'The Antiquities of the Jews' and 'The Wars of the Jews.' With 52 Illustrations and Maps. Two Vols., demy 8vo, half-cloth, 12s. 6d.

Kempt (Robert).—Pencil and Palette: Chapters on Art and Artists. Post 8vo, cloth limp, 2s. 6d.

Kershaw (Mark). — Colonial Facts and Fictions: Humorous Sketches. Post 8vo, illustrated boards, 2s. ; cloth, 2s. 6d.

King (R. Ashe), Novels by.
Post 8vo, illustrated boards, 2s. each.
'The Wearing of the Green.' | Passion's Slave. | Bell Barry.

A Drawn Game. Crown 8vo, cloth, 3s. 6d. ; post 8vo, illustrated boards, 2s.

Kipling Primer (A). Including Biographical and Critical Chapters, an Index to Mr. Kipling's principal Writings, and Bibliographies. By F. L. KNOWLES, Editor of 'The Golden Treasury of American Lyrics.' With Two Portraits. Crown 8vo, cloth, 3s. 6d.

Knight (William, M.R.C.S., and Edward, L.R.C.P.). — The Patient's Vade Mecum: How to Get Most Benefit from Medical Advice. Cr. 8vo, cloth, 1s. 6d.

Knights (The) of the Lion: A Romance of the Thirteenth Century. Edited, with an Introduction, by the MARQUESS OF LORNE, K.T. Crown 8vo, cloth extra, 6s.

Lamb's (Charles) Complete Works in Prose and Verse, including 'Poetry for Children' and 'Prince Dorus.' Edited, with Notes and Introduction, by R. H. SHEP-HERD. With Two Portraits and Facsimile of the 'Essay on Roast Pig.' Crown 8vo, cloth, 3s. 6d.
The Essays of Elia. Post 8vo, printed on laid paper and half-bound, 2s.
Little Essays: Sketches and Characters by CHARLES LAMB, selected from his Letters by PERCY FITZGERALD. Post 8vo, cloth limp, 2s. 6d.
The Dramatic Essays of Charles Lamb. With Introduction and Notes by BRANDER MAT-THEWS, and Steel-plate Portrait. Fcap. 8vo, half-bound, 2s. 6d.

Lambert (George).—The President of Boravia. Crown 8vo, cl., 3s. 6d.

Landor (Walter Savage).—Citation and Examination of William Shakspeare, &c. before Sir Thomas Lucy, touching Deer-stealing, 19th September, 1582. To which is added, **A Conference of Master Edmund Spenser** with the Earl of Essex, touching the State of Ireland, 1595. Fcap. 8vo, half-Roxburghe, 2s. 6d.

Lane (Edward William).—The Thousand and One Nights, commonly called in England **The Arabian Nights' Entertainments.** Translated from the Arabic, with Notes. Illustrated with many hundred Engravings from Designs by HARVEY. Edited by EDWARD STANLEY POOLE. With Preface by STANLEY LANE-POOLE. Three Vols., demy 8vo, cloth, 7s. 6d. ea.

Larwood (Jacob), Works by.
Anecdotes of the Clergy. Post 8vo, laid paper, half-bound, 2s.

Post 8vo, cloth limp, 2s. 6d. each.
Forensic Anecdotes. | **Theatrical Anecdotes.**

Lehmann (R. C.), Works by. Post 8vo, cloth, 1s. 6d. each.
Harry Fludyer at Cambridge.
Conversational Hints for Young Shooters: A Guide to Polite Talk.

Leigh (Henry S.).—Carols of Cockayne. Printed on hand-made paper, bound in buckram, 5s.

Leland (C. Godfrey). — A Manual of Mending and Repairing. With Diagrams. Crown 8vo, cloth, 5s.

Lepelletier (Edmond). — Madame Sans-Gène. Translated from the French by JOHN DE VILLIERS. Post 8vo, cloth, 3s. 6d.; picture boards, 2s.

Leys (John).—The Lindsays: A Romance. Post 8vo, illust. bds., 2s.

Lilburn (Adam).—A Tragedy in Marble. Crown 8vo, cloth, 3s. 6d.

Lindsay (Harry, Author of 'Methodist Idylls'), Novels by. Crown 8vo, cloth, 3s. 6d. each.
Rhoda Roberts.
The Jacobite: A Romance of the Conspiracy of 'The Forty.'

Linton (E. Lynn), Works by.
An Octave of Friends. Crown 8vo, cloth, 3s. 6d.
Crown 8vo, cloth extra, 3s. 6d. each; post 8vo, illustrated boards, 2s. each.

Patricia Kemball. | **Ione.**	**Under which Lord?** With 12 Illustrations.
The Atonement of Leam Dundas.	**'My Love!'** | **Sowing the Wind.**
The World Well Lost. With 12 Illusts.	**Paston Carew,** Millionaire and Miser.
The One Too Many.	**Dulcie Everton.** | **With a Silken Thread.**

The Rebel of the Family.
Post 8vo, cloth limp, 2s. 6d. each.
Witch Stories. | **Ourselves:** Essays on Women.
Freeshooting: Extracts from the Works of Mrs. LYNN LINTON.

Lowe (Charles, M.A.).—Our Greatest Living Soldiers. With 8 Portraits. Crown 8vo, cloth, 3s. 6d.

Lucy (Henry W.).—Gideon Fleyce: A Novel. Crown 8vo, cloth extra, 3s. 6d.; post 8vo, illustrated boards, 2s.

Macalpine (Avery), Novels by.
Teresa Itasca. Crown 8vo, cloth extra, 1s.
Broken Wings. With Six Illustrations by W. J. HENNESSY. Crown 8vo, cloth extra, 6s.

MacColl (Hugh), Novels by.
Mr. Stranger's Sealed Packet. Post 8vo, illustrated boards, 2s.
Ednor Whitlock. Crown 8vo, cloth extra, 6s.

Macdonell (Agnes).—Quaker Cousins. Post 8vo, boards, 2s.

MacGregor (Robert).—Pastimes and Players: Notes on Popular Games. Post 8vo, cloth limp, 2s. 6d.

Mackay (Charles, LL.D.). — Interludes and Undertones; or, Music at Twilight. Crown 8vo, cloth extra, 6s.

McCarthy (Justin), Works by.

A History of Our Own Times, from the Accession of Queen Victoria to the General Election of 1880. LIBRARY EDITION. Four Vols., demy 8vo, cloth extra, 12s. each.—Also a POPULAR EDITION, in Four Vols., crown 8vo, cloth extra, 6s. each.—And the JUBILEE EDITION, with an Appendix of Events to the end of 1886, in Two Vols., large crown 8vo, cloth extra, 7s. 6d. each.
A History of Our Own Times, from 1880 to the Diamond Jubilee. Demy 8vo, cloth extra, 12s. ; or crown 8vo, cloth, 6s.
A Short History of Our Own Times. One Vol., crown 8vo, cloth extra, 6s.—Also a CHEAP POPULAR EDITION, post 8vo, cloth limp, 2s. 6d.
A History of the Four Georges and of William the Fourth. By JUSTIN McCARTHY and JUSTIN HUNTLY McCARTHY. Four Vols., demy 8vo, cloth extra, 12s. each.
Reminiscences. With a Portrait. Two Vols., demy 8vo, cloth, 24s. [Vols. III. & IV. *shortly.*
Crown 8vo, cloth extra, 3s. 6d. each ; post 8vo, illustrated boards, 2s. each ; cloth limp, 2s. 6d. each.

The Waterdale Neighbours.	**Donna Quixote.** With 12 Illustrations.
My Enemy's Daughter.	**The Comet of a Season.**
A Fair Saxon. **Linley Rochford.**	**Maid of Athens.** With 12 Illustrations.
Dear Lady Disdain. **The Dictator.**	**Camiola :** A Girl with a Fortune.
Miss Misanthrope. With 12 Illustrations.	**Red Diamonds.** **The Riddle Ring.**

The Three Disgraces, and other Stories. Crown 8vo, cloth, 3s. 6d.
'The Right Honourable.' By JUSTIN McCARTHY and Mrs. CAMPBELL PRAED. Crown 8vo, cloth extra, 6s.

McCarthy (Justin Huntly), Works by.

The French Revolution. (Constituent Assembly, 1789-91). Four Vols., demy 8vo, cloth, 12s. each.
An Outline of the History of Ireland. Crown 8vo, 1s. ; cloth, 1s. 6d.
Ireland Since the Union : Sketches of Irish History, 1798-1886. Crown 8vo, cloth, 6s.
Hafiz in London : Poems. Small 8vo, gold cloth, 3s. 6d.
Our Sensation Novel. Crown 8vo, picture cover, 1s. ; cloth limp, 1s. 6d.
Doom : An Atlantic Episode. Crown 8vo, picture cover, 1s.
Dolly : A Sketch. Crown 8vo, picture cover, 1s. ; cloth limp, 1s. 6d.
Lily Lass : A Romance. Crown 8vo, picture cover, 1s. ; cloth limp, 1s. 6d.
A London Legend. Crown 8vo, cloth, 3s. 6d.
The Royal Christopher. Crown 8vo, cloth, 3s. 6d.

MacDonald (George, LL.D.), Books by.

Works of Fancy and Imagination. Ten Vols., 16mo, cloth, gilt edges, in cloth case, 21s. ; or the Volumes may be had separately, in Grolier cloth, at 2s. 6d. each.
Vol. I. WITHIN AND WITHOUT.—THE HIDDEN LIFE.
,, II. THE DISCIPLE.—THE GOSPEL WOMEN.—BOOK OF SONNETS.—ORGAN SONGS.
,, III. VIOLIN SONGS.—SONGS OF THE DAYS AND NIGHTS.—A BOOK OF DREAMS.—ROADSIDE POEMS.—POEMS FOR CHILDREN.
,, IV. PARABLES.—BALLADS.—SCOTCH SONGS.
,, V. & VI. PHANTASTES : A Faerie Romance. | Vol. VII. THE PORTENT.
,, VIII. THE LIGHT PRINCESS.—THE GIANT'S HEART.—SHADOWS.
,, IX. CROSS PURPOSES.—THE GOLDEN KEY.—THE CARASOYN.—LITTLE DAYLIGHT.
,, X. THE CRUEL PAINTER.—THE WOW O' RIVVEN.—THE CASTLE.—THE BROKEN SWORDS.—THE GRAY WOLF.—UNCLE CORNELIUS.
Poetical Works of George MacDonald. Collected and Arranged by the Author. Two Vols. crown 8vo, buckram, 12s.
A Threefold Cord. Edited by GEORGE MACDONALD. Post 8vo, cloth, 5s.
Phantastes : A Faerie Romance. With 25 Illustrations by J. BELL. Crown 8vo, cloth extra, 3s. 6d.
Heather and Snow : A Novel. Crown 8vo, cloth extra, 3s. 6d. ; post 8vo, illustrated boards, 2s.
Lilith : A Romance. SECOND EDITION. Crown 8vo, cloth extra, 6s.

Mackenna (Stephen J.) and J. Augustus O'Shea.—Brave Men in Action : Thrilling Stories of the British Flag. With 8 Illustrations by STANLEY L. WOOD. Small demy 8vo, cloth, gilt edges, 5s.

Maclise Portrait Gallery (The) of Illustrious Literary Characters : 85 Portraits by DANIEL MACLISE ; with Memoirs—Biographical, Critical, Bibliographical, and Anecdotal—illustrative of the Literature of the former half of the Present Century, by WILLIAM BATES, B.A. Crown 8vo, cloth extra, 3s. 6d.

Macquoid (Mrs.), Works by. Square 8vo, cloth extra, 6s. each.

In the Ardennes. With 50 Illustrations by THOMAS R. MACQUOID.
Pictures and Legends from Normandy and Brittany. 34 Illusts. by T. R. MACQUOID.
Through Normandy. With 92 Illustrations by T. R. MACQUOID, and a Map.
Through Brittany. With 35 Illustrations by T. R. MACQUOID, and a Map.
About Yorkshire. With 67 Illustrations by T. R. MACQUOID.

Magician's Own Book, The : Performances with Eggs, Hats, &c. Edited by W. H. CREMER. With 200 Illustrations. Crown 8vo, cloth extra, 4s. 6d.

Magic Lantern, The, and its Management : Including full Practical Directions. By T. C. HEPWORTH. With 10 Illustrations. Crown 8vo, 1s. ; cloth, 1s. 6d.

Magna Charta : An Exact Facsimile of the Original in the British Museum, 3 feet by 2 feet, with Arms and Seals emblazoned in Gold and Colours, 5s.

Mallory (Sir Thomas). — Mort d'Arthur : The Stories of King Arthur and of the Knights of the Round Table. (A Selection.) Edited by B. MONTGOMERIE RANKING. Post 8vo, cloth limp, 2s.

Mallock (W. H.), Works by.
The New Republic. Post 8vo, cloth, 3s. 6d.; picture boards, 2s.
The New Paul and Virginia: Positivism on an Island. Post 8vo, cloth, 2s. 6d.

Poems. Small 4to, parchment, 8s.
Is Life Worth Living? Crown 8vo, cloth extra, 6s.

Margueritte (Paul and Victor).—The Disaster. Translated by
FREDERIC LEES. Crown 8vo, cloth, 3s. 6d.

Marlowe's Works. Including his Translations. Edited, with Notes
and Introductions, by Colonel CUNNINGHAM. Crown 8vo, cloth extra, 3s. 6d.

Massinger's Plays. From the Text of WILLIAM GIFFORD. Edited
by Col. CUNNINGHAM. Crown 8vo, cloth extra, 3s. 6d.

Mathams (Walter, F.R.G.S.). — Comrades All. Fcp. 8vo, cloth
limp, 1s.; cloth gilt, 2s.

Matthews (Brander).—A Secret of the Sea, &c. Post 8vo, illus-
trated boards, 2s.; cloth limp, 2s. 6d.

Meade (L. T.), Novels by.
A Soldier of Fortune. Crown 8vo, cloth, 3s. 6d.; post 8vo, illustrated boards, 2s.

Crown 8vo, cloth, 3s. 6d. each.
The Voice of the Charmer. With 8 Illustrations.
In an Iron Grip. | On the Brink of a Chasm. | A Son of Ishmael.
The Siren. | The Way of a Woman. | An Adventuress.
Dr. Rumsey's Patient. By L. T. MEADE and CLIFFORD HALIFAX, M.D.
The Blue Diamond. Crown 8vo, cloth, gilt top, 6s.   [Shortly

Merivale (Herman C.).—Bar, Stage, and Platform: A Book of
Recollections. Demy 8vo, cloth, 12s.   [Shortly.

Merrick (Leonard), Novels by.
The Man who was Good. Post 8vo, picture boards, 2s.

Crown 8vo, cloth, 3s. 6d. each.
This Stage of Fools. | Cynthia: A Daughter of the Philistines.

Mexican Mustang (On a), through Texas to the Rio Grande. By
A. E. SWEET and J. ARMOY KNOX. With 265 Illustrations. Crown 8vo, cloth extra, 7s. 6d.

Middlemass (Jean), Novels by. Post 8vo, illust. boards, 2s. each.
Touch and Go. | Mr. Dorillion.

Miller (Mrs. F. Fenwick).—Physiology for the Young; or, The
House of Life. With numerous Illustrations. Post 8vo, cloth limp, 2s. 6d.

Milton (J. L.), Works by. Post 8vo, 1s. each; cloth, 1s. 6d. each.
The Hygiene of the Skin. With Directions for Diet, Soaps, Baths, Wines, &c.
The Bath in Diseases of the Skin.
The Laws of Life, and their Relation to Diseases of the Skin.

Minto (Wm.).—Was She Good or Bad? Crown 8vo, cloth, 1s. 6d.

Mitford (Bertram), Novels by. Crown 8vo, cloth extra, 3s. 6d. each.
The Gun-Runner: A Romance of Zululand. With a Frontispiece by STANLEY L. WOOD.
The Luck of Gerard Ridgeley. With a Frontispiece by STANLEY L. WOOD.
The King's Assegai. With Six full-page Illustrations by STANLEY L. WOOD.
Renshaw Fanning's Quest. With a Frontispiece by STANLEY L. WOOD.

Molesworth (Mrs.).—Hathercourt Rectory. Post 8vo, illustrated
boards, 2s.

Moncrieff (W. D. Scott-).—The Abdication: An Historical Drama.
With Seven Etchings by JOHN PETTIE, W. Q. ORCHARDSON, J. MACWHIRTER, COLIN HUNTER,
R. MACBETH and TOM GRAHAM. Imperial 4to, buckram, 21s.

Montagu (Irving).—Things I Have Seen in War. With 16 full-
page Illustrations. Crown 8vo, cloth, 6s.

Moore (Thomas), Works by.
The Epicurean; and Alciphron. Post 8vo, half-bound, 2s.
Prose and Verse; including Suppressed Passages from the MEMOIRS OF LORD BYRON. Edited
by R. H. SHEPHERD. With Portrait. Crown 8vo, cloth extra, 7s. 6d.

Morrow (W. C.).—Bohemian Paris of To-Day. With 106 Illustra-
tions by EDOUARD CUCUEL. Small demy 8vo, cloth, gilt top, 6s.

Muddock (J. E.) Stories by.
Crown 8vo, cloth extra, 3s. 6d. each.
Maid Marian and Robin Hood. With 12 Illustrations by STANLEY WOOD.
Basile the Jester. With Frontispiece by STANLEY WOOD.
Young Lochinvar. | The Golden Idol.

Post 8vo, illustrated boards, 2s. each.
The Dead Man's Secret. | From the Bosom of the Deep.
Stories Weird and Wonderful. Post 8vo, illustrated boards, 2s.; cloth, 2s. 6d.

Murray (D. Christie), Novels by.
Crown 8vo, cloth extra, 3s. 6d. each ; post 8vo, illustrated boards, 2s. each.

A Life's Atonement.
Joseph's Coat. 12 Illusts.
Coals of Fire. 3 Illusts.
Val Strange.
Hearts.
The Way of the World.

A Model Father.
Old Blazer's Hero.
Cynic Fortune. Frontisp.
By the Gate of the Sea.
A Bit of Human Nature.
First Person Singular.

Bob Martin's Little Girl.
Time's Revenges.
A Wasted Crime.
In Direst Peril.
Mount Despair.
A Capful o' Nails.

The Making of a Novelist : An Experiment in Autobiography. With a Collotype Portrait. Cr. 8vo, buckram, 3s. 6d.
My Contemporaries in Fiction. Crown 8vo, buckram, 3s. 6d.

Crown 8vo, cloth, 3s. 6d. each.
This Little World.
Tales in Prose and Verse. With Frontispiece by ARTHUR HOPKINS.
A Race for Millions.

Murray (D. Christie) and Henry Herman, Novels by.
Crown 8vo, cloth extra, 3s. 6d. each ; post 8vo, illustrated boards, 2s. each.
One Traveller Returns. | The Bishops' Bible.
Paul Jones's Alias, &c. With Illustrations by A. FORESTIER and G. NICOLET.

Murray (Henry), Novels by.
Post 8vo, cloth, 2s. 6d. each.
A Game of Bluff. | A Song of Sixpence.

Nisbet (Hume), Books by.
'Ball Up.' Crown 8vo, cloth extra, 3s. 6d.; post 8vo, illustrated boards, 2s.
Dr. Bernard St. Vincent. Post 8vo, illustrated boards, 2s.
Lessons in Art. With 21 Illustrations. Crown 8vo, cloth extra, 2s. 6d.

Norris (W. E.), Novels by. Crown 8vo, cloth, 3s. 6d. each ; post 8vo,
picture boards, 2s. each.
Saint Ann's.
Billy Bellew. With a Frontispiece by F. H. TOWNSEND.
Miss Wentworth's Idea. Crown 8vo, cloth, 3s. 6d.

Oakley (John).—A Gentleman in Khaki : A Story of the South
African War. Demy 8vo, picture cover, 1s.

O'Hanlon (Alice), Novels by. Post 8vo, illustrated boards, 2s. each.
The Unforeseen. | Chance? or Fate?

Ohnet (Georges), Novels by. Post 8vo, illustrated boards, 2s. each.
Doctor Rameau. | A Last Love.
A Weird Gift. Crown 8v cloth, 3s. 6d. ; post 8vo, picture boards, 2s.
Love's Depths. Translated by F. ROTHWELL. Crown 8vo, cloth, 3s. 6d.

Oliphant (Mrs.), Novels by. Post 8vo, illustrated boards, 2s. each.
The Primrose Path. | Whiteladies.
The Greatest Heiress in England.
The Sorceress. Crown 8vo, cloth, 3s. 6d.

O'Shaughnessy (Arthur), Poems by :
Fcap. 8vo, cloth extra, 7s. 6d. each.
Music and Moonlight. | Songs of a Worker.
Lays of France. Crown 8vo, cloth extra, 10s. 6d.

Ouida, Novels by. Cr. 8vo, cl., 3s. 6d. ea.; post 8vo, illust. bds., 2s. ea.
Held in Bondage.
Tricotrin.
Strathmore. | Chandos.
Cecil Castlemaine's Gage
Under Two Flags.
Puck. | Idalia.
Folle-Farine.

A Dog of Flanders.
Pascarel. | Signa.
Two Wooden Shoes.
In a Winter City.
Ariadne. | Friendship.
A Village Commune.
Moths. | Pipistrello.

In Maremma. | Wanda.
Bimbi. | Syrlin.
Frescoes. | Othmar.
Princess Napraxine.
Guilderoy. | Ruffino.
Two Offenders.
Santa Barbara.

POPULAR EDITIONS. Medium 8vo, 6d. each.
Under Two Flags. | Moths. | Held in Bondage. | Puck. [Shortly.
The Waters of Edera. Crown 8vo, cloth, 3s. 6d.
Wisdom, Wit, and Pathos, selected from the Works of OUIDA by F. SYDNEY MORRIS. Post 8vo, cloth extra, 5s.—CHEAP EDITION, illustrated boards, 2s.

Page (H. A.).—Thoreau : His Life and Aims. With Portrait. Post
8vo, cloth, 2s. 6d.

Pandurang Hari ; or, Memoirs o la Hindoo. With Preface by Sir
BARTLE FRERE. Post 8vo, illustrated boards, 2s.

Pascal's Provincial Letters. A New Translation, with Historical
Introduction and Notes by T. M'CRIE, D.D. Post 8vo, half-cloth, 2s.

Paul (Margaret A.).—Gentle and Simple. Crown 8vo, cloth, with
Frontispiece by HELEN PATERSON, 3s. 6d.; post 8vo, illustrated boards, 2s.

Payn (James), Novels by.
Crown 8vo, cloth extra, 3s. 6d. each ; post 8vo, illustrated boards, 2s. each.

Lost Sir Massingberd.
Walter's Word. | A County Family.
Less Black than We're Painted.
By Proxy. | For Cash Only.
High Spirits.
A Confidential Agent. With 12 Illusts.
A Grape from a Thorn. With 12 Illusts.

Holiday Tasks.
The Talk of the Town. With 12 Illusts.
The Mystery of Mirbridge.
The Word and the Will.
The Burnt Million.
Sunny Stories. | A Trying Patient.

Post 8vo illustrated boards, 2s. each.

Humorous Stories. | From Exile.
The Foster Brothers.
The Family Scapegrace.
Married Beneath Him.
Bentinck's Tutor.
A Perfect Treasure.
Like Father, Like Son.
A Woman's Vengeance.
Carlyon's Year. | Cecil's Tryst.
Murphy's Master. | At Her Mercy.
The Clyffards of Clyffe.

Found Dead. | Gwendoline's Harvest
Mirk Abbey. | A Marine Residence.
Some Private Views.
The Canon's Ward.
Not Wooed, But Won.
Two Hundred Pounds Reward.
The Best of Husbands.
Halves. | What He Cost Her.
Fallen Fortunes. | Kit: A Memory.
Under One Roof. | Glow-worm Tales.
A Prince of the Blood.

A Modern Dick Whittington ; or, A Patron of Letters. With a Portrait of the Author. Crown 8vo, cloth, 3s. 6d.
In Peril and Privation. With 17 Illustrations. Crown 8vo, cloth, 3s. 6d.
Notes from the 'News.' Crown 8vo, cloth, 1s. 6d.
By Proxy. POPULAR EDITION, medium 8vo, 6d.

Payne (Will).—Jerry the Dreamer. Crown 8vo, cloth, 3s. 6d.

Pennell (H. Cholmondeley), Works by. Post 8vo, cloth, 2s. 6d. ea.
Puck on Pegasus. With Illustrations.
Pegasus Re-Saddled. With Ten full-page Illustrations by G. DU MAURIER.
The Muses of Mayfair : Vers de Société. Selected by H. C. PENNELL.

Phelps (E. Stuart), Works by. Post 8vo, cloth, 1s. 6d. each.
An Old Maid's Paradise. | Burglars in Paradise.

Beyond the Gates. Post 8vo, picture cover, 1s. ; cloth, 1s. 6d.
Jack the Fisherman. Illustrated by C. W. REED. Crown 8vo, cloth, 1s. 6d.

Phil May's Sketch-Book. Containing 54 Humorous Cartoons. Crown folio, cloth, 2s. 6d.

Phipson (Dr. T. L.), Books by. Crown 8vo, art canvas, gilt top, 5s. ea.
Famous Violinists and Fine Violins.
Voice and Violin : Sketches, Anecdotes, and Reminiscences.

Planche (J. R.), Works by.
The Pursuivant of Arms. With Six Plates and 209 Illustrations. Crown 8vo, cloth, 7s. 6d.
Songs and Poems, 1819-1879. With Introduction by Mrs. MACKARNESS. Crown 8vo, cloth, 6s.

Plutarch's Lives of Illustrious Men. With Notes and a Life of Plutarch by JOHN and WM. LANGHORNE, and Portraits. Two Vols., demy 8vo, half-cloth 10s. 6d.

Poe's (Edgar Allan) Choice Works: Poems, Stories, Essays. With an Introduction by CHARLES BAUDELAIRE. Crown 8vo, cloth, 3s. 6d.

Pollock (W. H.).—The Charm, and other Drawing-room Plays. By Sir WALTER BESANT and WALTER H. POLLOCK. With 50 Illustrations. Crown 8vo, cloth gilt, 6s.

Pond (Major J. B.).—Eccentricities of Genius: Memories of Famous Men and Women of the Platform and the Stage. With 91 Portraits. Demy 8vo, cloth, 12s.

Pope's Poetical Works. Post 8vo, cloth limp, 2s.

Porter (John).—Kingsclere. Edited by BYRON WEBBER. With 19 full-page and many smaller Illustrations. Cheaper Edition. Demy 8vo, cloth, 7s. 6d.

Praed (Mrs. Campbell), Novels by. Post 8vo, illust. bds., 2s. each.
The Romance of a Station. | The Soul of Countess Adrian.

Crown 8vo, cloth, 3s. 6d. each ; post 8vo, boards, 2s. each.
Outlaw and Lawmaker. | Christina Chard. With Frontispiece by W. PAGET.
Mrs. Tregaskiss. With 8 Illustrations by ROBERT SAUBER.

Crown 8vo, cloth, 3s. 6d. each.
Nulma. | Madame Izan.
'As a Watch in the Night.' Crown 8vo, cloth, gilt top, 6s.

Price (E. C.), Novels by. Crown 8vo. cloth, 3s. 6d. each.
Valentina. | The Foreigners. | Mrs. Lancaster's Rival.

Princess Olga.—Radna: A Novel. Crown 8vo, cloth extra, 6s.

Proctor (Richard A.), Works by.

Flowers of the Sky. With 55 Illustrations. Small crown 8vo, cloth extra, 3s. 6d.
Easy Star Lessons. With Star Maps for every Night in the Year. Crown 8vo, cloth, 6s.
Familiar Science Studies. Crown 8vo, cloth extra, 6s.
Saturn and its System. With 13 Steel Plates. Demy 8vo, cloth extra, 10s. 6d.
Mysteries of Time and Space. With numerous Illustrations. Crown 8vo, cloth extra, 6s.
The Universe of Suns. &c. With numerous Illustrations. Crown 8vo, cloth extra, 6s.
Wages and Wants of Science Workers. Crown 8vo, 1s. 6d.

Pryce (Richard).—Miss Maxwell's Affections. Crown 8vo, cloth,
with Frontispiece by HAL LUDLOW, 3s. 6d.; post 8vo, illustrated boards, 2s.

Rambosson (J.).—Popular Astronomy. Translated by C. B. PITMAN.
With 10 Coloured Plates and 63 Woodcut Illustrations. Crown 8vo, cloth, 3s. 6d.

Randolph (Col. G.).—Aunt Abigail Dykes. Crown 8vo, cloth, 7s. 6d.

Read (General Meredith).—Historic Studies in Vaud, Berne,
and Savoy. With 31 full-page Illustrations. Two Vols., demy 8vo, cloth, 28s.

Reade's (Charles) Novels.

The New Collected LIBRARY EDITION, complete in Seventeen Volumes, set in new long primer type, printed on laid paper, and elegantly bound in cloth, price 3s. 6d. each.

1. **Peg Woffington; and Christie Johnstone.**	7. **Love Me Little, Love me Long.**
2. **Hard Cash.**	8. **The Double Marriage.**
3. **The Cloister and the Hearth.** With a Preface by Sir WALTER BESANT.	9. **Griffith Gaunt.**
4. **'It is Never Too Late to Mend.'**	10. **Foul Play.**
5. **The Course of True Love Never Did Run Smooth; and Singleheart and Doubleface.**	11. **Put Yourself in His Place.**
	12. **A Terrible Temptation.**
	13. **A Simpleton.**
	14. **A Woman-Hater.**
6. **The Autobiography of a Thief; Jack of all Trades; A Hero and a Martyr; and The Wandering Heir.**	15. **The Jilt, and other Stories; and Good Stories of Man and other Animals.**
	16. **A Perilous Secret.**
	17. **Readiana; and Bible Characters.**

In Twenty-one Volumes, post 8vo, illustrated boards, 2s. each.

Peg Woffington. | **Christie Johnstone.**	**Hard Cash.** | **Griffith Gaunt.**
'It is Never Too Late to Mend.'	**Foul Play.** | **Put Yourself in His Place.**
The Course of True Love Never Did Run Smooth.	**A Terrible Temptation.**
The Autobiography of a Thief; Jack of all Trades; and James Lambert.	**A Simpleton.** | **The Wandering Heir.**
Love Me Little, Love Me Long.	**A Woman-Hater.**
The Double Marriage.	**Singleheart and Doubleface.**
The Cloister and the Hearth.	**Good Stories of Man and other Animals.**
	The Jilt, and other Stories.
	A Perilous Secret. | **Readiana.**

POPULAR EDITIONS, medium 8vo, 6d. each.

'It is Never Too Late to Mend.'	**The Cloister and the Hearth.**
Peg Woffington; and Christie Johnstone.	**Hard Cash.**

Christie Johnstone. With Frontispiece. Choicely printed in Elzevir style. Fcap. 8vo, half-Roxb, 2s. 6d.
Peg Woffington. Choicely printed in Elzevir style. Fcap. 8vo, half-Roxburghe, 2s. 6d.
The Cloister and the Hearth. In Four Vols., post 8vo, with an Introduction by Sir WALTER BESANT, and a Frontispiece to each Vol., buckram, gilt top, 6s. the set.—Also the LARGE TYPE, FINE PAPER EDITION, pott 8vo, cloth, 2s. net; leather, 3s. net.
Bible Characters. Fcap. 8vo, leatherette, 1s.

Selections from the Works of Charles Reade. With an Introduction by Mrs. ALEX. IRELAND. Crown 8vo, buckram, with Portrait, 6s.; CHEAP EDITION, post 8vo, cloth limp, 2s. 6d.

Riddell (Mrs. J. H.), Novels by.

A Rich Man's Daughter. Crown 8vo, cloth, 3s. 6d.
Weird Stories. Crown 8vo, cloth extra, 3s. 6d.; post 8vo, illustrated boards, 2s.

Post 8vo, illustrated boards, 2s. each.

The Uninhabited House.	**Fairy Water.**
The Prince of Wales's Garden Party.	**Her Mother's Darling.**
The Mystery in Palace Gardens.	**The Nun's Curse.** | **Idle Tales.**

Rimmer (Alfred), Works by. Large crown 8vo, cloth, 3s. 6d. each.

Rambles Round Eton and Harrow. With 52 Illustrations by the Author.
About England with Dickens. With 58 Illustrations by C. A. VANDERHOOF and A. RIMMER.

Rives (Amelie, Author of 'The Quick or the Dead?'), Stories by.

Crown 8vo, cloth, 3s. 6d. each.

Barbara Dering.	**Meriel:** A Love Story.

Robinson Crusoe. By DANIEL DEFOE. With 37 Illustrations by
GEORGE CRUIKSHANK. Post 8vo, half-cloth, 2s.

Robinson (F. W.), Novels by.

Women are Strange. Post 8vo, illustrated boards, 2s.
The Hands of Justice. Crown 8vo, cloth extra, 3s. 6d.; post 8vo illustrated boards, 2s.
The Woman in the Dark. Crown 8vo, cloth, 3s. 6d.; post 8vo, illustrated boards, 2s.

Robinson (Phil), Works by. Crown 8vo, cloth extra, 6s. each.
The Poets' Birds. | The Poets' Beasts.
The Poets and Nature: Reptiles, Fishes, and Insects.

Roll of Battle Abbey, The: A List of the Principal Warriors who came from Normandy with William the Conqueror, 1066. Printed in Gold and Colours, 5s.

Rosengarten (A.).—A Handbook of Architectural Styles. Translated by W. COLLETT-SANDARS. With 630 Illustrations. Crown 8vo, cloth extra, 7s. 6d.

Ross (Albert).—A Sugar Princess. Crown 8vo, cloth, 3s. 6d.

Rowley (Hon. Hugh), Works by. Post 8vo, cloth, 2s. 6d. each.
Puniana: Riddles and Jokes. With numerous Illustrations.
More Puniana. Profusely Illustrated.

Runciman (James), Stories by. Post 8vo, cloth, 2s. 6d. each.
Grace Balmaign's Sweetheart. | Schools & Scholars.
Skippers and Shellbacks. Crown 8vo, cloth, 3s. 6d.

Russell (Dora), Novels by.
A Country Sweetheart. Post 8vo, picture boards, 2s.
The Drift of Fate. Crown 8vo, cloth, 3s. 6d.

Russell (Herbert).—True Blue; or, 'The Lass that Loved a Sailor.'
Crown 8vo, cloth, 3s. 6d.

Russell (W. Clark), Novels, &c., by.
Crown 8vo, cloth extra, 3s. 6d. each; post 8vo, illustrated boards, 2s. each; cloth limp, 2s. 6d. each.
Round the Galley-Fire. | An Ocean Tragedy.
In the Middle Watch. | My Shipmate Louise.
On the Fo'k'sle Head. | Alone on a Wide Wide Sea.
A Voyage to the Cape. | The Good Ship 'Mohock.'
A Book for the Hammock. | The Phantom Death.
The Mystery of the 'Ocean Star.' | Is He the Man? | The Convict Ship.
The Romance of Jenny Harlowe. | Heart of Oak. | The Last Entry.
The Tale of the Ten.
A Tale of Two Tunnels. Crown 8vo, cloth, 3s. 6d.
The Ship: Her Story. With 50 Illustrations by H. C. SEPPINGS WRIGHT. Small 4to, cloth, 6s.
The "Pretty Polly": A Voyage of Incident. With 12 Illustrations by G. E. ROBERTSON. Small demy 8vo, cloth, gilt edges, 5s.

Saint Aubyn (Alan), Novels by.
Crown 8vo, cloth extra, 3s. 6d. each; post 8vo, illustrated boards, 2s. each.
A Fellow of Trinity. With a Note by OLIVER WENDELL HOLMES and a Frontispiece.
The Junior Dean. | The Master of St. Benedict's. | To His Own Master.
Orchard Damerel. | In the Face of the World. | The Tremlett Diamonds.
Fcap. 8vo, cloth boards, 1s. 6d. each.
The Old Maid's Sweetheart. | Modest Little Sara.
Crown 8vo, cloth, 3s. 6d. each.
The Wooing of May. | A Tragic Honeymoon. | A Proctor's Wooing.
Fortune's Gate. | Gallantry Bower. | Bonnie Maggie Lauder.
Mary Unwin. With 8 Illustrations by PERCY TARRANT.
Mrs. Dunbar's Secret. Crown 8vo, cloth, gilt top. 6s.

Saint John (Bayle).—A Levantine Family. A New Edition.
Crown 8vo, cloth, 3s. 6d.

Sala (George A.).—Gaslight and Daylight. Post 8vo, boards, 2s.

Scotland Yard, Past and Present: Experiences of Thirty-seven Years. By Ex-Chief-Inspector CAVANAGH. Post 8vo, illustrated boards, 2s.; cloth, 2s. 6d.

Secret Out, The: One Thousand Tricks with Cards; with Entertaining Experiments in Drawing-room or 'White' Magic. By W. H. CREMER. With 300 Illustrations. Crown 8vo, cloth extra, 4s. 6d.

Seguin (L. G.), Works by.
The Country of the Passion Play (Oberammergau) and the Highlands of Bavaria. With Map and 37 Illustrations. Crown 8vo, cloth extra, 3s. 6d.
Walks in Algiers. With Two Maps and 16 Illustrations. Crown 8vo, cloth extra, 6s.

Senior (Wm.).—By Stream and Sea. Post 8vo, cloth, 2s. 6d.

Sergeant (Adeline), Novels by. Crown 8vo, cloth, 3s. 6d. each.
Under False Pretences. | Dr. Endicott's Experiment.

Shakespeare for Children: Lamb's Tales from Shakespeare.
With Illustrations, coloured and plain, by J. MOYR SMITH. Crown 4to, cloth gilt, 3s. 6d.

Shakespeare the Boy. With Sketches of the Home and School Life, the Games and Sports, the Manners, Customs, and Folk-lore of the Time. By WILLIAM J. ROLFE, Litt.D. A New Edition, with 42 Illustrations, and an INDEX OF PLAYS AND PASSAGES REFERRED TO. Crown 8vo, cloth gilt, 3s. 6d.

Sharp (William).—Children of To-morrow. Crown 8vo, cloth, 6s.

Shelley's (Percy Bysshe) Complete Works in Verse and Prose.
Edited, Prefaced, and Annotated by R. HERNE SHEPHERD. Five Vols., crown 8vo, cloth, 3s. 6d. each.
Poetical Works, in Three Vols.:
Vol. I. Introduction by the Editor; Posthumous Fragments of Margaret Nicholson; Shelley's Correspondence with Stockdale; The Wandering Jew; Queen Mab, with the Notes; Alastor, and other Poems; Rosalind and Helen; Prometheus Unbound; Adonais, &c.
  „ II. Laon and Cythna; The Cenci; Julian and Maddalo; Swellfoot the Tyrant; The Witch of Atlas; Epipsychidion; Hellas.
  „ III. Posthumous Poems; The Masque of Anarchy; and other Pieces.
Prose Works, in Two Vols.:
Vol. I. The Two Romances of Zastrozzi and St. Irvyne; the Dublin and Marlow Pamphlets; A Refutation of Deism; Letters to Leigh Hunt, and some Minor Writings and Fragments.
  II. The Essays; Letters from Abroad; Translations and Fragments, edited by Mrs. SHELLEY. With a Biography of Shelley, and an Index of the Prose Works.

Sherard (R. H.).—Rogues: A Novel. Crown 8vo, cloth, 1s. 6d.

Sheridan's (Richard Brinsley) Complete Works, with Life and
Anecdotes. Including his Dramatic Writings, his Works in Prose and Poetry, Translations, Speeches, and Jokes. Crown 8vo, cloth, 3s. 6d.
The Rivals, The School for Scandal, and other Plays. Post 8vo, half-bound, 2s.
Sheridan's Comedies: The Rivals and **The School for Scandal.** Edited, with an Introduction and Notes to each Play, and a Biographical Sketch, by BRANDER MATTHEWS. With Illustrations. Demy 8vo, half-parchment, 12s. 6d.

Shiel (M. P.).—The Purple Cloud. By the Author of "The Yellow
Danger." Crown 8vo, cloth, gilt top, 6s. [*Preparing.*

Sidney's (Sir Philip) Complete Poetical Works, including all
those in 'Arcadia.' With Portrait, Memorial-Introduction, Notes, &c., by the Rev. A. B. GROSART, D.D. Three Vols., crown 8vo, cloth boards, 3s. 6d. each.

Signboards: Their History, including Anecdotes of Famous Taverns and
Remarkable Characters. By JACOB LARWOOD and JOHN CAMDEN HOTTEN. With Coloured Frontispiece and 94 Illustrations. Crown 8vo, cloth extra, 3s. 6d.

Sims (George R.), Works by.
Post 8vo, illustrated boards, 2s. each; cloth limp, 2s. 6d. each.

The Ring o' Bells.	**Dramas of Life.** With 60 Illustrations.
Mary Jane's Memoirs.	**Memoirs of a Landlady.**
Tinkletop's Crime.	**My Two Wives.**
Zeph: A Circus Story, &c.	**Scenes from the Show.**
Tales of To-day.	**The Ten Commandments:** Stories.

Crown 8vo, picture cover, 1s. each; cloth, 1s. 6d. each.
The Dagonet Reciter and Reader: Being Readings and Recitations in Prose and Verse selected from his own Works by GEORGE R. SIMS.
The Case of George Candlemas. | **Dagonet Ditties.** (From *The Referee.*)
How the Poor Live; and **Horrible London.** With a Frontispiece by F. BARNARD. Crown 8vo, leatherette, 1s.
Dagonet Dramas of the Day. Crown 8vo, 1s.

Crown 8vo, cloth, 3s. 6d. each; post 8vo, picture boards, 2s. each; cloth limp, 2s. 6d. each.
Mary Jane Married. | **Rogues and Vagabonds.** | **Dagonet Abroad.**

Crown 8vo, cloth, 3s. 6d. each.
Once upon a Christmas Time. With 8 Illustrations by CHARLES GREEN, R.I.
In London's Heart: A Story of To-day.
Without the Limelight: Theatrical Life as it is.
The Small-part Lady, &c.

Sister Dora: A Biography. By MARGARET LONSDALE. With Four
Illustrations. Demy 8vo, picture cover, 4d.; cloth, 6d.

Sketchley (Arthur).—A Match in the Dark. Post 8vo, boards, 2s.

Slang Dictionary (The): Etymological, Historical, and Anecdotal.
Crown 8vo, cloth extra, 6s. 6d.

Smart (Hawley), Novels by.
Crown 8vo, cloth, 3s. 6d. each; post 8vo, picture boards, 2s. each.

Beatrice and Benedick.	**Long Odds.**
Without Love or Licence.	**The Master of Rathkelly.**

Crown 8vo, cloth, 3s. 6d. each.
The Outsider. | **A Racing Rubber.**
The Plunger. Post 8vo, picture boards, 2s.

Smith (J. Moyr), Works by.
The Prince of Argolis. With 130 Illustrations. Post 8vo, cloth extra, 3s. 6d.
The Wooing of the Water Witch. With numerous Illustrations. Post 8vo, cloth, 6s.

Snazelleparilla. Decanted by G. S. EDWARDS. With Portrait of
G. H. SNAZELLE, and 65 Illustrations by C. LYALL. Crown 8vo, cloth, 3s. 6d.

Society in London. Crown 8vo, 1s.; cloth, 1s. 6d.

Somerset (Lord Henry).—Songs of Adieu. Small 4to, Jap. vel., 6s.

⹂.ʌ.⹁uɪɪers, 111 St. Martin's Lane, Lon...

Dohl⹁...

Spalding (T. A., LL.B.).—Elizabethan Demonology: An Essay on the Belief in the Existence of Devils. Crown 8vo, cloth extra, 5s.

Speight (T.. W.), Novels by.
Post 8vo, illustrated boards, 2s. each.

The Mysteries of Heron Dyke.	The Loudwater Tragedy.
By Devious Ways, &c.	Burgo's Romance.
Hoodwinked; & Sandycroft Mystery.	Quittance in Full.
The Golden Hoop.	A Husband from the Sea.
Back to Life.	

Post 8vo, cloth limp, 1s. 6d. each.

A Barren Title.	Wife or No Wife?

Crown 8vo, cloth extra, 3s. 6d. each.

A Secret of the Sea. | The Grey Monk. | The Master of Trenance.
A Minion of the Moon: A Romance of the King's Highway.
The Secret of Wyvern Towers.
The Doom of Siva. | The Web of Fate.
The Strange Experiences of Mr. Verschoyle. Demy 8vo, 1s.

Spenser for Children. By M. H. TOWRY. With Coloured Illustrations by WALTER J. MORGAN. Crown 4to, cloth extra, 3s. 6d.

Spettigue (H. H.).—The Heritage of Eve. Crown 8vo, cloth, 6s.

Stafford (John), Novels by.
Doris and I. Crown 8vo, cloth, 3s. 6d.
Carlton Priors. Crown 8vo, cloth, gilt top, 6s.

Starry Heavens (The): A POETICAL BIRTHDAY BOOK. Royal 16mo, cloth extra, 2s. 6d.

Stedman (E. C.).—Victorian Poets. Crown 8vo, cloth extra, 9s.

Stephens (Riccardo, M.B.).—The Cruciform Mark: The Strange Story of RICHARD TREGENNA, Bachelor of Medicine (Univ. Edinb.) Crown 8vo, cloth, 3s. 6d.

Stephens (Robert Neilson).—Philip Winwood: A Sketch of the Domestic History of an American Captain in the War of Independence; embracing events that occurred between and during the years 1763 and 1786, in New York and London; written by His Enemy in War, HERBERT RUSSELL, Lieutenant in the Loyalist Forces. With Six Illustrations by E. W. D. HAMILTON. Crown 8vo, cloth, gilt top, 6s.

Sterndale (R. Armitage).—The Afghan Knife: A Novel. Post 8vo, cloth, 3s. 6d.; illustrated boards, 2s.

Stevenson (R. Louis), Works by.
Crown 8vo, buckram, gilt top, 6s. each; post 8vo, cloth limp, 2s. 6d. each.
Travels with a Donkey. With a Frontispiece by WALTER CRANE.
An Inland Voyage. With a Frontispiece by WALTER CRANE.

Crown 8vo, buckram, gilt top, 6s. each.

Familiar Studies of Men and Books.		
The Silverado Squatters. With Frontispiece by J. D. STRONG.		
The Merry Men.	Underwoods: Poems.	
Memories and Portraits.		
Virginibus Puerisque, and other Papers.	Ballads.	Prince Otto.
Across the Plains, with other Memories and Essays.		
Weir of Hermiston.	In the South Seas.	

A Lowden Sabbath Morn. With 27 Illustrations by A. S. BOYD. Fcap. 8vo, cloth, 6s.
Songs of Travel. Crown 8vo, buckram, 5s.
New Arabian Nights. Crown 8vo, buckram, gilt top, 6s.; post 8vo, illustrated boards, 2s.
—POPULAR EDITION, medium 8vo, 6d. [Shortly.
The Suicide Club; and The Rajah's Diamond. (From NEW ARABIAN NIGHTS.) With Eight Illustrations by W. J. HENNESSY. Crown 8vo, cloth, 3s. 6d.
The Stevenson Reader: Selections from the Writings of ROBERT LOUIS STEVENSON. Edited by LLOYD OSBOURNE. Post 8vo, cloth, 2s. 6d.; buckram, gilt top, 3s. 6d.

Stockton (Frank R.).—The Young Master of Hyson Hall. With numerous Illustrations by VIRGINIA H. DAVISSON and C. H. STEPHENS. Crown 8vo, cloth, 3s. 6d.

Storey (G. A., A.R.A.).—Sketches from Memory. With 93 Illustrations by the Author. Demy 8vo, cloth, gilt top, 12s. 6d.

Stories from Foreign Novelists. With Notices by HELEN and ALICE ZIMMERN. Crown 8vo, cloth extra 3s. 6d.

Strange Manuscript (A) Found in a Copper Cylinder. Crown 8vo, cloth extra, with 19 Illustrations by GILBERT GAUL, 3s. 6d.; post 8vo, illustrated boards, 2s.

Strange Secrets. Told by PERCY FITZGERALD, CONAN DOYLE, FLORENCE MARRYAT, &c. Post 8vo, illustrated boards, 2s.

Strutt (Joseph). — The Sports and Pastimes of the People of England: including the Rural and Domestic Recreations, May Games, Mummeries, Shows, &c., from the Earliest Period to the Present Time. Edited by WILLIAM HONE. With 140 Illustrations. Crown 8vo, cloth extra, 3s. 6d.

CHATTO & ....t).—**Handley, Cross; or, Mr. Jorrocks's Hunt.** ....ations by JOHN LEECH. A New Edition. Post 8vo, cloth, 2s.

Swift's (Dean) Choice Works, in Prose and Verse. With Memoir, Portrait, and Facsimiles of the Maps in 'Gulliver's Travels.' Crown 8vo, cloth, 3s. 6d.
Gulliver's Travels, and A Tale of a Tub. Post 8vo, half-bound, 2s.
Jonathan Swift: A Study. By J. CHURTON COLLINS. Crown 8vo, cloth extra, 8s.

Swinburne (Algernon C.), Works by.

Selections from the Poetical Works of A. C. Swinburne. Fcap. 8vo 6s.
Atalanta in Calydon. Crown 8vo, 6s.
Chastelard: A Tragedy. Crown 8vo, 7s.
Poems and Ballads. FIRST SERIES. Crown 8vo, or fcap. 8vo, 9s.
Poems and Ballads. SECOND SER. Cr.8vo,9s.
Poems & Ballads. THIRD SERIES. Cr.8vo, 7s.
Songs before Sunrise. Crown 8vo, 10s. 6d.
Bothwell: A Tragedy. Crown 8vo, 12s. 6d.
Songs of Two Nations. Crown 8vo, 6s.
George Chapman. (See Vol. II. of G. CHAPMAN'S Works.) Crown 8vo, 3s. 6d.
Essays and Studies. Crown 8vo, 12s.
Erechtheus: A Tragedy. Crown 8vo, 6s.
A Note on Charlotte Bronte. Cr. 8vo, 6s.
A Study of Shakespeare. Crown 8vo, 8s.
Songs of the Springtides. Crown 8vo, 6s.

Studies in Song. Crown 8vo, 7s.
Mary Stuart: A Tragedy. Crown 8vo, 8s.
Tristram of Lyonesse. Crown 8vo, 9s.
A Century of Roundels. Small 4to, 8s.
A Midsummer Holiday. Crown 8vo, 7s.
Marino Faliero: A Tragedy. Crown 8vo, 6s.
A Study of Victor Hugo. Crown 8vo, 6s.
Miscellanies. Crown 8vo, 12s.
Locrine: A Tragedy. Crown 8vo, 6s.
A Study of Ben Jonson. Crown 8vo, 7s.
The Sisters: A Tragedy. Crown 8vo, 6s.
Astrophel, &c. Crown 8vo, 7s.
Studies in Prose and Poetry. Cr. 8vo, 9s.
The Tale of Balen. Crown 8vo, 7s.
Rosamund, Queen of the Lombards: A Tragedy. SECOND EDITION, with a DEDICATORY POEM. Crown 8vo, 6s.

Syntax's (Dr.) Three Tours: In Search of the Picturesque, in Search of Consolation, and in Search of a Wife. With ROWLANDSON'S Coloured Illustrations, and Life of the Author by J. C. HOTTEN. Crown 8vo, cloth extra, 7s. 6d.

Taine's History of English Literature. Translated by HENRY VAN LAUN. Four Vols., small demy 8vo, cloth boards, 30s.—POPULAR EDITION, Two Vols., large crown 8vo, cloth extra, 15s.

Taylor (Bayard). — Diversions of the Echo Club: Burlesques of Modern Writers. Post 8vo, cloth limp, 2s.

Taylor (Tom).—Historical Dramas: 'JEANNE DARC,' ''TWIXT AXE AND CROWN,' 'THE FOOL'S REVENGE,' 'ARKWRIGHT'S WIFE,' 'ANNE BOLEYNE,' 'PLOT AND PASSION.' Crown 8vo, 1s. each.

Temple (Sir Richard, G.C.S.I.).—A Bird's-eye View of Picturesque India. With 32 Illustrations by the Author. Crown 8vo, cloth, gilt top, 6s.

Tennyson (Lord): A Biographical Sketch. By H. J. JENNINGS. With Portrait. Post 8vo, cloth, 1s. 6d.

Thackerayana: Notes and Anecdotes. With Coloured Frontispiece and Hundreds of Sketches by WILLIAM MAKEPEACE THACKERAY. Crown 8vo, cloth extra, 3s. 6d.

Thames, A New Pictorial History of the. By A. S. KRAUSSE. With 340 Illustrations. Post 8vo, cloth, 1s. 6d.

Thomas (Annie), Novels by.
The Siren's Web: A Romance of London Society. Crown 8vo, cloth, 3s. 6d.
Comrades True. Crown 8vo, cloth, gilt top, 6s.

Thomas (Bertha), Novels by.
Crown 8vo, cloth, 3s. 6d. each.
The Violin-Player. | The House on the Scar. [Preparing.
Crown 8vo, cloth, gilt top, 6s. each.
In a Cathedral City. | The Son of the House.

Thomson's Seasons, and The Castle of Indolence. With Introduction by ALLAN CUNNINGHAM, and 48 Illustrations. Post 8vo, half-bound, 2s.

Thornbury (Walter), Books by.
The Life and Correspondence of J. M. W. Turner. With Eight Illustrations in Colours and Two Woodcuts. New and Revised Edition. Crown 8vo, cloth, 3s. 6d.
Tales for the Marines. Post 8vo, illustrated boards, 2s.

Timbs (John), Works by. Crown 8vo, cloth, 3s. 6d. each.
Clubs and Club Life in London: Anecdotes of its Famous Coffee-houses, Hostelries, and Taverns. With 41 Illustrations.
English Eccentrics and Eccentricities: Stories of Delusions, Impostures, Sporting Scenes, Eccentric Artists, Theatrical Folk, &c. With 48 Illustrations.

Trollope (Anthony), Novels by.
Crown 8vo, cloth extra, 3s. 6d. each; post 8vo, illustrated boards, 2s. each.
The Way We Live Now. | Mr. Scarborough's Family.
Frau Frohmann. | Marion Fay. | The Land-Leaguers.
Post 8vo, illustrated boards, 2s. each.
Kept in the Dark. | The American Senator.
The Golden Lion of Granpere.

Trollope (Frances E.), Novels by.
Crown 8vo, cloth extra, 3s. 6d. each; post 8vo, illustrated boards, 2s. each.

Like Ships upon the Sea. | Mabel's Progress. | Anne Furness.

Trollope (T. A.).—Diamond Cut Diamond. Post 8vo, illust. bds., 2s.

Twain's (Mark) Books.
The Author's Edition de Luxe of the Works of Mark Twain, in 22 Volumes (limited to 600 Numbered Copies for sale in Great Britain and its Dependencies), price 12s. 6d. net per Volume, is now complete, and a detailed Prospectus may be had. The First Volume of the Set is SIGNED BY THE AUTHOR.

UNIFORM LIBRARY EDITION OF MARK TWAIN'S WORKS.
Crown 8vo, cloth extra, 3s. 6d. each.

Mark Twain's Library of Humour. With 197 Illustrations by E. W. KEMBLE.
Roughing It; and The Innocents at Home. With 200 Illustrations by F. A. FRASER.
The American Claimant. With 81 Illustrations by HAL HURST and others.
*The Adventures of Tom Sawyer. With 111 Illustrations.
Tom Sawyer Abroad. With 26 Illustrations by DAN BEARD.
Tom Sawyer, Detective, &c. With Photogravure Portrait of the Author.
Pudd'nhead Wilson. With Portrait and Six Illustrations by LOUIS LOEB.
*A Tramp Abroad. With 314 Illustrations.
*The Innocents Abroad; or, The New Pilgrim's Progress. With 234 Illustrations. (The Two Shilling Edition is entitled Mark Twain's Pleasure Trip.)
*The Gilded Age. By MARK TWAIN and C. D. WARNER. With 212 Illustrations.
*The Prince and the Pauper. With 190 Illustrations.
*Life on the Mississippi. With 300 Illustrations.
*The Adventures of Huckleberry Finn. With 174 Illustrations by E. W. KEMBLE.
*A Yankee at the Court of King Arthur. With 220 Illustrations by DAN BEARD.
*The Stolen White Elephant. | *The £1,000,000 Bank-Note.
The Choice Works of Mark Twain. Revised and Corrected throughout by the Author. With Life, Portrait, and numerous Illustrations.

⁎ The books marked * may be had also in post 8vo, picture boards, at 2s. each.

Crown 8vo, cloth, gilt top, 6s. each,
Personal Recollections of Joan of Arc. With Twelve Illustrations by F. V. DU MOND.
More Tramps Abroad.
The Man that Corrupted Hadleyburg, and other Stories and Sketches. With a Frontispiece.
Mark Twain's Sketches. Post 8vo, illustrated boards, 2s.

Tytler (C. C. Fraser-).—Mistress Judith: A Novel. Crown 8vo,
cloth extra, 3s. 6d.; post 8vo, illustrated boards, 2s.

Tytler (Sarah), Novels by.
Crown 8vo, cloth extra, 3s. 6d. each; post 8vo, illustrated boards, 2s. each.
Lady Bell. | Buried Diamonds. | The Blackhall Ghosts. | What She Came Through.

Post 8vo, illustrated boards, 2s. each.
Citoyenne Jacqueline. | The Huguenot Family.
The Bride's Pass. | Noblesse Oblige. | Disappeared.
Saint Mungo's City. | Beauty and the Beast.

Crown 8vo, cloth, 3s. 6d. each.
The Macdonald Lass. With Frontispiece. | Mrs. Carmichael's Goddesses.
The Witch-Wife. | Rachel Langton. | Sapphira. | A Honeymoon's Eclipse.
A Young Dragon.

Upward (Allen), Novels by.
A Crown of Straw. Crown 8vo, cloth, 6s.
Crown 8vo, cloth, 3s. 6d. each; post 8vo, picture boards, 2s. each.
The Queen Against Owen. | The Prince of Balkistan.
'God Save the Queen!' a Tale of '37. Crown 8vo, cloth, 2s.

Vandam (Albert D.).—A Court Tragedy. With 6 Illustrations by
J. BARNARD DAVIS. Crown 8vo, cloth, 3s. 6d.

Vashti and Esther. By 'Belle' of The World. Cr. 8vo, cloth, 3s. 6d.

Vizetelly (Ernest A.), Books by. Crown 8vo, cloth, 3s. 6d. each.
The Scorpion: A Romance of Spain. With a Frontispiece.
With Zola in England: A Story of Exile. With 4 Portraits.
A Path of Thorns. Crown 8vo, cloth, gilt top, 6s. [Shortly.

Wagner (Leopold).—How to Get on the Stage, and how to
Succeed there. Crown 8vo, cloth, 2s. 6d.

Walford's County Families of the United Kingdom (1900).
Containing Notices of the Descent, Birth, Marriage, Education, &c., of more than 12,000 Distinguished Heads of Families, their Heirs Apparent or Presumptive, the Offices they hold or have held, their Town and Country Addresses, Clubs, &c. Royal 8vo, cloth gilt, 50s.

Waller (S. E.).—Sebastiani's Secret. With 9 Illusts. Cr. 8vo, cl., 6s.

Walton and Cotton's Complete Angler. With Memoirs and Notes
by Sir HARRIS NICOLAS, and 61 Illustrations. Crown 8vo, cloth antique, 7s. 6d.

Walt Whitman, Poems by. Edited, with Introduction, by WILLIAM
M. ROSSETTI. With Portrait. Crown 8vo, hand-made paper and buckram, 6s.

Warden (Florence).—Joan, the Curate. Crown 8vo, cloth, 3s. 6d.

Warman (Cy).—The Express Messenger, and other Tales of the Rail. Crown 8vo, cloth, 3s. 6d.

Warner (Charles Dudley).—A Roundabout Journey. Crown 8vo, cloth extra, 6s.

Wassermann (Lillias).—The Daffodils. Crown 8vo, cloth, 1s. 6d.

Warrant to Execute Charles I. A Facsimile, with the 59 Signatures and Seals. Printed on paper 22 in. by 14 in. 2s.
Warrant to Execute Mary Queen of Scots. A Facsimile, including Queen Elizabeth's Signature and the Great Seal. 2s.

Weather, How to Foretell the, with the Pocket Spectroscope. By F. W. CORY. With Ten Illustrations Crown 8vo, 1s.; cloth, 1s. 6d.

Westall (William), Novels by.
Trust Money. Crown 8vo, cloth, 3s. 6d.; post 8vo, illustrated boards, 2s.

Crown 8vo, cloth, 6s. each.

As a Man Sows.	A Red Bridal.	As Luck would have it.

Crown 8vo, cloth 3s. 6d. each.

A Woman Tempted Him.	Nigel Fortescue.	The Phantom City.
For Honour and Life.	Ben Clough. | Birch Dene.	Ralph Norbreck's Trust.
Her Two Millions.	The Old Factory.	A Queer Race.
Two Pinches of Snuff.	Sons of Belial.	Red Ryvington.
	With the Red Eagle.	

Roy of Roy's Court. With 6 Illustrations. Crown 8vo, cloth, 3s. 6d.
Strange Crimes. (True Stories.) Crown 8vo, cloth, 3s. 6d.
The Old Factory. POPULAR EDITION. Medium 8vo, 6d.

Westbury (Atha).—The Shadow of Hilton Fernbrook: A Romance of Maoriland. Crown 8vo, cloth, 3s. 6d.

White (Gilbert).—The Natural History of Selborne. Post 8vo, printed on laid paper and half-bound, 2s.

Wilde (Lady). — The Ancient Legends, Mystic Charms, and Superstitions of Ireland; with Sketches of the Irish Past. Crown 8vo, cloth, 3s. 6d.

Williams (W. Mattieu, F.R.A.S.), Works by.
Science in Short Chapters. Crown 8vo, cloth extra, 7s. 6d.
A Simple Treatise on Heat. With Illustrations. Crown 8vo, cloth, 2s. 6d.
The Chemistry of Cookery. Crown 8vo, cloth extra, 6s.
A Vindication of Phrenology. With Portrait and 43 Illusts. Demy 8vo, cloth extra, 12s. 6d.

Williamson (Mrs. F. H.).—A Child Widow. Post 8vo, bds., 2s.

Wills (C. J.), Novels by.
An Easy-going Fellow. Crown 8vo, cloth, 3s. 6d. | His Dead Past. Crown 8vo, cloth, 6s.

Wilson (Dr. Andrew, F.R.S.E.), Works by.
Chapters on Evolution. With 259 Illustrations. Crown 8vo, cloth extra, 7s. 6d.
Leaves from a Naturalist's Note-Book. Post 8vo, cloth limp, 2s. 6d.
Leisure-Time Studies. With Illustrations. Crown 8vo, cloth extra, 6s.
Studies in Life and Sense. With 36 Illustrations. Crown 8vo, cloth, 3s. 6d.
Common Accidents: How to Treat Them. With Illustrations. Crown 8vo, 1s.; cloth, 1s. 6d
Glimpses of Nature. With 35 Illustrations. Crown 8vo, cloth extra, 3s. 6d.

Winter (John Strange), Stories by. Post 8vo, illustrated boards, 2s. each; cloth limp, 2s. 6d. each.
Cavalry Life. | Regimental Legends.
Cavalry Life and Regimental Legends. LIBRARY EDITION, set in new type and handsomely bound. Crown 8vo, cloth, 3s. 6d.
A Soldier's Children. With 34 Illustrations by E. G. THOMSON and E. STUART HARDY. Crown 8vo, cloth extra, 3s. 6d.

Wissmann (Hermann von). — My Second Journey through Equatorial Africa. With 92 Illustrations. Demy 8vo, cloth, 16s.

Wood (H. F.), Detective Stories by. Post 8vo, boards, 2s. each.
The Passenger from Scotland Yard. | The Englishman of the Rue Cain.

Woolley (Celia Parker).—Rachel Armstrong; or, Love and Theology. Post 8vo, cloth, 2s. 6d.

Wright (Thomas, F.S.A.), Works by.
Caricature History of the Georges; or, Annals of the House of Hanover. Compiled from Squibs, Broadsides, Window Pictures, Lampoons, and Pictorial Caricatures of the Time. With over 300 Illustrations. Crown 8vo, cloth, 3s. 6d.
History of Caricature and of the Grotesque in Art, Literature, Sculpture, and Painting. Illustrated by F. W. FAIRHOLT, F.S.A. Crown 8vo, cloth, 7s. 6d.

Wynman (Margaret).—My Flirtations. With 13 Illustrations by J. BERNARD PARTRIDGE. Post 8vo, cloth limp, 2s.

'ZZ' (L. Zangwill).—A Nineteenth Century Miracle. Cr. 8vo, 3s. 6d.

Zola (Emile), Novels by. Crown 8vo, cloth extra, 3s. 6d. each.

The Fortune of the Rougons. Edited by ERNEST A. VIZETELLY.
Abbe Mouret's Transgression. Edited by ERNEST A. VIZETELLY.
The Conquest of Plassans. Edited by ERNEST A. VIZETELLY.
Germinal; or, Master and Man. Edited by ERNEST A. VIZETELLY. [Jan.
His Excellency (Eugene Rougon). With an Introduction by ERNEST A. VIZETELLY.
The Dram-Shop (L'Assommoir). With Introduction by E. A. VIZETELLY.
The Fat and the Thin. Translated by ERNEST A. VIZETELLY.
Money. Translated by ERNEST A. VIZETELLY.
The Downfall. Translated by E. A. VIZETELLY.
The Dream. Translated by ELIZA CHASE. With Eight Illustrations by JEANNIOT.
Doctor Pascal. Translated by E. A. VIZETELLY. With Portrait of the Author.
Lourdes. Translated by ERNEST A. VIZETELLY.
Rome. Translated by ERNEST A. VIZETELLY.
Paris. Translated by ERNEST A. VIZETELLY.
Fruitfulness (Fécondité). Translated and Edited, with an Introduction, by E. A. VIZETELLY.

With Zola in England. By ERNEST A. VIZETELLY. With Four Portraits. Crown 8vo, cloth, 3s. 6d.

SOME BOOKS CLASSIFIED IN SERIES.

** For fuller cataloguing, see alphabetical arrangement, pp. 1–26.

The Mayfair Library. Post 8vo, cloth limp, 2s. 6d. per Volume.

Quips and Quiddities. By W. D. ADAMS.
The Agony Column of 'The Times.'
A Journey Round My Room. By X. DE MAISTRE. Translated by HENRY ATTWELL
Poetical Ingenuities. By W. T. DOBSON.
The Cupboard Papers. By FIN-BEC.
W. S. Gilbert's Plays. Three Series.
Songs of Irish Wit and Humour.
Animals and their Masters. By Sir A HELPS.
Social Pressure. By Sir A. HELPS.
Autocrat of Breakfast-Table. By O. W. HOLMES.
Curiosities of Criticism. By H. J. JENNINGS.
Pencil and Palette. By R. KEMPT.
Little Essays: from LAMB'S LETTERS.
Forensic Anecdotes. By JACOB LARWOOD.
Theatrical Anecdotes. By JACOB LARWOOD.
Ourselves. By E. LYNN LINTON.
Witch Stories. By E. LYNN LINTON.
Pastimes and Players. By R. MACGREGOR.
New Paul and Virginia. By W. H. MALLOCK.
Muses of Mayfair. Edited by H. C. PENNELL
Thoreau: His Life and Aims. By H. A. PAGE.
Puck on Pegasus. By H. C. PENNELL.
Pegasus Re-saddled. By H. C. PENNELL.
Puniana. By Hon. HUGH ROWLEY.
More Puniana. By Hon. HUGH ROWLEY.
By Stream and Sea. By WILLIAM SENIOR.
Leaves from a Naturalist's Note-Book. By Dr. ANDREW WILSON.

The Golden Library. Post 8vo, cloth limp, 2s. per Volume.

Songs for Sailors. By W. C. BENNETT.
Lives of the Necromancers. By W. GODWIN.
The Autocrat of the Breakfast Table. By OLIVER WENDELL HOLMES.
Tale for a Chimney Corner. By LEIGH HUNT.
Scenes of Country Life. By EDWARD JESSE.
La Mort d'Arthur: Selections from MALLORY.
The Poetical Works of Alexander Pope.
Diversions of the Echo Club. BAYARD TAYLOR.

Handy Novels. Fcap. 8vo, cloth boards, 1s. 6d. each.

Dr. Palliser's Patient. By GRANT ALLEN
Monte Carlo Stories. By JOAN BARRETT.
Black Spirits and White. By R. A. CRAM.
Seven Sleepers of Ephesus. M. E. COLERIDGE.
The Old Maid's Sweetheart. By A. ST. AUBYN.
Modest Little Sara. By ALAN ST. AUBYN.

My Library. Printed on laid paper, post 8vo, half-Roxburghe, 2s. 6d. each.

The Journal of Maurice de Guerin.
The Dramatic Essays of Charles Lamb.
Citation and Examination of William Shakspeare. By W. S. LANDOR.
Christie Johnstone. By CHARLES READE.
Peg Woffington. By CHARLES READE.

The Pocket Library. Post 8vo, printed on laid paper and hf.-bd., 2s. each.

Gastronomy. By BRILLAT-SAVARIN.
Robinson Crusoe. Illustrated by G. CRUIKSHANK
Autocrat of the Breakfast-Table and The Professor at the Breakfast-Table. By O. W. HOLMES.
Provincial Letters of Blaise Pascal.
Whims and Oddities. By THOMAS HOOD.
Leigh Hunt's Essays. Edited by E. OLLIER.
The Barber's Chair. By DOUGLAS JERROLD.
The Essays of Elia. By CHARLES LAMB.
Anecdotes of the Clergy. By JACOB LARWOOD.
The Epicurean, &c. By THOMAS MOORE.
Plays by RICHARD BRINSLEY SHERIDAN.
Gulliver's Travels, &c. By Dean SWIFT.
Thomson's Seasons. Illustrated.
White's Natural History of Selborne.

POPULAR SIXPENNY NOVELS.

New Arabian Nights. R. L. STEVENSON. [Jan.
Puck. By OUIDA. [Feb.
A Son of Hagar. By HALL CAINE. [Mar.
All Sorts and Conditions of Men. By WALTER BESANT.
The Golden Butterfly. By WALTER BESANT and JAMES RICE.
The Deemster. By HALL CAINE.
The Shadow of a Crime. By HALL CAINE.
Antonina. By WILKIE COLLINS.
The Moonstone. By WILKIE COLLINS
The Woman in White. By WILKIE COLLINS.
The Dead Secret. By WILKIE COLLINS.
The New Magdalen. By WILKIE COLLINS.
Held in Bondage. By OUIDA.
Moths. By OUIDA.
Under Two Flags. By OUIDA.
By Proxy. By JAMES PAYN.
Peg Woffington; and Christie Johnstone. By CHARLES READE. [READE.
The Cloister and the Hearth. By CHARLES
Never Too Late to Mend. By CHARLES READE.
Hard Cash. By CHARLES READE.
The Old Factory. By WILLIAM WESTALL.

THE PICCADILLY NOVELS.

LIBRARY EDITIONS OF NOVELS, many Illustrated, crown 8vo, cloth extra, 3s. 6d. each.

By Mrs. ALEXANDER.

Valerie's Fate. | Barbara.
A Life Interest. | A Fight with Fate.
Mona's Choice. | A Golden Autumn.
By Woman's Wit. | Mrs. Crichton's Creditor.
The Cost of Her Pride. | The Step-mother.

By F. M. ALLEN.—Green as Grass.

By GRANT ALLEN.

Philistia. | Babylon. | The Great Taboo.
Strange Stories. | Dumaresq's Daughter.
For Maimie's Sake. | Duchess of Powysland.
In all Shades. | Blood Royal.
The Beckoning Hand. | I. Greet's Masterpiece.
The Devil's Die. | The Scallywag.
This Mortal Coil. | At Market Value.
The Tents of Shem. | Under Sealed Orders.

By M. ANDERSON.—Othello's Occupation.

By EDWIN L. ARNOLD.

Phra the Phœnician. | Constable of St. Nicholas.

By ROBERT BARR.

In a Steamer Chair. | A Woman Intervenes.
From Whose Bourne. | Revenge!

By FRANK BARRETT.

Woman of Iron Bracelets. | Under a Strange Mask.
Fettered for Life. | A Missing Witness.
The Harding Scandal. | Was She Justified?

By 'BELLE.'—Vashti and Esther.

By Sir W. BESANT and J. RICE.

Ready-Money Mortiboy. | By Celia's Arbour.
My Little Girl. | Chaplain of the Fleet.
With Harp and Crown. | The Seamy Side.
This Son of Vulcan. | The Case of Mr. Lucraft.
The Golden Butterfly. | In Trafalgar's Bay.
The Monks of Thelema. | The Ten Years' Tenant.

By Sir WALTER BESANT.

All Sorts & Conditions. | Armorel of Lyonesse.
The Captains' Room. | S. Katherine's by Tower
All in a Garden Fair. | Verbena Camellia, &c.
Dorothy Forster. | The Ivory Gate.
Uncle Jack. | Holy Rose | The Rebel Queen.
World Went Well Then. | Dreams of Avarice.
Children of Gibeon. | In Deacon's Orders.
Herr Paulus. | The Master Craftsman.
For Faith and Freedom. | The City of Refuge.
To Call Her Mine. | A Fountain Sealed.
The Revolt of Man. | The Changeling.
The Bell of St. Paul's. | The Charm.

By AMBROSE BIERCE—In Midst of Life.

By HAROLD BINDLOSS, Ainslie's Ju-Ju.

By M. McD. BODKIN.—Dora Myrl.

By PAUL BOURGET.—A Living Lie.

By J. D. BRAYSHAW.—Slum Silhouettes.

By ROBERT BUCHANAN.

Shadow of the Sword. | The New Abelard.
A Child of Nature. | Matt. | Rachel Dene
God and the Man. | Master of the Mine.
Martyrdom of Madeline | The Heir of Linne.
Love Me for Ever. | Woman and the Man.
Annan Water. | Red and White Heather.
Foxglove Manor. | Lady Kilpatrick.
The Charlatan.

R. W. CHAMBERS.—The King in Yellow.

By J. M. CHAPPLE.—The Minor Chord.

By HALL CAINE.

Shadow of a Crime. | Deemster. | Son of Hagar.

By AUSTIN CLARE.—By Rise of River.

By ANNE COATES.—Rie's Diary.

By MACLAREN COBBAN.

The Red Sultan. | The Burden of Isabel.

By MORT. & FRANCES COLLINS.

Blacksmith & Scholar. | You Play me False.
The Village Comedy. | Midnight to Midnight.

By WILKIE COLLINS.

Armadale. | After Dark. | The Woman in White.
No Name. | Antonina | The Law and the Lady.
Basil. | Hide and Seek. | The Haunted Hotel.
The Dead Secret. | The Moonstone.
Queen of Hearts. | Man and Wife.
My Miscellanies. | Poor Miss Finch.

By WILKIE COLLINS—continued.

Miss or Mrs.? | Jezebel's Daughter.
The New Magdalen. | The Black Robe.
The Frozen Deep. | Heart and Science.
The Two Destinies. | The Evil Genius.
'I Say No.' | The Legacy of Cain.
Little Novels. | A Rogue's Life.
The Fallen Leaves. | Blind Love.

M. J. COLQUHOUN.—Every Inch Soldier.

By E. H. COOPER.—Geoffory Hamilton.

By V. C. COTES.—Two Girls on a Barge.

C. E. CRADDOCK.—His Vanished Star.

By H. N. CRELLIN.

Romances of the Old Seraglio.

By MATT CRIM.

The Adventures of a Fair Rebel.

By S. R. CROCKETT and others.

Tales of Our Coast.

By B. M. CROKER.

Diana Barrington. | The Real Lady Hilda.
Proper Pride. | Married or Single?
A Family Likeness. | Two Masters.
Pretty Miss Neville. | In the Kingdom of Kerry
A Bird of Passage. | Interference.
'To Let.' | Mr. Jervis. | A Third Person.
Village Tales. | Beyond the Pale.
Some One Else. | Jason. | Miss Balmaine's Past.
| Infatuation.

By W. CYPLES.—Hearts of Gold.

By ALPHONSE DAUDET.

The Evangelist; or, Port Salvation.

H. C. DAVIDSON.—Mr. Sadler's Daughters.

By E. DAWSON.—The Fountain of Youth.

By J. DE MILLE.—A Castle in Spain.

By J. LEITH DERWENT.

Our Lady of Tears. | Circe's Lovers.

By HARRY DE WINDT.

True Tales of Travel and Adventure.

By DICK DONOVAN.

Man from Manchester. | Tales of Terror.
Records of Vincent Trill | Chronicles of Michael
The Mystery of | Danevitch. | Detective.
Jamaica Terrace. | Tyler Tatlock, Private

By RICHARD DOWLING.

Old Corcoran's Money.

By A. CONAN DOYLE.

The Firm of Girdlestone.

By S. JEANNETTE DUNCAN.

A Daughter of To-day. | Vernon's Aunt.

By A. EDWARDES.—A Plaster Saint.

By G. S. EDWARDS.—Snazelleparilla.

By G. MANVILLE FENN.

Cursed by a Fortune. | A Fluttered Dovecote.
The Case of Ailsa Gray. | King of the Castle
Commodore Junk. | Master of Ceremonies.
The New Mistress. | Eve at the Wheel, &c.
Witness to the Deed. | The Man with a Shadow
The Tiger Lily. | One Maid's Mischief.
The White Virgin. | Story of Antony Grace.
Black Blood. | This Man's Wife.
Double Cunning. | In Jeopardy. [ning.
Bag of Diamonds, &c. | A Woman Worth Win-

By PERCY FITZGERALD.—Fatal Zero?

By R. E. FRANCILLON.

One by One. | Ropes of Sand.
A Dog and his Shadow. | Jack Doyle's Daughter.
A Real Queen.

By HAROLD FREDERIC.

Seth's Brother's Wife. | The Lawton Girl.

By GILBERT GAUL.

A Strange Manuscript Found in a Copper Cylinder

By PAUL GAULOT.—The Red Shirts.

By CHARLES GIBBON.

Robin Gray. | The Golden Shaft.
Loving & Dream. | The Braes of Yarrow.
Of High Degree

By E. GLANVILLE.

The Lost Heiress. | The Golden Rock.
Fair Colonist | Fossicker | Tales from the Veld.

THE PICCADILLY (3/6) NOVELS—*continued.*

By E. J. GOODMAN.
The Fate of Herbert Wayne.

By Rev. S. BARING GOULD.
Red Spider. | Eve.

CECIL GRIFFITH.—Corinthia Marazion.

By A. CLAVERING GUNTER.
A Florida Enchantment.

By OWEN HALL.
The Track of a Storm. | Jetsam.

By COSMO HAMILTON.
Glamour of Impossible. | Through a Keyhole.

By THOMAS HARDY.
Under the Greenwood Tree.

By BRET HARTE.
A Waif of the Plains. | A Protégée of Jack
A Ward of the Golden | Hamlin's.
Gate. [Springs. | Clarence.
A Sappho of Green | Barker's Luck.
Col. Starbottle's Client. | Devil's Ford. [celsior.'
Susy. | Sally Dows. | The Crusade of the 'Ex-
Bell-Ringer of Angel's. | Three Partners.
Tales of Trail and Town | Gabriel Conroy.

By JULIAN HAWTHORNE.
Garth. | Dust. | Beatrix Randolph.
Ellice Quentin. | David Poindexter's Dis-
Sebastian Strome. | appearance.
Fortune's Fool. | Spectre of Camera.

By Sir A. HELPS.—Ivan de Biron.
By I. HENDERSON.—Agatha Page.
By G. A. HENTY.
Dorothy's Double. | The Queen's Cup.

By HEADON HILL.
Zambra the Detective.

By **JOHN HILL.** The Common Ancestor.

By TIGHE HOPKINS.
'Twixt Love and Duty. | Nugents of Carriconna.
The Incomplete Adventurer.

VICTOR HUGO.—The Outlaw of Iceland.

FERGUS HUME.—Lady from Nowhere.

By Mrs. HUNGERFORD.
A Mental Struggle. | A Maiden all Forlorn.
Lady Verner's Flight. | The Coming of Chloe.
The Red-House Mystery | Nora Creina.
The Three Graces. | An Anxious Moment.
Professor's Experiment. | April's Lady.
A Point of Conscience. | Peter's Wife. | Lovice.

By Mrs. ALFRED HUNT.
The Leaden Casket. | Self-Condemned.
That Other Person. | Mrs. Juliet.

By C. J. CUTCLIFFE HYNE.
Honour of Thieves.

By R. ASHE KING.—A Drawn Game.

By GEORGE LAMBERT.
The President of Boravia.

By EDMOND LEPELLETIER.
Madame Sans-Gêne.

By **ADAM LILBURN.**—A Tragedy in Marble
By HARRY LINDSAY.
Rhoda Roberts. | The Jacobite.

By HENRY W. LUCY.—Gideon Fleyce.

By E. LYNN LINTON.
Patricia Kemball. | The Atonement of Leam
Under which Lord? | Dundas.
'My Love!' | Ione. | The One Too Many.
Paston Carew. | Dulcie Everton.
Sowing the Wind. | Rebel of the Family.
With a Silken Thread. | An Octave of Friends.
The World Well Lost.

By JUSTIN McCARTHY.
A Fair Saxon. | Donna Quixote.
Linley Rochford. | Maid of Athens.
Dear Lady Disdain. | The Comet of a Season.
Camiola. | The Dictator.
Waterdale Neighbours. | Red Diamonds.
My Enemy's Daughter. | The Riddle Ring.
Miss Misanthrope. | The Three Disgraces.

By JUSTIN H. McCARTHY.
A London Legend. | The Royal Christopher

By GEORGE MACDONALD.
Heather and Snow. | Phantastes.

W. H. MALLOCK.—The New Republic.

P. & V. MARGUERITTE.—The Disaster.

By L. T. MEADE.
A Soldier of Fortune. | On Brink of a Chasm.
In an Iron Grip. | The Siren.
Dr. Rumsey's Patient. | The Way of a Woman.
The Voice of the Charmer | A Son of Ishmael.
An Adventuress.

By LEONARD MERRICK.
This Stage of Fools. | Cynthia.

By BERTRAM MITFORD.
The Gun-Runner. | The King's Assegai.
Luck of Gerard Ridgeley. | Rensh. Fanning's Quest.

By J. E. MUDDOCK.
Maid Marian and Robin Hood. | Golden Idol.
Basile the Jester. | Young Lochinvar.

By D. CHRISTIE MURRAY.
A Life's Atonement. | The Way of the World.
Joseph's Coat. | Bob Martin's Little Girl
Coals of Fire. | Time's Revenges.
Old Blazer's Hero. | A Wasted Crime.
Val Strange. | Hearts. | In Direst Peril.
A Model Father. | Mount Despair.
By the Gate of the Sea. | A Capful o' Nails.
A Bit of Human Nature. | Tales in Prose & Verse.
First Person Singular. | A Race for Millions.
Cynic Fortune. | This Little World.

By MURRAY and HERMAN.
The Bishops' Bible. | Paul Jones's Alias.
One Traveller Returns.

By HUME NISBET.—'Bail Up!'

By W. E. NORRIS.
Saint Ann's. | Billy Bellew.
Miss Wentworth's Idea.

By G. OHNET.
A Weird Gift. | Love's Depths.

By Mrs. OLIPHANT.—The Sorceress.

By OUIDA.
Held in Bondage. | In a Winter City.
Strathmore. | Chandos. | Friendship.
Under Two Flags. | Moths. | Ruffino.
Idalia. | [Gage. | Pipistrello. | Ariadne.
Cecil Castlemaine's | A Village Commune.
Tricotrin. | Puck. | Bimbi. | Wanda.
Folle Farine. | Frescoes. | Othmar.
A Dog of Flanders. | In Maremma.
Pascarel. | Signa. | Syrlin. | Guilderoy.
Princess Napraxine. | Santa Barbara.
Two Wooden Shoes. | Two Offenders.
The Waters of Edera.

By MARGARET A. PAUL.
Gentle and Simple.

By JAMES PAYN.
Lost Sir Massingberd. | The Talk of the Town.
A County Family. | Holiday Tasks.
Less Black than We're | For Cash Only.
Painted. | The Burnt Million.
A Confidential Agent. | The Word and the Will.
A Grape from a Thorn. | Sunny Stories.
In Peril and Privation. | A Trying Patient.
Mystery of Mirbridge. | A Modern Dick Whit-
Walter's Word. | tington.
High Spirits. | By Proxy.

By WILL PAYNE.—Jerry the Dreamer.

By Mrs. CAMPBELL PRAED.
Outlaw and Lawmaker. | Mrs. Tregaskiss.
Christina Chard. | Nulma. | Madame Izan.

By E. C. PRICE.
Valentina. | Foreigners. | Mrs. Lancaster's Rival.

By RICHARD PRYCE.
Miss Maxwell's Affections.

By Mrs. J. H. RIDDELL.
Weird Stories. | A Rich Man's Daughter.

By AMELIE RIVES.
Barbara Dering. | Meriel.

By F. W. ROBINSON.
The Hands of Justice. | Woman in the Dark.

By ALBERT ROSS.—A Sugar Princess.

By HERBERT RUSSELL. True Blue.

The Captains' Room.
All in a Garden Fair.
Dorothy Forster.
Uncle Jack.
The World Went Very Well Then.
Children of Gibeon.
Herr Paulus.
For Faith and Freedom.
To Call Her Mine.
The Master Craftsman.

The Ivory Mode.
Armorel of Lyonesse.
S.Katherine's by Tower
Verbena Camellia Stephanotis.
The Ivory Gate.
The Rebel Queen.
Beyond the Dreams of Avarice.
The Revolt of Man.
In Deacon's Orders.
The City of Refuge.

By AMBROSE BIERCE.
In the Midst of Life.

BY BRET HARTE.
Californian Stories.
Gabriel Conroy.
Luck of Roaring Camp.
An Heiress of Red Dog.

Flip. | Maruja.
A Phyllis of the Sierras.
A Waif of the Plains.
Ward of Golden Gate.

By ROBERT BUCHANAN.
Shadow of the Sword.
A Child of Nature.
God and the Man.
Love Me for Ever.
Foxglove Manor.
The Master of the Mine.
Annan Water.

The Martyrdom of Madeline.
The New Abelard.
The Heir of Linne.
Woman and the Man.
Rachel Dene. | Matt.
Lady Kilpatrick.

By BUCHANAN and MURRAY.
The Charlatan.

By HALL CAINE.
The Shadow of a Crime. | The Deemster.
A Son of Hagar.

By Commander CAMERON.
The Cruise of the 'Black Prince.'

By HAYDEN CARRUTH.
The Adventures of Jones.

By AUSTIN CLARE.
For the Love of a Lass.

By Mrs. ARCHER CLIVE.
Paul Ferroll.
Why Paul Ferroll Killed his Wife.

By MACLAREN COBBAN.
The Cure of Souls. | The Red Sultan.

By C. ALLSTON COLLINS.
The Bar Sinister.

By MORT. & FRANCES COLLINS.
Sweet Anne Page.
Transmigration.
From Midnight to Midnight.
A Fight with Fortune.

Sweet and Twenty.
The Village Comedy.
You Play me False.
Blacksmith and Scholar
Frances.

By WILKIE COLLINS.
Armadale. | AfterDark.
No Name.
Antonina.
Basil.
Hide and Seek.
The Dead Secret.
Queen of Hearts.
Miss or Mrs.?
The New Magdalen.
The Frozen Deep.
The Law and the Lady
The Two Destinies.
The Haunted Hotel.
A Rogue's Life.

My Miscellanies.
The Woman in White.
The Moonstone.
Man and Wife.
Poor Miss Finch.
The Fallen Leaves.
Jezebel's Daughter.
The Black Robe.
Heart and Science.
'I Say No!'
The Evil Genius.
Little Novels.
Legacy of Cain.
Blind Love.

'To Let.'
A Bird of Passage.
Proper Pride.
A Family Likeness.
A Third Person.

Two Masters.
Mr. Jervis.
The Real Lady Hilda.
Married or Single?
Interference.

By ALPHONSE DAUDET.
The Evangelist; or, Port Salvation.

By DICK DONOVAN.
The Man-Hunter.
Tracked and Taken.
Caught at Last!
Wanted!
Who Poisoned Hetty Duncan?
Man from Manchester.
A Detective's Triumphs
The Mystery of Jamaica Terrace.
The Chronicles of Michael Danevitch.

In the Grip of the Law.
From Information Received.
Tracked to Doom.
Link by Link
Suspicion Aroused.
Dark Deeds.
Riddles Read.

By Mrs. ANNIE EDWARDES.
A Point of Honour. | Archie Lovell.

By EDWARD EGGLESTON.
Roxy.

By G. MANVILLE FENN.
The New Mistress.
Witness to the Deed.

The Tiger Lily.
The White Virgin.

By PERCY FITZGERALD.
Bella Donna.
Never Forgotten.
Polly.
Fatal Zero.

Second Mrs. Tillotson.
Seventy-five Brooke Street.
The Lady of Brantome

By P. FITZGERALD and others.
Strange Secrets.

By R. E. FRANCILLON.
Olympia.
One by One.
A Real Queen.
Queen Cophetua.

King or Knave?
Romances of the Law.
Ropes of Sand.
A Dog and his Shadow

By HAROLD FREDERIC.
Seth's Brother's Wife. | The Lawton Girl.

Prefaced by Sir BARTLE FRERE.
Pandurang Hari.

By GILBERT GAUL.
A Strange Manuscript.

By CHARLES GIBBON.
Robin Gray.
Fancy Free.
For Lack of Gold.
What will World Say?
In Love and War.
For the King.
In Pastures Green.
Queen of the Meadow.
A Heart's Problem.
The Dead Heart.

In Honour Bound.
Flower of the Forest.
The Braes of Yarrow.
The Golden Shaft.
Of High Degree.
By Mead and Stream.
Loving a Dream.
A Hard Knot.
Heart's Delight.
Blood-Money.

By WILLIAM GILBERT.
James Duke.

By ERNEST GLANVILLE.
The Lost Heiress.
A Fair Colonist.

The Fossicker

TWO-SHILLING NOVELS—*continued.*

By Rev. S. BARING GOULD.
Red Spider. | Eve.

By HENRY GREVILLE.
Nikanor.

By ANDREW HALLIDAY.
Every-day Papers.

By THOMAS HARDY.
Under the Greenwood Tree.

By JULIAN HAWTHORNE.
Garth. | Beatrix Randolph.
Ellice Quentin. | Love—or a Name.
Fortune's Fool. | David Poindexter's Dis-
Miss Cadogna. | appearance.
Sebastian Strome. | The Spectre of the
Dust. | Camera.

By Sir ARTHUR HELPS.
Ivan de Biron.

By G. A. HENTY.
Rujub the Juggler.

By HEADON HILL.
Zambra the Detective.

By JOHN HILL.
Treason Felony.

By Mrs. CASHEL HOEY.
The Lover's Creed.

By Mrs. GEORGE HOOPER.
The House of Raby.

By Mrs. HUNGERFORD.
A Maiden all Forlorn. | Lady Verner's Flight.
In Durance Vile. | The Red-House Mystery
Marvel. | The Three Graces.
A Mental Struggle. | Unsatisfactory Lover.
A Modern Circe. | Lady Patty.
April's Lady. | Nora Creina.
Peter's Wife. | Professor's Experiment.

By Mrs. ALFRED HUNT.
Thornicroft's Model. | Self-Condemned.
That Other Person. | The Leaden Casket.

By HARRIETT JAY.
The Dark Colleen. | Queen of Connaught.

By MARK KERSHAW.
Colonial Facts and Fictions.

By R. ASHE KING.
A Drawn Game. | Passion's Slave.
'The Wearing of the | Bell Barry.
Green.'

By EDMOND LEPELLETIER.
Madame Sans-Gene.

By JOHN LEYS.
The Lindsays.

By E. LYNN LINTON.
Patricia Kemball. | The Atonement of Leam
The World Well Lost. | Dundas.
Under which Lord? | Rebel of the Family.
Paston Carew. | Sowing the Wind.
'My Love!' | The One Too Many.
Ione. | Dulcie Everton.
With a Silken Thread.

By HENRY W. LUCY.
Gideon Fleyce.

By JUSTIN McCARTHY.
Dear Lady Disdain. | Donna Quixote.
Waterdale Neighbours. | Maid of Athens.
My Enemy's Daughter | The Comet of a Season.
A Fair Saxon. | The Dictator.
Linley Rochford. | Red Diamonds.
Miss Misanthrope. | The Riddle Ring.
Camiola.

By HUGH MACCOLL.
Mr. Stranger's Sealed Packet.

By GEORGE MACDONALD.
Heather and Snow.

By AGNES MACDONELL.
Quaker Cousins.

By W. H. MALLOCK.
The New Republic.

By BRANDER MATTHEWS.
A Secret of the Sea.

By L. T. MEADE.
A Soldier of Fortune.

By LEONARD MERRICK.
The Man who was Good.

By JEAN MIDDLEMASS.
Touch and Go. | Mr. Dorillion.

By Mrs. MOLESWORTH.
Hathercourt Rectory.

By J. E. MUDDOCK.
Stories Weird and Won- | From the Bosom of the
derful. | Deep.
The Dead Man's Secret. |

By D. CHRISTIE MURRAY.
A Model Father. | A Bit of Human Nature.
Joseph's Coat. | First Person Singular.
Coals of Fire. | Bob Martin's Little Girl.
Val Strange. | Hearts. | Time's Revenges.
Old Blazer's Hero. | A Wasted Crime.
The Way of the World. | In Direst Peril.
Cynic Fortune. | Mount Despair.
A Life's Atonement. | A Capful o' Nails
By the Gate of the Sea. |

By MURRAY and HERMAN.
One Traveller Returns. | The Bishops' Bible.
Paul Jones's Alias. |

By HUME NISBET.
'Bail Up!' | Dr. Bernard St. Vincent.

By W. E. NORRIS.
Saint Ann's. | Billy Bellew.

By ALICE O'HANLON.
The Unforeseen. | Chance? or Fate?

By GEORGES OHNET.
Dr. Rameau. | A Weird Gift.
A Last Love. |

By Mrs. OLIPHANT.
Whiteladies. | The Greatest Heiress in
The Primrose Path. | England.

By OUIDA.
Held in Bondage. | Two Lit. Wooden Shoes.
Strathmore. | Moths.
Chandos. | Bimbi.
Idalia. | Pipistrello.
Under Two Flags. | A Village Commune.
Cecil Castlemaine's Gage | Wanda.
Tricotrin. | Othmar.
Puck. | Frescoes.
Folle Farine. | In Maremma.
A Dog of Flanders. | Guilderoy.
Pascarel. | Ruffino.
Signa. | Syrlin.
Princess Napraxine. | Santa Barbara.
In a Winter City. | Two Offenders.
Ariadne. | Ouida's Wisdom, Wit,
Friendship. | and Pathos.

By MARGARET AGNES PAUL.
Gentle and Simple.

By Mrs. CAMPBELL PRAED.
The Romance of a Station.
The Soul of Countess Adrian.
Outlaw and Lawmaker. | Mrs. Tregaskiss
Christina Chard. |

TWO-SHILLING NOVELS—*continued.*

By RICHARD PRYCE.
Miss Maxwell's Affections.

By JAMES PAYN.

Bentinck's Tutor.	The Talk of the Town.
Murphy's Master.	Holiday Tasks.
A County Family.	A Perfect Treasure.
At Her Mercy.	What He Cost Her.
Cecil's Tryst.	A Confidential Agent.
The Clyffards of Clyffe.	Glow-worm Tales.
The Foster Brothers.	The Burnt Million.
Found Dead.	Sunny Stories.
The Best of Husbands.	Lost Sir Massingberd.
Walter's Word.	A Woman's Vengeance.
Halves.	The Family Scapegrace.
Fallen Fortunes.	Gwendoline's Harvest.
Humorous Stories.	Like Father, Like Son.
£200 Reward.	Married Beneath Him.
A Marine Residence.	Not Wooed, but Won.
Mirk Abbey	Less Black than We're
By Proxy.	Painted.
Under One Roof.	Some Private Views.
High Spirits.	A Grape from a Thorn.
Carlyon's Year.	The Mystery of Mir-
From Exile.	bridge.
For Cash Only.	The Word and the Will.
Kit.	A Prince of the Blood.
The Canon's Ward.	A Trying Patient.

By CHARLES READE.

It is Never Too Late to	A Terrible Temptation.
Mend.	Foul Play.
Christie Johnstone.	The Wandering Heir.
The Double Marriage.	Hard Cash.
Put Yourself in His	Singleheart and Double-
Place	face.
Love Me Little, Love	Good Stories of Man and
Me Long.	other Animals.
The Cloister and the	Peg Woffington.
Hearth.	Griffith Gaunt.
Course of True Love.	A Perilous Secret.
The Jilt.	A Simpleton.
The Autobiography of	Readiana.
a Thief.	A Woman-Hater.

By Mrs. J. H. RIDDELL.

Weird Stories.	The Uninhabited House.
Fairy Water.	The Mystery in Palace
Her Mother's Darling.	Gardens.
The Prince of Wales's	The Nun's Curse.
Garden Party.	Idle Tales.

By F. W. ROBINSON.

Women are Strange.	The Woman in the Dark
The Hands of Justice.	

By W. CLARK RUSSELL.

Round the Galley Fire.	An Ocean Tragedy.
On the Fo'k'sle Head.	My Shipmate Louise.
In the Middle Watch.	Alone on Wide Wide Sea.
A Voyage to the Cape.	Good Ship 'Mohock.'
A Book for the Ham-	The Phantom Death.
mock.	Is He the Man?
The Mystery of the	Heart of Oak.
'Ocean Star.'	The Convict Ship.
The Romance of Jenny	The Tale of the Ten.
Harlowe.	The Last Entry.

By DORA RUSSELL.
A Country Sweetheart.

By GEORGE AUGUSTUS SALA.
Gaslight and Daylight.

By GEORGE R. SIMS.

The Ring o' Bells.	Zeph.
Mary Jane's Memoirs.	Memoirs of a Landlady.
Mary Jane Married.	Scenes from the Show.
Tales of To-day.	The 10 Commandments.
Dramas of Life.	Dagonet Abroad.
Tinkletop's Crime.	Rogues and Vagabonds.
My Two Wives.	

By ARTHUR SKETCHLEY.
A Match in the Dark.

By HAWLEY SMART.

Without Love or Licence.	The Plunger.
Beatrice and Benedick.	Long Odds.
The Master of Rathkelly.	

By T. W. SPEIGHT.

The Mysteries of Heron	Back to Life.
Dyke.	The Loudwater Tragedy.
The Golden Hoop.	Burgo's Romance.
Hoodwinked.	Quittance in Full.
By Devious Ways.	A Husband from the Sea

By ALAN ST. AUBYN.

A Fellow of Trinity.	Orchard Damerel.
The Junior Dean.	In the Face of the World.
Master of St. Benedict's	The Tremlett Diamonds.
To His Own Master.	

By R. A. STERNDALE.
The Afghan Knife.

By R. LOUIS STEVENSON.
New Arabian Nights.

By ROBERT SURTEES.
Handley Cross.

By BERTHA THOMAS.
The Violin-Player.

By WALTER THORNBURY.
Tales for the Marines.

By T. ADOLPHUS TROLLOPE.
Diamond Cut Diamond.

By F. ELEANOR TROLLOPE.

Like Ships upon the	Anne Furness.
Sea.	Mabel's Progress.

By ANTHONY TROLLOPE.

Frau Frohmann.	The American Senator.
Marion Fay.	Mr. Scarborough's
Kept in the Dark.	Family.
The Way We Live Now.	Golden Lion of Granpere
The Land-Leaguers.	

By MARK TWAIN.

A Pleasure Trip on the	Stolen White Elephant.
Continent.	Life on the Mississippi.
The Gilded Age.	The Prince and the
Huckleberry Finn.	Pauper.
Mark Twain's Sketches.	A Yankee at the Court
Tom Sawyer.	of King Arthur.
A Tramp Abroad.	£1,000,000 Bank- Note.

By C. C. FRASER-TYTLER.
Mistress Judith.

By SARAH TYTLER.

Bride's Pass	Lady Bell	The Huguenot Family
Buried Diamonds.	The Blackhall Ghosts
St. Mungo's City.	What She Came Through
Noblesse Oblige.	Beauty and the Beast.
Disappeared.	Citoyenne Jaqueline.

By ALLEN UPWARD.
The Queen against Owen. | Prince of Balkistan.
'God Save the Queen!'

By WILLIAM WESTALL.
Trust-Money.

By Mrs. P. H. WILLIAMSON.
A Child Widow.

By J. S. WINTER.
Cavalry Life. | Regimental Legends.

By H. F. WOOD.
The Passenger from Scotland Yard.
The Englishman of the Rue Cain.

UNWIN BROTHERS, Printers, 27, Pilgrim Street, London, E.C.